"DO EVERYTHING" REFORM

Frances E. Willard. 1890. Photo courtesy of The Frances E.
Willard Archives, Evanston, Illinois.

"DO EVERYTHING" REFORM

The Oratory of Frances E. Willard

Richard W. Leeman

Foreword by Bernard K. Duffy

Great American Orators, Number 15

Bernard K. Duffy and Halford R. Ryan,
Series Advisers

Greenwood Press
New York • Westport, Connecticut • London

Library of Congress Cataloging-in-Publication Data

Leeman, Richard W.
  "Do everything" reform : the oratory of Frances E. Willard /
Richard W. Leeman ; foreword by Bernard K. Duffy.
    p. cm.—(Great American orators, ISSN 0898-8277 ; no. 15)
  Includes bibliographical references and index.
  ISBN 0-313-27487-8 (alk. paper)
  1. Willard, Frances Elizabeth, 1839-1898. 2. Women social
reformers—United States—Biography. 3. Woman's Christian
Temperance Union. I. Title. II. Series.
HV5232.W6L44 1992
322.4'4'092—dc20   91-35714
  [B]

British Library Cataloguing in Publication Data is available.

Library of Congress Catalog Card Number: 91-35714
ISBN: 0-313-27487-8
ISSN: 0898-8277

First published in 1992

Greenwood Press, 88 Post Road West, Westport, CT 06881
An imprint of Greenwood Publishing Group, Inc.

Printed in the United States of America

The paper used in this book complies with the
Permanent Paper Standard issued by the National
Information Standards Organization (Z39.48-1984).

10 9 8 7 6 5 4 3 2 1

The author and publisher gratefully acknowledge permission to use extracts
from the following material.

"Everybody's War," circa 1874; "Home Protection," 1879; "Annual Address,"
1881; "Tenth Annual Address," 1889; "A White Life for Two," 1890; and
"President's Address," 1897 by Frances E. Willard, and various archival
material are used courtesy of the National Woman's Christian Temperance
Union.

Karlyn Kohrs Campbell, *Man Cannot Speak for Her*, vol. 1 (Greenwood Press,
Westport, CT, 1989), pp. 122-129 & 131, *passim*. Copyright © 1989 by Karlyn
Kohrs Campbell. Reprinted with permission.

Contents

Series Foreword

The idea for a series of books on great American orators grew out of a recognition that there is a paucity of book-length studies on individual orators and their speeches. Apart from a few notable exceptions, the study of American public address has been pursued in scores of articles published in professional journals. As helpful as these studies have been, none has or can provide a complete analysis of a speaker's rhetoric. Book-length studies, such as those in this series, will help fill the void that has existed in the study of American public address and its related disciplines of politics and history, theology and sociology, communication and law. In books, the critic can explicate a broader range of a speaker's persuasive discourse than reasonably could be treated in articles. The comprehensive research and sustained reflection that books require will undoubtedly yield many original and enduring insights concerning the nation's most important voices.

Public address has been a fertile ground for scholarly investigation. No matter how insightful their intellectual forebears, each generation of scholars must reexamine its universe of discourse, while expanding the compass of its researches and redefining its purpose and methods. To avoid intellectual torpor new scholars cannot be content simply to see through the eyes of those who have come before them. We hope that this series of books will stimulate important new understanding of the nature of persuasive discourse and provide additional opportunities for scholarship in the history and criticism of American public address.

This series examines the role of rhetoric in the United States. American speakers shaped the destiny of the colonies, the young republic, and the mature nation. During each stage of the intellectual, political, and religious development of the United States, great orators, standing at the rostrum, on the stump, and in the pulpit, used words and gestures to influence their audiences. Usually striving for the noble, sometimes achieving the base, they urged their fellow citizens toward a more perfect Union. The books in this series chronicle and explain the accomplishments of representative American leaders as orators.

A series of book-length studies on American persuaders honors the role men and women have played in U.S. history. Previously, if one desired to assess the impact of a speaker or a speech upon history, the path was, at best, not well marked and, at worst, littered with obstacles. To be sure, one might turn to biographies and general histories to learn about an orator, but for the public address scholar these sources often prove unhelpful. Rhetoric topics, such as speech invention, style, delivery, organizational strategies, and persuasive effect, are often treated in passing, if mentioned at all. Authoritative speech texts are often difficult to locate and the problem of textual accuracy is frequently encountered. This is especially true for those figures who spoke one or two hundred years ago, or for those whose persuasive role, though significant, was secondary to other leading lights of the age.

Each book in this series is organized to meet the needs of scholars and students of the history and criticism of American public address. Part I is a critical analysis of the orator and his or her speeches. Within the format of a case study, one may expect considerable latitude. For instance, in a given chapter an author might explicate a single speech or a group of related speeches, or examine orations that comprise a genre of rhetoric such as forensic speaking. But the critic's focus remains on the rhetorical considerations of speaker, speech, occasion, and effect. Part II contains the texts of the important addresses that are discussed in the critical analysis that precedes it. To the extent possible, each author has endeavored to collect authoritative speech texts, which have often been found through original research in collections of primary source material. In a few instances, because of the extreme length of a speech, texts have been edited, but the authors have been careful to delete material that is least important to the speech, and these deletions have been held to a minimum.

In each book there is a chronology of major speeches that serves more purposes than may be apparent at first. Pragmatically, it lists all of the orator's known speeches and addresses. Places and dates of the speeches are also listed, although this is information that is sometimes difficult to determine precisely. But in a wider sense, the chronology attests to the scope of rhetoric in the United States. Certainly in quantity, if not always in quality, Americans are historically talkers and listeners.

Because of the disparate nature of the speakers examined in the series, there is some latitude in the nature of the bibliographical materials that have been included in each book. But in every instance, authors have carefully described original historical materials and collections and gathered critical studies, biographies and autobiographies, and a variety of secondary sources that bear on the speaker and the oratory. By combining in each book bibliographical materials, speech texts, and critical chapters, this series notes that text and research sources are interwoven in the act of rhetorical criticism.

May the books in this series serve to memorialize the nation's greatest orators.

Bernard K. Duffy
Halford R. Ryan

Foreword

A work of traditional rhetorical criticism, Richard Leeman's carefully crafted book on Frances Willard will serve to remind rhetorical critics of the rich legacy of critical techniques they hold in common. A good index to the quality of this work is the degree to which it draws the reader to Willard's speeches. Unlike historical narrative, Leeman's analysis, although satisfying on its own, is not wholly complete unless one reads the speeches that are the focus of his analysis. Professor Leeman's explication of several of Willard's best speech texts is the result of a careful and sustained examination as sensitive to questions of rhetorical scene as to the instrumentalities of language and argument Willard enlisted on behalf of her causes. Because of her prodigious speaking and the quality of her addresses, Willard deserves to be considered among the ranks of notable American orators. Although temperance was a Quixotic cause, Willard's oratory gave voice to an array of topics, apart from temperance, that significantly advanced the cause of women in society and helped spur progressive reforms. As an issue temperance was a touchstone for the revelation of many other social injustices.

Willard identified alcoholism with the disruption of domestic life and the subjugation of women. The evils of alcoholism bore witness to the social and political dependency of women and children upon men. Willard was acutely aware that without suffrage, women were perpetually minors, unable to assert direct influence to change society. In her advocacy of prohibition she discovered themes popular with social reformers of her day, including opposition to immoral behavior, prostitution, bad hygiene, pornography, and "impure art." She also helped promote a fear of immigrants, whom she alleged preferred the saloon to the church. Much of her rhetoric suggests the straight-laced, high collared moralism of the Gilded Age. It was, as she admitted and Leeman affirms, too diffuse, interlacing clearly related topics with some others that bore little relation to temperance or suffrage. Like many reformers, Willard's enthusiasm for reform seemed unbounded by any one interest. Her rhetoric tended toward the Manichean, and consequently her perceptual world was created of as many assembled evils as assembled goods. Her Manichean tendencies were of a piece with her rhetoric, whose synecdoches, images, and metaphors of social evil were made more vivid in being contrasted with their opposites.

Perhaps most interesting among Willard's speeches were those that preached Christian socialism, the so-called "Social Gospel." By considering the plight of women from the standpoint of socialism, Willard was able to discern the importance of shared property rights, the male domination of scientific knowledge about contraception, and the need for co-education. Willard, whose fertile mind conceived many impressive metaphors, called for a "moral evolution" to match the physical evolution that Darwin had pronounced. To the existing tide of Christian millenialism Willard added a strong current that pushed for reforms in the role and status of women.

J.A.C. Brown in *Techniques of Persuasion* comments that the temperance movement is a remarkable example of one which, though effective for a time, was undermined by the fundamental currents of society (77). This is certainly true when one considers prohibition alone, but Willard's rhetoric succeeded in securing permanent improvements in the social and political status of women. Paradoxically, Willard's rhetoric, though it set the stage for successful reforms, has gone unremembered and largely ignored by historians. For some of the very reasons Willard might have anticipated, she does not enjoy the fame of her male counterparts. One cannot help but think that if Willard had been a man her place in history would be materially improved. Her oratory is no less impressive in substance or style than the oratory of men in the same era. Women were doomed to be outsiders agitating against the establishment while male reformers mounted platforms in culturally sanctioned political arenas that amplified their rhetoric and gave it greater historical permanence. Without asking us to walk the line of political correctness recently laid down by a new generation of reformers, Leeman wants us to see that Willard is an important orator when judged by a genderless standard of oratorical significance.

Of course, the canon of American public address cannot be enlarged without such groundbreaking work as Leeman's; a case must be made for Willard and those like her. Quite apart from the satisfaction this book should give those who believe the canon of American public address should be reconstituted to include forgotten women and minority members, the guild of rhetorical critics should find this book a strong validation of the intellectual efficacy of its traditional tools and

techniques. I trust this book will cause scholars to rethink the place of
this important American.

Bernard K. Duffy

Acknowledgments

Few tasks are harder than acknowledging the debt an author owes to fellow scholars, archivists, editors, family and friends. Words, as students of rhetoric are especially aware, are often insufficient to express one's sense of gratitude to those who have helped nurture, sustain, challenge, and assist. While those errors certain to be discovered within these pages are unquestionably the result of my own failings, any successes also found are the result of the collaborative effort of many, whom I here sincerely thank. Those acknowledged below are simply those whose contributions are most easily identified.

My appreciation goes first of all to Bernie Duffy and Halford Ryan, the series editors, for having the courage and openness to accept and endorse my study of an orator that many had forgotten. Similar appreciation goes to Mildred Vasan, senior editor for Social and Behavioral Sciences at Greenwood, for accepting the series editors' recommendation on behalf of a young scholar and a little known orator. I also wish to thank Bernie for his helpful comments on the manuscript, and at Greenwood, Mildred Vasan, Editor, Politics and Law, and Catherine Lyons, production editor, helped bring the manuscript to publication.

I am also indebted to the National Woman's Christian Temperance Union for their generous cooperation in providing copyright permissions. The president of the National W.C.T.U., Rachel Kelly, was especially helpful. I also thank Al Goldstein, chief librarian at the Frances E. Willard Memorial Library, maintained by the W.C.T.U., for choosing the photograph used for the frontispiece.

I wish also to acknowledge my intellectual debt to those scholars of history and rhetoric whose earlier efforts made possible my own. I not only appreciated but thoroughly enjoyed the works of Rachel

Strachey, Mary Earhart, Susan Earl Dyes Lee, Ida Tetreault Miller, and Ruth Bordin. Their scholarly investigations of Willard's life and work provided much of the inspiration and motivation for my own. I also appreciate the work of the Ohio Historical Society in microfilming the Temperance Papers of the W.C.T.U. This book would not have reached completion when it did without the availability of those records.

At the University of North Carolina at Charlotte, the staff of the Interlibrary Loan department were indispensably helpful. They procured virtually everything I requested, from microfilmed archives to century old newspapers to obscure editions of Willard's own books.

My colleagues in the Communication Studies program and the Department of English at UNCC were supportive in the extreme. The department gave me additional released time to devote to researching and writing, and Mark West lent his expertise in literature to help track down some of Willard's more obscure literary references. Of my colleagues, I especially thank Bill Hill for his careful reading of the manuscript as it unfolded.

Of all those for whom words are insufficient to express my gratitude, greatest among them are the thanks I owe to my wife, Carol. She was supportive, concerned, interested, and inquisitive, all in the proper measure. She listened without complaint to unending discussions of the work and she tolerated my obsession, but she also helped me leave it "at the office" when the time came for that, too. For her patience and her love, and with heartfelt appreciation, I dedicate this book to Carol Bibby Leeman.

I
CRITICAL ANALYSIS

1
The "Do Everything" Reformer

If one were, like Cicero, to outline the ideal course of development by which a person might grow to be an orator, such a resume would probably resemble the life of Frances E. Willard. She was raised in a household that instilled in her the value of education and, within a clearly demarcated code of conduct, formulated a habit of independent thought. She began her professional life as an educator, and there she first developed the skill of speaking in public on a variety of subjects to audiences of diverse backgrounds. She became the head of a woman's college, a position that taught her skills in administration, organization, fundraising, and community relations.

After resigning her position as dean in 1874, she turned to temperance work, which included giving lectures whenever and wherever invitations and local customs allowed. She joined the Lyceum Bureau for a time, which provided opportunities for addressing a wider variety of audiences. Her development as a speaker culminated in her position as president of the Woman's Christian Temperance Union. From that post, for nineteen years until her death, Frances Willard delivered literally thousands of speeches on a wealth of topics. During that time she never stopped developing herself as an orator speaking to the nation's ills. Her yearly presidential addresses reveal an evolution of thought and reflect an active habit of inquiry. That Frances Willard experienced considerable opportunities to nurture her talents as an orator is the subject of this chapter. What she did with those opportunities will be the subject of this book.

GROWING UP

Frances E. Willard was born on September 28, 1839, the fourth of five children, of whom only three survived past infancy. The eldest daughter of Josiah and Mary Willard, Frances joined an older brother, Oliver, and was followed by a younger sister, Mary. A successful farmer and businessman in Churchville, New York, Josiah sold his farm in 1841 and moved the family to Oberlin, Ohio, in order to prepare for the ministry. Oberlin College offered two attractions: its president—the great revivalist Charles G. Finney—and coeducational classes. The latter offered Frances's mother, a schoolteacher until she married at age 26, the opportunity to also attend classes at the college. In 1846 Frances' father displayed symptoms of tuberculosis, and the family moved once again, this time to Janesville, Wisconsin, following the doctor's recommendation that Josiah pursue the "clean air" of farming.

At Janesville, Josiah was elected to the state legislature and pursued business interests in addition to farming. Their farm, which they named Forest Home, was located in relative isolation. Janesville was fifteen miles away, the closest neighbor, a mile. Besides domestic help, farmhands, and an occasional itinerant teacher for the children, Frances's social and intellectual development were limited to what the family unit provided. Mother Willard gave rudimentary instruction in reading and writing, but much of the education was self-supplied. Frances's autobiography mentions access to an array of reading materials, including Methodist and Free Will Baptist Sunday books, Anti-slavery Society volumes, biographies and English poetry, to name a few.[1] She kept a faithful and extensive journal, which is much quoted in her autobiography. Around the Willard household, Frances was also the instigator and ringleader of frequent games and clubs, such as the Artist Club, the Rustic Club, and Fort City, which was Forest Home re-organized into a make-believe city. For each new club, Frances took the lead in creating constitutions, bylaws, rules, and offices.

In addition to providing lessons in civics and writing, these clubs helped form an independence of character that Frances carried throughout her career as an orator. Called "Frank" throughout her life by family and friends, it was Frances who decided which club it would be this time, drew up the rules, held the major office, and directed the activities. Her brother Oliver sometimes joined these games, but did so as an equal. Ability and native talents, not gender, were what distinguished one's contributions to the club. Other opportunities encouraged this independence as well. Frances disliked sewing, cooking, or cleaning, and Mother Willard did little to force these domestic chores upon her. Instead Frances rode horseback, hunted with Oliver, made and shot crossbows, and fashioned most of her own toys with her father's carpentry tools.[2]

That Mother Willard allowed Frances to grow up in tomboy fashion was probably due in part to her generally permissive attitude toward childrearing. Within a strictly bounded code of morals, Mother Willard encouraged her children to develop as individuals. There is also a strong sense from Frances's autobiography and her mother's journals that Mother Willard experienced a deep frustration as a result of her own arrested development.[3] From college classes at Oberlin to isolation on a Wisconsin farm was as great a psychological distance as it was geographic. Mother Willard relished visiting her hometown in New York, with its increased intellectual opportunities. Back in Janesville, she seems to have projected many of her ambitions onto Frances. As she later put it, "I had many ambitions but I disappeared from the world that I might reappear at some future day in my children."[4]

Her father, too, influenced Frances's development. He was a stern disciplinarian, particularly regarding matters of religion. Although he never did enter the ministry, and church was too distant for regular Sunday attendance, he rigidly enforced the Sabbath. Physical exertion was limited to walks around the farm; reading was restricted to Scripture and similar religious fare. He allowed his children to read certain fiction, such as *Robinson Crusoe* and *Swiss Family Robinson,* but "miserable love stories"—such as *Jane Eyre*—were banned.[5] Despite his stubborn streak, he was a caring, if not demonstrative, parent. In her autobiography, Frances relates a telling anecdote about publicly reading *Ivanhoe* on the day she turned eighteen.

Father was opposed to reading story books, and on coming in he scanned this while his brow grew cloudy.

"I thought I told you not to read novels, Frances," he remarked seriously.

"So you did, father, and in the main I've kept faith with you in this; but you forget what day it is."

"What day, indeed! I should like to know if the day has anything to do with the deed!"

"Indeed it has—I am eighteen—I am of age—I am now to do what *I* think right, and to read this fine historical story is, in my opinion, a right thing for me to do."

My father could hardly believe his ears. He was what they call "dumbfounded." At first he was inclined to take the book away, but that would do harm, he thought, instead of good, so he concluded to see this novel action from the funny side, and laughed heartily over the situation, Oliver doing the same, and both saying in one breath, "A chip of [sic] the old block."[6]

Frances obviously took pride not only in her determined independence, but in her father's fair-mindedness. She also took pride in having inherited some of his resoluteness for herself.

Frances and Mary's formal schooling began in 1854, under the instigation of Mother Willard. Oliver was sent to Beloit College, and

Josiah organized the building of a nearby schoolhouse so that the girls could attend. In the winter of 1855, the entire family—save Oliver—entered in Janesville so that they could send the girls to Mrs. Fonda's School. In 1857, Frances and Mary enrolled in the Milwaukee Female College, where their Aunt Sarah taught.

Throughout this period of formal and informal schooling, the range of Frances's studies was impressive. One visiting tutor specialized in botany, and often sent the girls out to collect specimens. Frances's father was a "fact-finder", that is, a weather watcher, for the Smithsonian Institution. When away on his duties as a state legislator, he would have Frances and Mary do his observations for him, and so they learned some rudimentary meteorology. Physiology, geology, history, composition, anatomy, music—at various times in her life Frances studied all of these. If she ever endured them, she reports no lessons on etiquette, sewing, or managing a household. She either did not have them, or they did not interest her.

In the spring of 1858, after one term at Milwaukee Female College, Josiah Willard transferred his daughters to the Northwestern Female College in Evanston, Illinois. Despite Aunt Sarah's employment at Milwaukee, Josiah was disappointed in the Congregationalist school's apparent—from his point of view—irreligiosity. Northwestern, affiliated with the Methodist church, had a religious atmosphere more to his liking. However, even Methodist affiliation was not enough to allay Josiah's concerns, and the family moved once again to be near the girls, this time to Evanston.

Northwestern Female College seems to have played an enormous role in molding Frances's character. In her autobiography she scarcely mentions her term at Milwaukee, but devotes considerable attention to her year and a half at Northwestern. At college Frances excelled in her studies. She was obviously a good, multitalented student. From the first, her speeches displayed a command of language that was impressive, a facility begun with her early reading and journal-keeping but refined in her college years. Her college years were also a time of becoming a leader among women. Just as at Forest Home, Frances was the one who thought of things to do, organized them and carried them out. It was also a time of independence. In her autobiography she writes that there were the "E'er-do-wells," of whom sister Mary was one, and the "Ne'er-do-wells," a group more to Frances's liking. At Northwestern she often skipped Sunday services, resisted salvation, and generally challenged her professors.

Frances's religious skepticism ended in the spring of 1859, as she was nearing graduation. Sick with typhoid fever, she underwent a serious examination of her religious views and decided to convert to the Methodist faith. Her account of this decision suggests, however, that this was more than a "deathbed" conversion. Rather, it seems as if, once she had asserted her independence and withstood both family

and professorial pressure to announce her salvation, she was willing to
arrive at the decision by her own reasoning rather than that of others.
She had decided herself to "come to the Lord," others had not
"converted" her. She graduated in June of 1859, but the lingering
effects of her fever prevented her from delivering the valedictorian
address. Indeed, she spent the next full year just recuperating from her
fever. Then, in the summer of 1860, she began her teaching career.

EDUCATOR

Frances Willard's early career as an educator was a peripatetic
one. In the summer of 1860 she taught in a one-room schoolhouse in
Harlem, a district located in Cook County, Illinois. That fall she took
what looked like a better, though similar, position in Kankakee,
Illinois. She did not care for her clientele there, however, and so in
the Spring of 1861 returned to Harlem, where she taught for the
subsequent year.

Typical of the period, social occasions for young, unmarried
females such as Frances were limited primarily to church, family, and
friends. Frances spent most holidays at home, and her family made
occasional Sunday visits of their own. Wherever she went, she seemed
to make friends easily, and her journal entries speak fondly of walks
with Clara, the daughter of the family she boarded with in Harlem, or
merry evenings of song and conversation with her "adopted family" in
Kankakee.[7] Much of her time outside the classroom was also spent
preparing for the next day and making daily entries in her journal.
There she made some note of the Civil War, but in general the war
was far away, geographically and personally. By nature and upbringing she was opposed to war, and what she does write is largely
concerned with expressions of sympathy for the returning wounded and
the bereaved widows and mothers. She was, however, very Republican and very anti-slavery in her convictions, and her journal entries
celebrate Lincoln's Emancipation Proclamation.[8] Later references to
the war in her speeches invariably recall the righteousness of the cause
and analogize it to the temperance movement.[9] Although her social
life was full enough, romance seemed not to touch her until the spring
of 1861 when her brother brought the Reverend Charles Fowler with
him on a visit to see Frances. For several months Fowler courted her,
and they became engaged in June of that year. Nine months later, she
inexplicably broke off the engagement. Biographers have subsequently
forwarded several guesses regarding the reason. Rachel Strachey and
Mary Earhart argue that Fowler was a man of no small intelligence,
who held his opinions highly and strongly. Initially attracted by this
quality, Willard came to realize that she could not yield her opinions
in favor of his simply because nineteenth-century customs demanded

it.[10]   Ruth Bordin argues that it may have been less a matter of independence and more a matter of intimacy.   In the fashion of the times, over the years Willard had several close friendships with other women, of which intimacy was an integral part.   Willard may have been unable to conceptualize marriage without intimacy, although such unions were prevalent in the era and Charles Fowler was not likely to be an intimate man.[11]   In either event, her diary entry indicates something of her state of mind, and, more strongly, suggests a nonconformist view of marriage.   "For a woman to marry a man whom she does not love, is to make one man as good in her sight, as another; hence it is prostitution. . . .   If I go alone and hungry to my grave, and spinster is written on my tombstone, I will at least stand before God in the next life, and tell him that I am guiltless of the crime [that] attends a marriage of convenience."[12]   After her break with Fowler, Frances entertained one more suitor in 1866, but of shorter duration and less seriously than Fowler.[13]

In 1862, Frances was several weeks into the spring term at Harlem when her sister, Mary, contracted consumption.   Frances left school to help tend her ailing sister, but in June of that year Mary Willard died at nineteen years of age.   Frances was devastated by Mary's death, and this may also account for the general inattention to the war in her journals.   She took the position as preceptress of natural sciences at her alma mater, Northwestern, but in the spring of 1863 took advantage of an offer to teach at the Pittsburgh Female College.   Evanston and Northwestern simply held too many memories of Mary, and so she tried a change of locale.   Although the change helped, in the spring of 1864 she left Pittsburgh in order to finish writing *Nineteen Beautiful Years*, a memoir of and memorial to her sister Mary.

During the next two years Frances wrote, taught a year at Grove School in Evanston, and journeyed to New York to arrange for the publication of her book.   She also experienced her first public work outside the academy.   In the fall of 1865 she was elected the corresponding secretary of the American Methodist Ladies Centenary Association.   In that position she helped raise money for the Garrett Biblical Institute.   The following year Frances had to move again, this time because Grove School was closed down.   Along with Kate Jackson, another teacher from Grove, Frances was hired to be preceptress of Genesee Wesleyan Seminary in Lima, New York.   There, in addition to her duties as administrator and counselor, she gave instruction in such diverse subjects as physiology, literature, and rhetoric.   At the end of the school year she was informally invited to speak at commencement, to be held in the chapel.   As Willard recalled it, "I stoutly declined, saying that while I would rejoice to speak were I a man, such a beatitude was not for women, and I would not face the grim visage of public prejudice."[14]

Willard took a hiatus from teaching for the next several years. Kate Jackson's father, owner of the New Jersey Locomotive Works, agreed to underwrite a tour of Europe by the two women. The trip was delayed until 1868 because of Josiah Willard's declining health, which finally failed him in January of that year. Biographer Ruth Bordin argues that although he acquiesced to Frances's pursuit of a teaching career, he had never really accepted or supported the decision. Her father's death, Bordin writes, finally freed Frances to pursue her independence with wholeheartedness, an independence that first manifested itself in the trip to Europe.[15]

From the spring of 1868 until the fall of 1870, Frances and Kate toured Europe and the Middle East. They attended lectures at the College de France, studied several European languages, visited numerous galleries, churches, cathedrals, and great displays of public art and architecture. They toured the Kremlin and the Nile, Athens, Damascus, Beirut, and Jerusalem. Supported primarily by James Jackson's largesse, Frances also earned some income by writing travel pieces for American magazines and newspapers. In retrospect, her travels provided her with a sense of sophistication and a larger perspective on the world. Although most of her journal entries are devoted to the sights seen and the personages met, she also noted the appalling poverty and the demeaning status of women in many of the cultures she encountered.[16] Indeed, her first public speaking experience outside the classroom and college would come in 1871, with a lecture entitled "The New Chivalry," in which she contrasted the treatment of women in America with that of other countries.[17]

In early 1871, Frances was asked to become the president of a proposed new college, the Evanston College for Ladies. This suited not only her plan to reestablish her career in education, but her desire to do her part regarding "the woman question." Even before opening, Evanston College for Ladies became part of Northwestern University, supplanting the less-than-successful Northwestern Female College, Willard's alma mater. However, although affiliated with Northwestern, the new college was separately administered, even having its own board of trustees, and segregated classes were offered where appropriate. With such independence, Willard exerted significant influence over the education of "her girls." Probably her most significant contribution in this regard was a system of self-government. That is, she replaced Northwestern Female College's extensive list of rules and regulations with an honor system. Rather than giving specific directions, Willard expected each student to act with "a sense of their own individual responsibility."[18] So novel was the system that Willard presented a paper on the subject to a meeting of the Woman's Congress, held in New York City in October of 1873.[19]

By all accounts, Frances was happy in her position with the college. She was challenged by the administrative and fund-raising duties involved, and she enjoyed playing a major role in the formation of young women's lives. She taught a variety of classes that drew on her European travels as well as her previous studies. This happiness came despite continuing financial pressures. Although affiliated with Northwestern University, the college was expected to be self-supporting. Despite high enrollments, from the very beginning the college was plagued by poor financing. A disadvantageous lease and meager fund-raising because of the Great Chicago fire of 1871 kept the college in dangerous financial straits.

In October of 1872, Bishop Erastus O. Haven, always supportive of Frances's work, resigned as president of Northwestern. His replacement was the Reverend Charles Fowler, Willard's former suitor. Whether for personal or professional reasons, Fowler was at odds with much of what Frances was trying to accomplish. Taking advantage of the college's tenuous financial footing, Fowler had it absorbed fully into the university. Frances was demoted to dean of the Women's College of Northwestern, and her ability to administer the women's college was correspondingly reduced. She suffered the situation for a full year, but finally in June of 1874 tendered her resignation.[20] Although she probably did not realize it at the time, her career as a professional educator had reached its conclusion.

TEMPERANCE LEADER

It is not at all clear that Frances Willard intended to become a temperance leader when she resigned as dean of the Women's College. She was, it seems, simply frustrated at the limited role women were given to play in education. She had flourished under Bishop Haven's supportive allowance of autonomy, but the lesson she learned from his resignation was clear. In the existing educational atmosphere, she would ultimately have to answer to male authority. Her reticence to take on yet a twelfth position in education—offered by a school in New York—was compounded by her reluctance to move her mother out of Evanston. She wanted local employment, but in what she was not sure. She moved quickly and easily, however, into the field of temperance.

Willard's decision to work in the temperance movement must be understood within the context of 1874. During the spring of that year, temperance had become *the* women's issue. In Hillsboro, Ohio, Dr. Diocletian Lewis had delivered a lecture urging the women of the town to shut down the town's saloons by going directly to them, to demonstrate and pray. This kind of women's action had been tried sporadically in the past, and Lewis himself had delivered the same basic lecture many times previously, but for some reason—perhaps economic, perhaps social—the spark became a flame and the flame became a fire.

The Hillsboro women demonstrated, prayed, and, within a fortnight, managed to shut down all the town's saloons. News of their success spread, and the women of neighboring towns took up the challenge. The Crusade captured women's imaginations in the Midwestern states, while fewer New England women and almost no Southern women participated in such physical demonstrations. In all, the Woman's Crusade was tangibly felt in some 435 towns, mostly located throughout the Midwest.[21]

One of those women was Frances Willard. During the spring she made several temperance speeches to groups gathered at local churches. In fact, she records the second of these as "the first and last time I read my speech." A clergyman called it a "school-girl essay," and Willard admitted the truth of his estimation. She was even then refining her oratorical skills, however. She wrote in her autobiography that for her next speech she eschewed having a manuscript or even a detailed outline, limiting her notes to topic "heads."[22]   It is clear from newspaper accounts, however, that from speech to speech Willard repeated phrases, sentences, or entire sections. In point of fact, her delivery was probably half memorized, half extemporaneous, much like paid lecturers or political stump speeches of our own day.[23]

After her resignation from Northwestern, Willard travelled east. At the Woman's Congress she had made friends with influential men and women involved with the woman's question. Through these acquaintances she met leaders of the temperance movement, particularly of women's temperance societies. She attended the Old Orchard Beach temperance camp in August. There she met Neal Dow, for whom Maine's prohibitory legislation of 1856 was named, and Francis Murphy, leader of the temperance meeting. On her return trip to Evanston, she paused in Boston for an audience with Diocletian Lewis. In her autobiography she records him as a "kind old gentleman," but thought naive his belief that "if the women would go to the saloons they could soon close them up forever."[24]   She also stopped over in Pittsburgh, to visit old friends. There she experienced her only active participation in the Crusade, as she joined with local women to hold prayer meetings in some of the city's saloons. To her as well as other women, however, it was apparent that only organized pressure could effect the purpose of the Crusade. Too many saloons had reopened once the Crusade had left town. Prayer meetings and physical protests were too emotionally exhausting to be sustained indefinitely.[25]

In the summer of 1874, a conference of Sunday school teachers meeting in Chatauqua issued a call for a temperance convention with only women as participants. They announced that the meeting would be held in Cleveland, Ohio, in November. In preparation for that conference, local societies met to choose delegates and begin organizing their temperance activities. Shortly after her return to Evanston, Willard was elected president of the Chicago Woman's Christian

Temperance Union. At the Illinois state convention, she was chosen
to be secretary and one of the state's delegates to the national convention. Between the state and national conventions, the second National
Congress of Women met in Chicago. There she was elected secretary
of the congress and delivered one of two temperance addresses given
at the meeting.[26] By the time of the National Woman's Christian
Temperance Union (WCTU) convention, Willard had already demonstrated the organizational and oratorical abilities which established her
as an energetic and respected temperance leader.

The first National WCTU convention was held in November of
1874 in Cleveland, Ohio. Willard declined nomination for the
presidency of the organization, saying that she preferred for the time
being to gain greater experience in the movement before taking on a
job of that magnitude. Significantly, within organizations to which she
belonged, Frances always exhibited a marked tendency to avoid
controversy. Just as she had resigned her position at Northwestern
rather than cause bad blood within the school's administration, so she
deferred at this convention to more established temperance leaders.
One, Annie Wittenmeyer, was elected president on the second ballot.
Willard accepted a subsequent nomination for the office of corresponding secretary and gained election on the first ballot.

During the next year of temperance, Willard was heavily involved
in local WCTU work in Chicago, frequently speaking and, as corresponding secretary, writing on behalf of the National WCTU to anyone
who expressed an interest in establishing their own local WCTU
chapter. Bordin credits Willard with doing the organizing which
allowed the National WCTU to grow from eighty delegates in 1874 to
200 in 1875, representing twenty-one states and 7,500 dues-paying
members.[27]

At first Willard drew no salary for all her labors, earning income
only by taking up collections at her lectures. She later recalled that
"the first of these collections was at Princeton in October of 1874 and
amounted to seven dollars, for I had small reputation and audiences in
proportion."[28] She developed a tendency at this time to look at the
Chicago WCTU's finances as her own. Money given to her for "the
work" would sometimes be used to pay for heating the home or putting
food on the table. This would be a habit which she would indulge as
president of the National WCTU as well, obviously feeling that
providing subsistence for herself and her mother benefitted the
organization. To her credit, there is ample evidence that Willard never
used the money for other than subsistence. She and her mother lived
simply, and what she took from the organization she more than
returned by way of services rendered. Indeed, Rest Cottage, still her
home in Evanston, became a kind of unofficial headquarters for the
WCTU. Meetings were held, visitors came and went, her personal
secretary boarded there, yet no money was ever collected from the

organization for this official use of her home. If some of her contemporaries criticized Willard on this account, it was because they felt she should have provided a more careful accounting of her finances, not that she did not deserve the financial support of the union.[29]

Through the time of the second National WCTU convention, Willard was content to work as an organizer, traveler, and occasional lecturer. In the summer of 1875 she visited Annie Wittenmeyer in Philadelphia for a month, working on WCTU business. She attended the National Temperance Camp Meeting, the New York State WCTU convention, and the Third Woman's Congress. The second National WCTU convention came and went uneventfully. That winter, however, she had Anna Dickinson, a well-known member of the lyceum circuit, address a gathering in Evanston. Dickinson was Willard's guest at Rest Cottage, and the two became good friends. More and more Willard became interested and involved in platform speaking. Always a voluminous and able writer, she began receiving voice lessons from the director of the School of Oratory at Northwestern.[30] Besides dozens of temperance lectures at various churches, Willard spoke that year at the Centennial Exposition in Philadelphia, the temperance conference at Chatauqua, and Henry Ward Beecher's Plymouth Church in Brooklyn. Wrote John Heyl Vincent, founder of Chatauqua, to Willard, "[I do not] care for women speakers generally. . . . You are one of the magnificent exceptions."[31]

In addition to feeling the allure of the audience, Willard also felt a broadened sense of purpose. Always pro-suffrage, Willard at first gave only temperance talks. In the spring of 1876, however, she wrote to Wittenmeyer, expressing her desire to begin speaking on suffrage as well. Wittenmeyer instructed her to limit herself to temperance matters, and at first Willard complied. In August 1876, however, Willard gave her first suffrage address, entitled "The Home Protection Ballot," at the Old Orchard Beach temperance camp meeting. She delivered the speech again at the Fourth Women's Congress, and a third time at the National WCTU convention. In her autobiography she recalled Wittenmeyer's disapproval. "At the close [of the speech] I was applauded beyond my hopes. The dignified chairman [Wittenmeyer] came forward saying, 'I wish it clearly understood that the speaker represents herself and not the Woman's Christian Temperance Union, for we do not propose to trail our skirts through the mire of politics.' . . . As we left the hall my honored chief whispered regretfully, 'You might have been a leader, but now you'll be only a scout.'"[32] Their differences on suffrage created a permanent rupture between Wittenmeyer and Willard, and a temporary one between Willard and the National WCTU.

Although she never left the WCTU itself, between 1876 and 1879 Willard increasingly distanced herself from the organization's executive leadership. Early in 1877 she resigned as president of the Chicago

WCTU and joined Dwight Moody's revival in Boston. There she gave daily gospel talks to women's prayer meetings. Moody took exception to Frances's temperance work outside the revival, however, and especially to the presence of her frequent platform partner, Mary Livermore. In Moody's estimation, Livermore was an unacceptable fellow speaker because she was a Unitarian, and, in addition to her temperance work, was active in woman's suffrage. Willard curtailed her lectures outside the revival, but could not long tolerate such a restriction on her speaking. In September of 1877 she resigned her position with Moody, returning to Illinois.

At the 1877 National WCTU convention, Willard delivered the welcoming address, in which she resigned as Corresponding Secretary. Her dispute with Wittenmeyer over women's suffrage had become more heated, especially since she had taken over editorship of *Our Union*, the WCTU's newspaper. Until 1876, *Our Union* had languished, editorially as well as financially. Willard volunteered to try putting it on a more solid financial footing. As editor, however, she repeatedly printed articles that supported women's suffrage. Although Willard made it clear that such articles did not necessarily reflect the official views of the WCTU, Wittenmeyer as well as other conservative members objected to any such publication. Willard strategically resigned as corresponding secretary, but retained the more influential position of editor.

In 1878, friends suggested she join the Lyceum Lecture Bureau, in order to establish a regular schedule of speaking engagements and earn a surer income for herself. "In an evil hour I listened to the siren's voice," she later wrote.[33] For those interested in her view of oratory, her account of that period is illuminating, sounding much like those recounted by present day campaigners on the political trail.

> To go from the genial, breezy, out-doorsy temperance meeting, the warm, tender, exalted gospel meeting, . . . into a human snow-bank of folks who have "paid to get in" and are reckoning quietly, as one proceeds, whether or not they are really going "to get their money's worth," is an experience not to be endured with equanimity by anybody who can slip his head out of its noose. To have a solemn "Lyceum Committee" of men meet you at the train, take you to a hotel of funereal dreariness and cooked-over cuisine; to march upon a realistic stage that no woman's hand has beautified or brightened; to have no heartsome music or winsome prayer preceding you and tuning your weary spirit to the high ministry for which you came; to face the glare of footlights; and after you have "gone through" your speech and are feeling particularly "gone," to hear the jeremiad of the treasurer that "they had n't sold so many tickets as they hoped," or "the weather was against them," or "counter attractions had proved too powerful;" all this is "nerve-wear" to no purpose.[34]

When she quit the Lyceum Bureau, she wrote that she thought her manager was as glad to see her go as she was to leave.[35]

Her brother Oliver died in March of 1878, and for a time she and her mother attempted to run his newspaper, the *Chicago Post*. She also appeared before the Illinois state legislature and the U.S. House of Representatives, appealing for the Home Protection Ballot—that is, to grant limited suffrage to women on issues related to the licensing of saloons. At the 1878 convention she delivered yet another suffrage speech, which won endorsement for her publication of suffrage articles in *Our Union*. Although nominated for the presidency, she lost to Wittenmeyer by ten votes.

Throughout 1879 Willard focused her attention in Illinois, campaigning for passage of the Home Protection ballot. Although the effort failed that year, gathering 180,000 signatures and gaining House sponsorship of the bill were indices of how far the movement had come politically. When Willard went to the 1879 convention in Indianapolis, she did so with immense personal popularity, considerable fame, and, as an active leader in the movement, having successfully filled an array of posts at a variety of levels. Although the National WCTU would not endorse the Home Protection ballot until 1881, the delegates elected the ballot's most vocal advocate as their president. In 1879, Willard gained election over Wittenmeyer by 99 votes to 40.

PRESIDENT

Frances Willard's tenure as president can be divided into two distinct periods. From 1879 until 1892 she was an activist president, working almost frenetically to bring the WCTU specifically, and women generally, into the political arena. She attempted to ally her organization with the Prohibition party and the Knights of Labor, and she increasingly broadened the sphere of its interests beyond temperance itself. In 1892 she became more reserved, projecting a more philosophical, less political attitude toward reform. She died in 1898 still the president of the WCTU, but a very different president from the one she had been in 1879. Significantly, her oratory marked much of her evolution from temperance organizer to philosopher of reform.

Willard began her presidency with a series of administrative changes. First, she procured a change in the rules whereby only dues-paying members elected delegates to the National WCTU. This gave greater incentive to the state and local WCTUs to keep as many members current with their dues as possible, which in turn put the entire organization on a sounder financial footing. Second, Willard decentralized the organization, allowing state and local WCTUs to determine their own agendas. This allowed greater freedom for the local chapters to adapt to their membership. Southern WCTUs could, for example, ignore the National WCTU's endorsement of the Home Protection ballot, while Midwestern WCTUs could petition for full, rather than limited, suffrage. Finally, she replaced the committee system with departments, which were headed by superintendents. A partial list of departments included Heredity and Hygiene, Scientific Temperance Instruction, Legislation and Petition, and Social Purity. To each superintendent Willard delegated great authority, thus giving herself the freedom to travel the country, speaking on behalf of the organization and the cause.

And travel Frances Willard did. In 1881, she toured the South. Her visit helped organize the WCTU in that region, an area suspicious of Northern reformers generally. The subsequent convention was the first attended by delegates from the South. From 1882 to 1883, she engaged in what she called the "Round-Up," in which she brought the temperance message to every state and territory. In 1884 she personally attended the conventions of each of the four major parties—Democratic, Republican, Greenback, and Prohibition—urging at each the adoption of prohibition and suffrage planks. She helped organize and spoke at the First International Council of Women in 1888, where she was elected president of the U.S. National Council of Women, with Susan B. Anthony as vice-president. She attempted to be a fraternal visitor to numerous national church conferences—for example, the Presbyterian General Assembly meeting at Madison, Wisconsin; the General Conference of the Methodist Church meeting at Cincinnati—but, because of her gender, was often refused the opportunity to speak.[36] Despite such occasions when she could not address her audience, during the first ten years of her presidency Frances Willard managed to speak at an average of one meeting per day.[37]

According to many of those in her audience, Willard coupled an eloquent quality with the quantity of her speaking. Many deemed her "eloquent," "persuasive," and "silver-tongued."[38] The *Des Moines (IA) Daily Leader* supplied this description of her speaking style in 1880.

In personal appearance she is rather prepossessing, but would never be taken for handsome. She is apparently about thirty-seven years of age, average height, thin, nervous and intellectual looking. The contour of her face is good but she is near-sighted and too spare of flesh. Her complexion is fair and her hair almost red. When in repose her countenance has the sad appearance indicative of a thinker, but when she smiles in the animation of argument that face lights up until it makes her seem almost beautiful. As a speaker she is rapid in enunciation, jerky in gesture, and has the absolute command of all the words necessary for any effect. She is an orator of practical knowledge, and burrows into the heart of her hearers even to the inmost recess. A fluent tongue, vivid imagination and fervid utterance is the compound that does effective work, and they are each possessed by Miss Willard in a marked degree. The combination makes her as striking a figure as has appeared to a Des Moines audience.[39]

The reported effects of her speaking are remarkably consistent, and much like those described after a lecture in Galveston: "She spoke for one hour in the grand cause [of temperance]. . . . [And] from the commencement to the close of the lecture the attention of the large audience was riveted upon her, and not one word was lost."[40]

In addition to speaking on behalf of the "grand cause" of temperance, Willard continued to support suffrage, but more and more began addressing a variety of other reforms. At the 1881 convention she charged the WCTU members to "do everything." "Recognizing the fact that varying conditions in communities must, in large measure, determine our line of action, wisdom dictates the do-everything policy."[41] Although the phrase originally applied only to methods—do whatever you are fitted to do in the service of temperance—it evolved over the years to indicate the connectedness of temperance with other reforms.[42] In her presidential address of 1883, she endorsed free kindergarten for children. In 1886, she urged that a delegation be sent with greetings to the convention of the Knights of Labor and she supported the eight-hour day. Her presidential address of 1888 endorsed arbitration and special consideration of working conditions for women laborers. As superintendent of the Department of Social Purity, the only department she retained direct control over, she worked to raise the legal age of consent, toughen the laws on rape, and remove the double standard from laws against prostitution, insisting that the patron should be punished as well as the prostitute. Concerned about prison reform, especially regarding the treatment of women convicts, in 1887 she spoke to the Commission on Charities and Corrections, an association with which she had been active for several years. Within that organization as well as the WCTU, she worked to improve prison conditions.

Just as her reform interests grew during this time period, so did her involvement in politics. In 1880, Willard encouraged members to "be involved" in the presidential campaign, and she personally endorsed the Republican candidate, James Garfield. Garfield and the Republicans, however, were cool to the petitions of the WCTU, and in

1881 Willard declared herself a supporter of the Prohibition Party. In 1883, Willard sponsored a resolution that was a thinly veiled endorsement of the Prohibition party. It asked members to support the party—"by whatever name called"—that most closely endorsed the temperance and suffrage positions of the WCTU. The following year, at the Prohibition party's convention, Willard gave the speech that seconded the nomination of John St. John for president.

Opposition to such political involvement was intense, however. J. Ellen Foster, president of the National Association of Republican Women's Clubs, objected to Willard's partisanship. Willard presented a vigorous defense in her 1884 presidential address, "Gospel Politics." At that convention, Willard proposed and the WCTU passed a stronger resolution endorsing the Prohibition party. Foster led the challenge to that resolution in each of the following years until the presidential election of 1888. Frustrated at Willard's formidable hold on the national membership, in 1889 Foster formed the Non-partisan WCTU.

By 1888, Frances Willard was a major player in the Prohibition party. For the first time, she managed to have a suffrage plank included in the party's platform. The party, however, suffered a convincing defeat in the general election. Willard called for a congress of the major reform parties of the time: the Prohibition, Greenback, Union Labor, National Reform, and Farmers' Alliance parties. This Congress, and another in 1892, laid the groundwork for the Populist party. The 1892 meeting, however, declared suffrage a "state and local issue," a clear defeat for Frances Willard's agenda and marking her last active involvement in the political arena.

The year 1892 was something of a watershed for Frances Willard's career as president of the WCTU. She had suffered a major political defeat with the Populist Party. In August of that year, her mother, and lifelong confidant, Mary Willard, died. Frances had met Lady Henry Somerset, president of the British Women's Temperance Association, at the first World's WCTU convention in 1891, and, upon Mother Willard's death, Lady Henry invited Frances to come visit her in England. Frances accepted the invitation, and from 1892 until her death in 1898 she spent more than half her time in England, where she became far more engaged in advocating reform generally, and much less engaged with directing the American temperance movement specifically.

In England, Willard became interested in a variety of new ideas. She investigated phrenology and psychic phenomenon. She wrote pamphlets advocating bicycle riding and clothing reform for women.

She was attracted to the Christian socialist philosophy of the Fabians. She toured England and the continent, delivering temperance and reform lectures. In 1896 she was in Marseilles, working to find temporary housing for the Armenian refugees. She helped agitate to have Turkey admit the Red Cross to Armenia. During this decade, she was also became the first president of the World's WCTU. First elected in 1891, she continued in that office until her death in 1898.

As always, her presidential addresses to the National WCTU provided a remarkably accurate mirror of her year's activities. In 1893, pleading ill health, Willard sent Lady Henry to read her address to the national convention. The speech was a comprehensive defense of the "Do Everything" policy. Significantly, that policy was no longer controversial in America—but it was in England. In her 1894 and 1895 addresses, Willard for the first time suggested that poverty may be the root cause of intemperance, rather than intemperance the cause of poverty. This constituted a fundamental shift in attitude, implying that such reforms as prohibition were ill-founded. If her new formulation of the problem were correct, then alcohol abuse would only be alleviated by reducing poverty, not by outlawing the sale of liquor. Willard's 1895 presidential address illustrated her global concerns, making reference to the Polyglot Petition which, begun eleven years previously, was a petition to be signed by women around the world for presentation to every government. In her final presidential address, at the 1897 convention, Willard openly declared herself to be a Christian Socialist.

Throughout this period, despite her absences and her change of philosophy, Frances Willard was re-elected president of the National WCTU by overwhelming majorities. Rumors permeated the WCTU, however. Miss Willard was not really ill, they said, she was more taken with helping Lady Henry than with her own WCTU, and in England she and Lady Henry drank wine at the dinner table. Her absence was most keenly felt, however, in regard to the Temple project. The Temple was an office tower built by the National WCTU in downtown Chicago. Initially, Willard allowed the Temple project to be run like one of the departments, with great control going to its director, Matilda Carse. Carse's inexperience with complex financial matters was exacerbated by the financial Panic of 1893, and, for some years, the project's debt was a serious drain on the organization's finances. Support for maintaining ownership of the building became a test of loyalty to Frances Willard herself. However, in the deepest year of the crisis, 1893, when the challenge to Willard was most pronounced, only ten votes were recorded against her reelection as president.

Exhausted by her nonstop travels of the 1880s, health problems bothered Frances throughout the 1890s. In 1897 she toured America once more, but concentrated on visiting those places most significant during her life: Churchville, Oberlin, Janesville, and, of course, Rest Cottage in Evanston. To many around her it seemed to be a farewell tour, and her 1897 presidential address sounded like a retrospective on her life. In January of 1898 she went to New York City, hoping from there to sail for England. She fell ill, however, and, on February 17, 1898, she died.

CONCLUSION

Frances Willard was an active, influential orator. Her preparation for the task matched her desire to master the art. She was well-educated and well-read, and was taught early in life to think for herself. She spoke to classrooms full of children long before taking on the public audience. She studied the art of oratory, and taught it. Early in her speaking career, she delivered revival talks and toured the lecture circuit. Given a national audience in 1879, Willard was well prepared to address the serious issues that concerned American women and America generally. Those issues, and her oratorical skill in addressing them, can be grouped roughly into three categories: temperance and suffrage, Gospel Politics, and Christian Socialism. The next three chapters examine these three general periods of her speaking.

NOTES

1. Frances E. Willard, *Glimpses of Fifty Years* (Chicago: Woman's Temperance Publication Association, 1889) 7, 8, 87.

2. Ibid, 25.

3. A sense which is commented upon by almost every biographer. See Ruth Bordin, *Frances Willard: A Biography* (Chapel Hill: University of North Carolina Press, 1986) 18-19; and Ida Tetreault Miller, "Frances Elizabeth Willard: Religious Leader and Social Reformer," diss. Boston University, 1978, 23-24.

4. As quoted in Anna Gordon, *The Beautiful Life of Frances E. Willard, A Memorial Volume* (Chicago: Woman's Temperance Publishing, 1898) 10.

5. Willard, *Glimpses of Fifty Years*, 51, 87.

6. Ibid, 72.

7. Mary Earhart, *Frances Willard: From Prayer to Politics* (Chicago: University of Chicago Press, 1944) 53, 72-75.

8. See Ray (Rachel) Strachey, *Frances Willard: Her Life and Work* (London: T. Fisher Unwin, 1912) 78-113.

9. The exception would be her speeches delivered for Southern audiences, such as those given during her tour of the South in 1881 and 1882. In those speeches, war references were only to the necessity of both sides to join together for common cause.

10. Strachey, *Frances Willard*, 78-113; and Earhart, *Frances Willard*, 55-57.

11. Bordin, *Frances Willard*, 34-37.

12. Willard's diary, 27 Feb. 1862, as quoted in Bordin, *Frances Willard*, 36.

13. Bordin, *Frances Willard*, 37. Willard's autobiography does, however, allude to a mysterious romantic interest. "Of the real romance of my life, unguessed save by a trio of close friends, these pages may not tell. When I have passed from sight I would be glad to have it known, for I believe it might contribute to a better understanding between good men and women." Her "trio of close friends," however, never revealed the person to whom the passage refers. Willard, *Glimpses of Fifty Years*, 645.

14. Willard, *Glimpses of Fifty Years*, 196.

15. Bordin, *Frances Willard*, 48.

16. See, for example, Willard's diary, 13 Mar. 1870 and 6 Apr. 1870, as quoted in Willard, *Glimpses of Fifty Years*, 295-298, 301-303.

17. An anonymously authored synopsis of the speech can be found in "The New Chivalry," "Woman's Christian Temperance Series," *Temperance and Prohibition Papers*, microfilm ed. (hereafter cited WCTU Series), reel 26, folder 112. See also *Chicago Evening Journal*, 22 Mar. 1871.

18. Isabella Parks, as quoted in Gordon, *The Life. of Frances E. Willard*, 63.

19. *Woman's Journal*, 1 Nov. 1873: 352.

20. The fullest discussion of the controversy may be found in Earhart, *Frances Willard*.

21. Susan Earls Dye Lee, "Evangelical Domesticity: The Origins of the Woman's National Christian Temperance Union under Frances E. Willard," diss., Northwestern University, 1980, 122.

22. Willard, *Glimpses of Fifty Years*, 336-337.

23. For additional discussion of Willard's style of delivery, see Chapter 2, notes 6 and 21.

24. Willard, *Glimpses of Fifty Years,* 338.

25. Lee, "Evangelical Domesticity," 111-112, 166-175, 200-201.

26. A synopsis of Willard's speech, a "lengthy paper," is given in the *Chicago Tribune* 18 Oct. 1874: 10.

27. Bordin, *Frances Willard,* 79.

28. Willard, *Glimpses of Fifty Years,* 343.

29. Bordin, *Frances Willard,* 77.

30. WCTU Series, reel 27, folder 114. See also, R. L. Cunnock to Anna Gordon, 2 Apr. 1898, WCTU Series, reel 27, folder 114.

31. John Heyl Vincent to Willard, 6 June 1877, WCTU Series, Reel 11.

32. Willard, *Glimpses of Fifty Years*, 352.

33. Ibid, 362.

34. Ibid.

35. Ibid, 363.

36. As a response to these rebuffs, Willard wrote *Woman in the Pulpit,* (Boston: D. Lothrop, 1888). Elected in 1887 to be a delegate to the General Conference of the Methodist Church, she was denied her rightful seat by a vote of the conference. Aware that organized opposition to her election existed, she did not attend, preferring to avoid conflict within the church. Characteristically, rather than physically confront her opposition, she chose to respond in her 1888 presidential address. She continued to campaign for admittance of women, a campaign not won until a vote at the 1896 conference allowed women to be delegates to the 1904 conference. See Bordin, *Frances Willard*, 163-168.

37. Bordin, *Frances Willard,* 112.

38. See, for example, *Williamsport (PA) Daily Sun and Banner,* 9 Oct. 1882: np, Scrapbook 7, WCTU Series, reel 30; *Adrian (MI) Times and Expositor,* 9 Feb. 1880: np, Scrapbook 14, WCTU Series, reel 32; and *Minutes of the National WCTU 1877,* 139, WCTU Series, reel 1.

39. *Des Moines (IA) Daily Leader* 26, Jan. 1880: np, Scrapbook 14, WCTU Series, reel 32. The *Washington Evening Star* has a similar description. See 26 Oct. 1881: 4.

40. *The Galveston News* 1 Mar. 1882: np, Scrapbook 7, WCTU Series, reel 30.

41. *Minutes of the National Woman's Christian Temperance Union, 1881 convention,* 43, WCTU Series, reel 1.

42. See Ruth Bordin, *Frances Willard,* 130.

2
Protecting the Home

From her vantage point in Evanston, Illinois, Frances Willard watched the Women's Crusade catch fire in Ohio and then blaze across the Midwest and into Chicago in the winter of 1873-74. Prayer meetings were held, saloons occupied, and petitions presented to the city's leaders, but, as Willard recalled in her autobiography, "there were fewer writers and speakers among women then than now."[1] She continued, "Some missionary and educational addresses of mine made within the two years past caused certain Methodist friends to name me as a possible speaker; and so to my quiet home eleven miles up the lake-shore came Mrs. Charles H. Case, a leading Congregational lady of the city, asking me to go and try."[2] Acting upon this invitation, Frances Willard delivered her first temperance address at Clark Street Church on April 7, 1874. "For myself," she wrote, "I was frightened by the crowd and overwhelmed by a sense of my own emptiness and inadequacy. What I said I do not know except that I was with the women heart, hand and soul, in this wonderful new 'Everybody's War.'"[3]

After resigning her position as Dean of the Woman's College at Northwestern in June of 1874, Willard began devoting all her energies to the temperance cause. In September, she traveled east to attend the Old Orchard Beach temperance camp in Maine. Willard had already heard the great temperance speaker John Gough, but on this tour she was exposed to the lectures of many other noted temperance orators, including Francis Murphy, William H. Boole, Neal Dow, Diocletian Lewis, and Lillian Stevens.[4] In November, at the first convention of the National Woman's Christian Temperance Union, she heard more temperance speeches, delivered this time by women from the Midwestern, New England, and Middle Atlantic states.

Throughout most of the fall and winter of 1874, however, Willard worked in Chicago and its neighboring environs as a temperance lecturer, organizer, and president of the city's WCTU. Her lectures were designed to alert her audience to the dangers of alcohol, promote the adoption of prohibition, and encourage membership in the WCTU. "Everybody's War" was one such lecture. As one of Willard's earliest efforts, it was heavily influenced by those lecturers she had heard in Chicago as well as at Old Orchard Beach, and as such typifies the temperance speeches of the time. For Willard, as for many others, however, temperance was a "women's issue" because women and children were the innocent victims of men's intemperance. Over time, other women's issues—especially suffrage—came to be included in the standard temperance fare. As a means of combining temperance with suffrage concerns, Willard coined the term "Home Protection." As a phrase, Home Protection united the educational and suasory elements of her 1874 address with a call for women's suffrage in regard to the licensing or prohibition of alcohol. First introduced in an 1876 speech, by 1879 Willard had refined her call for the Home Protection ballot in a speech entitled simply "Home Protection." When contrasted with "Everybody's War," "Home Protection" illustrates Willard's transformation from a minor, imitative temperance speaker to a creative orator of significant note.

EVERYBODY'S WAR

Frances Willard probably delivered "Everybody's War" sometime in late October or early November of 1874.[5] Interestingly, it fits all the particulars of Willard's account of what she called her second temperance speech, except chronology. As Willard reports it, she read the speech straight from her manuscript, a practice she claims to have abandoned immediately thereafter.[6] Significantly, "Everybody's War" is the only extant manuscript of a speech to be found in the WCTU's archives of Willard's papers. In her autobiography, Willard recalled that the Reverend Dr. L. T. Chamberlain called her speech a "schoolgirl essay," and she agreed with that characterization.[7] It is indeed rough-hewn in parts, with some awkward construction and inappropriate use of style. However, it also contains seeds of her later eloquence. Fundamentally, though, it is representative of the genre, the "temperance speech," as given by literally hundreds of lecturers of the day.[8]

The speech begins in a manner typical of temperance lectures, with the story of a "poor fellow" who had led an obviously "dissolute life." Temperance speakers often began their talks with a story illustrating the wastefulness of a life gone to drink. Some speakers, like John Gough, would reveal to the audience that the "poor fellow" was in fact the speaker himself. Those not afforded the rhetorical flourish of confessing themselves a drunkard would, like Willard, often provide some melodramatic twist to the story. In "Everybody's War," Willard reverses the more usual story of the *reformed* drunkard by comparing the *non-reformed* drinker to his earlier self, before drink took its toll. The twist is underscored by irony—as the drunkard says that he has not proved to be much of a friend to himself—again, a rhetorical device typical of the genre.

Willard does manage to incorporate an element of confession in her speech, however. She cannot confess to drunkenness, but it is strategic for her to confess to apathy, for it provides an avenue for identification with her audience and makes her an example to them. Before the Woman's Crusade against alcohol, "I never cared," she says, "it was nothing to me." Unfortunately, however, this ethos-building device is used six paragraphs *after* challenging her audience's apathy, rather than *before,* an error of arrangement rarely seen in later Willard speeches.

Willard's other stories are similarly typical of temperance talks, and each illustrates a common temperance theme. For example, temperance lecturers usually warned their audiences that drinking was an addictive habit. The life of the drunkard began innocently enough—with a "few drinks"—but "the taste" for alcohol would grow until it seized the drinker, and made his life one of misery and dependence.[9] Willard's hypothetical story of "this man who [as a boy] was taught in our Sunday schools," who "got in the way of going" to saloons, illustrates that moral. So, too, do the story of Tim, a "graduate of a seven years course in a saloon," and the opening story of the "poor fellow." A story with a contrasting moral is that of the reformed board of trade member, who turns away from the "occasional" drink "just" in time. The story also illustrates the importance of each individual act of temperate behavior.

Through such stories, Willard and other temperance speakers introduced their audiences to the saloon. While most people had some passing acquaintance with the institution, many of their listeners, and especially the women, had never been inside a saloon. These stories—real and hypothetical—took the audience on a vicarious journey into the land of the "drunkard." Even for those well acquainted with that territory, the stories supplied the audience with the speaker's perspective of the saloon and its product. Even a little drinking was habit forming; those who formed the habit were destructive of themselves and their families; and, though personally responsible for those first steps on the path of destruction, the drinker was also a victim.

Saloons were a temptation, alcohol a deceiver, and liquor the tool of the devil. Willard purposely shocked her audience with the revelation that, in the saloons, Christ was considered a fraud. To describe Christianity and the saloon as "insurmountable and unassailable foes" in an "irrepressible conflict" was Willard's particular language, but it incorporated a dichotomous worldview typical of the temperance reformer. Willard is not unusual when she juxtaposes the image of the rum shops with that of Christ upon the cross. Blending phrases from prayers and hymns into one's text is also typical: "We are taught to pray, 'Thy kingdom come, thy will be done' where? 'On earth.' . . . How is [Christ] going to rule until we get all the rum shops out of the way?" Biblical quotations, metaphorically applied to the question of temperance, are also common to the genre: "How long, O God, how long?"

Like that of other temperance speakers, Willard's use of biblical language, lessons, and imagery works to reinforce a Manichean conception of alcohol and Christianity.[10] Temperance reform is the war of Christianity against alcohol: "We are outgeneraled by the people who keep the rum shops—we who keep the Sunday school and church." Her argument is literal: Until those working for temperance "get all the rum shops out of the way," Christ cannot return to rule on earth. Thus, Willard can say of herself that she believes she is "on the errand I believe God sent me to go upon."

Other references and stylistic devices in "Everybody's War" similarly echo the temperance genre. It was typical phrasing to say that one would "taste a drunkard's death," or that a drunkard had "got in the way of going there," and "the habit grew upon him." Analogizing the temperance reform with the abolitionist movement and the Civil War, as Willard does with her allusion to the "irrepressible conflict," was also common. Willard's particular use of statistics is also representative. Infrequently used, statistics typically supported two points for the temperance speaker: the growing drinking problem in America and the economic toll incurred by the liquor trade. In "Everybody's War" statistical evidence serves both ends. Willard enumerates the number of drinkers who die each year and the number of steady, moderate, and occasional drinkers in America, all ready to march "to a drunkard's tomb." She also compares the $70 million raised in excise taxes on alcohol with a figure of $90 million which, because of alcoholism, is spent on police, prisons, hospitals, and homes for the friendless.

Finally, "Everybody's War" typifies the usual temperance lecture because of its antiforeigner undercurrent. The "alcohol problem" was frequently portrayed as one caused by the influx of immigrants. In 1874, the two major classes of immigrants were the Irish and the Germans. The former were stereotypically associated with drinking whiskey, the latter with beer. So strong was this theme that Joseph Gusfield, in *The Symbolic Crusade*, argues that Prohibition was primarily a struggle of the rural, Protestant, native population to exert its influence in an America that was increasingly becoming urban,

Catholic, and immigrant.[11]   Others have questioned this conclusion, but Gusfield's observation that the temperance movement contained significant antiforeign sentiment is accurate.[12]

Willard's speech is representative in that regard, as she makes clear almost immediately. "This sort of thing [drinking] might do for others—for other lands, but it will not do for the land of the star spangled banner." She juxtaposes the rum shop's "series of lessons, international if you please," with those of the Sunday school. Her dismissal of the Eskimo, Polynesians, and American Indians as "such people" is typically ethnocentric. Her rhetorical decision to compare America's system of government with that of Germany is purposeful. In later speeches her condemnation of Germans and their "habits and drinking customs" becomes somewhat more muted. She never, however, completely abandons the rhetorical tack of associating foreign cultures with the affliction of alcohol.

These imitative qualities of "Everybody's War" betray Willard's oratorical inexperience. Later speeches, although sounding familiar temperance themes, are far more original in their language, evidence, and arguments. Similarly, there are other significant features of "Everybody's War" which mark it as an early effort in Willard's career as an orator. For example, Willard sometimes sounds like the schoolteacher she had been, addressing her audience in condescending tones. Some of this occurs because children were present in the audience, although one wonders whether even they might have been offended by parts of it. "Let me tell you young people the way I seem to see it [the temperance movement] now. You just reflect." When addressing the adults, the effect is worse. "I don't suppose everybody who is listening to me knows what all these drinks are made out of." This condescending undertone, however, would not be repeated in later speeches.

Willard's organization and transitions also indicate a beginning speech writer at work. Several times she raises points of discussion only to dismiss them peremptorily with a "I shall not dwell on that" or a "There is no use in stopping to dwell longer."   She begins her conclusion early, with two awkward transition sentences: "I want to say a few words more before I close. I want to say just this one thing more on this subject." She then goes on to discuss five more points: men's votes, donating to the cause in hard times, boys' responsibilities, young ladies' responsibilities, and the story of her sister Mary.

There are other organizational problems. For example, she needlessly repeats her portrait of the inebriate who "staggers up to the polls and drops in the ballot on election day." Or, she says, "I was going to talk about the harm the liquor traffic does to the country and flag we love so well, for I tell you I always loved the flag," which suggests that she changed her mind about what to talk about while writing the speech and never revised her transition. The sentence makes no sense, however, because she has at this point of the speech already described some of that harm. Her occasionally awkward or inartistic transitions—for example, the use of "another thing"—also suggest the organizational deficiencies of the speech.

While its organization is generally awkward, "Everybody's War" reveals Willard's early love of composition and her habitual search for the well-turned phrase. She typically enjoys the use of parallel construction; for example, "and between these two (church and school) are institutions called a saloon, equally guaranteed by our laws—equally fostered by our nation; and more than equally patronized by our people." Using *gradatio*, Willard often arranges her parallel constructions climactically; for example, whisky shops grind out destruction "all the days of every week, all the weeks of every month, and all the months of every year." Metaphors are plentiful: taxpayers are a cat's paw; drunkards' votes are bleared ballots; the world is awake; and the temperance movement is on the enemy's track.

While most of her rhetorical figures are simple in formulation, others are more artfully constructed. There is a sense of irony, for example, in saying that Tim is a "graduate in a seven years course in a saloon." Her alliterative "fevered fancy of woman's dreams" subtly attributes to the liquor industry a dismissive attitude toward women, and her anthimeria[13] "we are outgeneraled [by the rum dealers]" quickly connotes the considerable task which confronts the temperance movement.

In "Everybody's War," however, Willard's reach for eloquence sometimes exceeds her grasp. For example, when she asks her audience "to fathom the unfathomable," it sounds more like a mundane contradiction of terms than a poetic use of oxymoron. Similarly, she appears to strain when reaching for antanaclasis[14] when she asks, "What fruits can we expect but salary grabbers, credit rings, whisky rings, post tradership rings, and every sort of ring except the ring of true metal?" Because the term "true metal" lacks an antecedent definition, the double use of "ring"—as metal artifact and type of sound—appears artificial, even by nineteenth-century standards.

Willard's use of the rhetorical question yields similar conclusions. Early in the speech she challenges her audience by asking, "I want to ask you now, if you have not formed before in this work [temperance], hadn't you better in the name of these boys and girls sitting here? Hadn't you better?" The directness of her question as well as her repetition of the key phrase helps make this rhetorical question effective. Later in the speech, however, she asks a series of ill-defined, ill-formed questions which diffuse the focus of her argument rather than sharpen it.

I am here to ask you just this simple question. Is all this anything at all to you? How do you stand affected by it? How are you toward the temperance reform? How are you in the sentiments you cherish in your hearts, that is it. You know what Mrs. Stowe said about it. If you can't say anything about it, you can feel right. How are you in the sentiments you express? How are you on election day, when aldermen are to be elected? How are you when a notice comes for a primary? How do you stand on the question of New Year's Day? How do you stand in the social sanctity? Let me tell you it makes all the difference in the world how you *stand*, though you never say one word or give one dollar toward our cause. If you only just care.

In addition to using too many questions, which scatter thought rather than focus it, she weakens the effect of her argument by saying she is here to ask "a simple question." Such a preview might be effective if there were a sense of irony intended, but here it simply appears to be an editorial oversight. Similarly, whereas in the earlier example Willard was content to let the audience answer "hadn't you better," in this later section Willard feels compelled to assert the answer twice.

Finally, Willard's use of metaphor reveals a speaker sometimes struggling too hard for effect. While many of her metaphors are well-formulated, others seem ill-chosen. For example, to make her financial plea by saying that temperance workers cannot, "like King Midas," turn everything they touch into gold seems a trite comparison. Or, in another instance, she analogizes the temperance workers' devotion to that of Hannibal, a metaphor which invites the conclusion that temperance is a lost, albeit noble, cause. After all, Hannibal led his troops to defeat—an association Willard probably does not mean to evoke.

In this speech, Willard's reach for style often exceeds her grasp, and at other junctures in the speech she fails to take advantage of opportunities to achieve eloquence. In the following passage, for example, climactic structure would effectively add texture to her argument; instead, the passage trails off with its reference to "book-stores": "I tell you my eyes have been opened with wonder to see things I didn't use to see at all. I saw dear friends going up and down our streets. I saw things I liked to see. I saw [undecipherable] and homes on every side of the way. I saw churches which are suggestive of immortal hope. I saw bookstores at once honey hives of thought."

Similarly, in another passage Willard mitigates the impact of her comparison by vacillating about the number of saloons, barkeepers, and times that churches are open: "There are in this city, for instance, a number of churches and for every church there are from twenty-five to thirty whisky shops. There are for every minister twenty-five or thirty barkeepers, and while the churches only meet and open their blessed doors once or twice, or at most four or five times a week, the whisky shops grind on their mill of destruction all the days of every week, all the weeks of every month, and all the months of every year." In later speeches, Willard would rarely miss the opportunity to usefully employ climactic arrangement, nor would she distract attention from her central argument by unnecessarily qualifying her statistics.

A comparison here will illustrate the difference between this early speech of Willard's and her later efforts. In "Everybody's War" she describes the "war" thusly: "We have an irrepressible conflict, a war to the knife and the knife to the hilt. Only one can win, the question is which one is it going to be." In this description, she includes a graphic metaphor—war to the knife and the knife to the hilt—in order to convey her sense of the life-threatening nature of the struggle against alcohol. It is a workable though unimpressive use of the metaphor. Five years later, however, she resurrects the metaphor in "Home Protection." There, rather than employ it neutrally, she uses it specifically to characterize the war being waged *by* the liquor interests *against* the WCTU.

> Yet a few men and women, densely ignorant about [the Home Protection] movement, have been heard to say: "Who knows that women will vote right?" . . . Have distillers, brewers, and saloon-keepers, then, more confidence in women's sense and goodness than she has herself? They have a very practical method of exhibiting their faith. They declare war to the knife and the knife to the hilt against the Home Protection Movement. By secret circulars, by lobbyists and attorneys, by the ridicule of their newspaper organs, and threats of personal violence to such women of their families as sign our petition, they display their confidence in womankind.

By using the metaphor to denounce the opponent rather than describe the general conflict, it becomes more vivid, more threatening, and more strongly condemnatory of the liquor industry.

It overstates the case, however, to say that in "Everybody's War" Willard's oratory was purely in its embryonic stages. As noted above, the speech includes some artistic use of parallel construction, irony, rhetorical question, and metaphor. The speech also reveals Willard's use of some rhetorical devices which would characterize her oratory throughout her temperance career. These include her use of synecdoche,[15] maxims, and her ability to directly address her audience.

From the start, Willard demonstrates a proclivity and an ability to summarize her arguments in a name, phrase or slogan. As president of the WCTU she would campaign for Home Protection and a "white life for two," and give to the organization its motto: "For God and Home and Native Land."[16] In this early temperance speech Willard attempts to rally her audience to fight in "Everybody's War," and at times uses such synecdochic phrasing in clear, well-defined terms. For example, her use of personification makes vivid the two temptations of alcohol: "let us go in [to the saloon] with some friend and see this transaction. Behind the counter stands avarice, before the counter appetite, and between the two a transaction that puts a few dimes into the till of the proprietor and throws voluntary insanity into the brain of the patron." Similarly, she pithily dismisses the "keep liquor legal so we can tax it" argument by calling it "that old financial basis."

Strategically, however, she attaches that label only *after* reviewing the numbers which justify its dismissal.

At other times, Willard cannily employs ambiguity in her terms. For example, she says that there is a war about "that sort of thing which changes men so that their mothers . . . would not know them." There is an ambiguity in the phrase "that sort of thing" which invites the audience to analogize alcohol to any and all evils that would estrange men from their mothers in the fashion Willard describes. Similarly, Willard reminds the men in her audience that "when you go to the election you represent more than you did once. You represent more thoughts, more work, more prayers." The ambiguity in her phrasing invites the men to supply enthymematically which thoughts, which work, and which prayers they "represent" when voting.[17] Whether ambiguous or clearly defined, Willard strategically uses synecdoche and naming to invite her audience to new conclusions about old issues.

In addition to synecdoche, Willard uses maxims to elicit new perspectives from her audience.[18] Syllogistically, she announces that "men are only boys grown tall." She has already set out what men should do for the temperance cause: vote right and act right. The boys, therefore, can deduce her instructions to them: grow up in such a fashion that, upon reaching manhood, you will be able to vote right and act right. Willard uses other maxims analogically; for example, to contrast Germany, where "they know who is to be the next king," with America, where "every man is King," and "ballots are bayonets."

Maxims such as these allow Willard not only to establish common ground with her audience, but, because the maxims are peculiarly her own—or employed within a context of her choosing—the common ground is molded out of *Willard's* perspective. For example, to associate the maxims "every man a king" with America and "where they know who is to be the next king" with Germany is to characterize distinctly these countries' respective political systems. These characterizations, of course, hide as much as they reveal. To mention only Germany's kaiser is to oversimplify its political system, even in 1874. To say that in America "every man [is] a king" similarly exaggerates the degree of equality present there. However, because each of the maxims is more true for the one country than it is for the other, Willard's comparison invites certain perceptions and discourages others. Moreover, because these perceptions are couched as maxims, they acquire the rhetorical power of a truism. Such a move allows Willard to focus the debate beyond these initial maxims and onto other issues (for example, how to counter the "problem" of giving the vote to foreigners acculturated to non-democratic political systems).

Finally, to the degree that her audience accepts her maxims as true, Willard's use of them enhances her ethos as a speaker. As Aristotle noted, maxims are typically considered the product of acquired wisdom and long experience. When credible and appropriate, they confer those traits upon the speaker who employs them. Throughout her career, Willard would use maxims for just these effects.

Willard also displays an ability to directly address and involve her audience in her speech. As noted above, at times this effort comes off badly, as her tone is sometimes condescending. At other times, however, she achieves the effect of engaging in a dialogue with the audience. She seems to confront them honestly, though without rancor, when she says, "Ladies of the north side, I am sad but frank to say it, there has not been so much interest in this quarter of the city as in others." She seems honestly disclosive when she tells her audience that "I am here to ask you just this simple question." Her use of rhetorical questions and first person plural pronouns both work to include the audience in her discussion: "We are outnumbered, or are we not?" She uses the imperative to command their engagement in the dialogue: "Remember it is simply a matter of fact. . . . Let us go in with this man who was taught in our Sunday schools." Combined with her use of maxims, these directed statements, rhetorical questions, first-person pronouns, and imperatives all work to create a dialogue between speaker and audience. When condescension is eliminated, Willard successfully gives hearers the impression that she talks directly to each and every one of them.

In sum, "Everybody's War" represents Willard's speaking early in her oratorical career. She is at places imitative, simply echoing other temperance speakers she has heard. She does not exhibit full command of her rhetorical figures and arguments. At times, her style is too ornate, while at other times it is not ornate enough. Still, it is obvious that Willard is aware of rhetorical style and its importance, as she sometimes achieves the effect she desires. Finally, this early speech shows evidence of certain elements that endure throughout her career—her use of synecdoche, maxims, and her ability to directly address her audience.

HOME PROTECTION

For two years, Frances Willard's temperance speeches continued to sound the call for "Everybody's War," although it is unclear how closely subsequent lectures resembled the address just discussed.[19] In the summer of 1876, she merged woman suffrage with temperance reform in a speech she later called "My First Home Protection Address."[20] Delivered at least three times in 1876 alone, in that speech Willard argued that suffrage for the purpose of granting or denying licenses for saloons was properly within the woman's sphere of interest. Nineteenth-century America subscribed to the doctrine that men and women each had natural spheres of interest. Men were instinctually the leaders in business, war, and politics. Conversely, women's interests were centered on the home and church. Some, such as Susan B. Anthony and Elizabeth Cady Stanton, directly challenged these fundamental beliefs, and were generally dismissed as "radicals" in an age when the term carried considerable pejorative connotations.[21] Willard defended suffrage by claiming that it was needed to protect the home—in which women had a rightful and natural interest. Alcohol, Willard and others argued, posed a singular threat to the home—it made men abusive, drained household finances, and lured mothers' children into lives of crime and dissolution. Thus, the ballot was particularly needed regarding the licensing, regulation, and prohibition of alcohol. Such votes would be Home Protection ballots.

Three years after her 1876 "First Home Protection Address," Willard was giving a different speech entitled "Home Protection." Delivered many times in various forms, Willard used this basic speech from the summer of 1879 through the spring of 1880.[22] The version included in this volume is an early one, delivered in 1879 as a Fourth of July oration at Woodstock, Connecticut. Willard had it reprinted in her *Home Protection Manual*, published later that year. Significantly, in this speech Willard provides a justification for women's suffrage generally, although she allows her audience to decide which type of suffrage—general or limited—they wish to work for.

Contrasting this speech with "Everybody's War," Willard's oratorical development is apparent. To some degree, this is probably the inevitable result of experience. Between 1874 and 1879, Willard had delivered hundreds and probably thousands of lectures and speeches. However, in addition to, or perhaps because of, her increased experience, a clearer sense of purpose in her speeches helped account for much of her improvement. In "Everybody's War," Willard had little focus in her speech, speaking instead on behalf of temperance and prohibition in rather broad terms. The first half of her conclusion called the audience to multiple actions: be temperate, vote right, support the boys, grow up properly, give money to the cause if you can. Her peroration was even less definite, simply admonishing everyone to "be good." In "Home Protection," however, her purpose is focused: The speech is designed to persaude the audience that they should petition for and lobby on behalf of women's suffrage, limited or general. With this purpose as the driving force of the speech, Willard's style is crisper, her arguments more convincing, and her persona as a speaker more pronounced.

Many of the elements characteristic of Willard's style in 1874 are displayed in her 1879 address as well, but they are used here more effectively. Her storytelling, her figures of speech, her use of

synecdoche and metaphors, her impressive vocabulary—all are
evidenced in "Home Protection" just as they were in "Everybody's
War." They are used in better measure, however, because they are
employed for a purpose other than simple adornment.

Willard relates three notable stories in "Home Protection," one
allegorical, one actual, and one a hybrid of the two. As in "Everybody's War," Willard uses a story for her introduction. However,
rather than begin with a trite, pathos-laden story of a drunkard, Willard
uses an allegory for the purpose of characterizing American political
culture. She names her characters King Majority and King Alcohol.
The former is the true ruler of America, a "potentate of [a] million
hands and myriad voices." The latter is the *chief* ambassador of his
Satanic Majesty, a "skeleton at our patriotic banquet" who wishes to
dupe King Majority by offering tribute called "Internal Revenue," that
is, the liquor excise tax. The story has no dialogue, little plot, and no
conclusion. It does, however, permit Willard to reify the problem
which her speech attempts to solve: "How can we rouse the stolid
giant, King Majority? How light in those sleepy eyes the fires of a
holy and relentless purpose?"

Willard's other two stories are similarly pointed, directly serving
the purpose of her speech. The "factual" story briefly relates the
Woman's Crusade of 1873. The moral of the story is found in the
apocryphal tale that, because of financial and political interests,
husbands and fathers supported the women quietly, saying that "the
women of America must solve this problem." Because Willard holds
that the problem can only be "solved" at the ballot box, the story
effectively completes her syllogism: women must solve the problem,
the problem can only be solved through ballots, therefore women must
be allowed the ballot. Willard's final story about "Mrs. Pellucid" is
grounded in her actual experience of petitioning the Illinois legislature
for the Home Protection ballot. She uses allegorical names—Mrs.
Pellucid, Mr. Teutonius, Mr. Politicus—to make obvious the story's
moral. It is a lengthy story, complete with characters and dialogue,
but it all works to a single conclusion: prohibition will not be sanctioned until the majority of voters desire it, a condition that will only
occur once women receive suffrage.

Like her storytelling, Willard's use of rhetorical figures seems
improved by the clear focus of her speech. Combining parallel and
climactic structure with polyptoton, Willard effectively summarizes the
work to date of the temperance movement and juxtaposes its work with
that of the liquor industry.[23] "While they brew beer we are brewing
public sentiment; while they distill whisky we are distilling facts; while
they rectify brandy we are rectifying political constituencies; and ere
long their fuming tide of intoxicating liquor shall be met and driven
back by the overwhelming flood of enlightened sentiment and divinely
aroused energy." Similarly, antithesis is used to contrast the situation

of men with that of women, and of the liquor industry's interests with those of women. "Ere long our brothers, hedged about by temptations, even as we are by safeguards, shall thus match force with force; shall set over against the dealer's avarice our timid instinct of self-protection, and match the drinker's love of liquor by our love of him." Aside from parallel structure, rhetorical questions are the figures most common in "Home Protection," and perhaps best illustrate the point that Willard's clearly defined purpose invites a sharper style. Willard seems more self-assured, generally allowing the audience to answer the question for themselves. Questions asked in a series are constructed purposefully, designed to build one upon the other. "But you say 'Maine is different from any other state.' Why so? Are not its citizens of like passions with other men?" Questions are used as transitional as well as enthymematic devices. As noted above, her opening story ends with several questions which frame the entire speech. A later section of the speech begins with a question: "Yet a few men and women, densely ignorant about this movement, have been heard to say: 'Who knows that women would vote right?'" Finally, Willard poses questions tinged with irony as well: "Have distillers, brewers, and saloon-keepers, then, more confidence in woman's sense and goodness than she has herself?"

Willard seems similarly self-assured in her use of synecdoche. Many of her synecdochic figures are casual, inserting a visual part for the more abstract whole. Cunard wharves, Castle Garden, Hamburg and Cork are all synecdochic in this passage: "Go with me to the Cunard wharves of Boston and to Castle Garden of New York, and as the long procession of emigrants steps across the gangway, you will find *three times as many men as women*. How can we offset their vote? . . . [B]y counting in the home vote to offset that of Hamburg and Cork . . . the opinion of [women]." Willard is just as quick to employ synecdochic phrases which summarize larger, more fully developed arguments. "Home Protection" is the most obvious example. "Tremble, King Alcohol!" is another such slogan, used early in the speech to predict the ultimate demise of liquor through the education of children. In another passage, to call women's ballots "whiter" infers purity, morality, and temperance, and enthymematically recalls the similar synecdochic use of the white ribbon to symbolize the WCTU.

Perhaps her most artful, and representative, use of synecdoche is in her allegorically true story of Mrs. Pellucid. The ultimate moral of the story is that each politician is the puppet of "the folks that voted him in." To change the politician, one must change the "folks," for example, allow women to vote. Willard foreshadows the moral in her opening story, and repeats it in various phrases in this later tale. "I've got to represent the men that voted me in," she has Mr. Politicus say. As for the women, "you hain't got any votes." Willard even uses her phrase when later filing a disclaimer, humorously reminding the audience of the story's moral even while acknowledging that the National WCTU does not officially support her position. "In speaking thus I am aware that I transcend the present purpose of my constituency, and represent myself rather than 'the folks that voted me in!'"

Like her use of synecdoche to vivify her speech, Willard uses metaphors and analogies with apparent ease. Her range of metaphors is wide—from the biblical "Damascus blade" to the colloquial "Old dog Tray's ever faithful." Saloons are being opened in "the *shadow* of the church and public school," Maine adopted prohibition after a "*thirty years' war*," the liquor traffic is a "*pirate* on the *high seas* of trade."[24] In this national war of words—and votes—"*bullets* will be molded into printers' type . . . . [and the] *Gatling guns* will be the pulpit and the platform."[25] Maine was "*sown* knee-deep with temperance literature before we *reaped* the harvest of prohibition."[26]

Willard's metaphors also benefit from the clearer focus of her speech. They are not simply adornment in "Home Protection"; they are integral parts of her argument. For example, she knows that a substantial portion of her audience believes that temperance should be promoted through education, not prohibition. Willard's metaphor of the millstone suggests the futility of adopting only one course of action or the other. "[In Maine], the majority came to believe that, between the *upper and nether mill-stones* of starving out saloons, on the one hand, and voting them out, on the other, they could be *pounded to death*; and they have so *pounded* them."[27] Millstones, as the audience knew well, only work in pairs. So, too, did the nation need both temperance education and prohibition.

The sharper sense of purpose in "Home Protection" enhances much of Willard's general use of rhetorical figures. It seems to give her a yardstick by which to determine which stylistic devices to use, and how to fashion them for best effect. For similar reasons, this clearer purpose appears to improve some of those stylistic elements which announce the speech so clearly as *hers*: her easy use of religious allusions, her maxims, and her manner of directly addressing her audience.

While "Everybody's War" broadly exhibits Willard's deeply held religious beliefs, "Home Protection" contains noticeably more allusions to specific Biblical passages. The extracted passages and emergent themes are typically taken from the Old Testament, and emphasize sin, punishment, and repentance. "Lord, what wouldst thou have me to do?" Willard asks. She has God reply, "Make a chain, for the land is full of bloody crimes and the city is full of violence." Other references to Christianity are frequent: quoting hymns, calling politicians and liquor interests an "unholy alliance," juxtaposing churches and saloons, and contrasting religious teachings with those of the liquor traffic.

One biblical quotation in "Everybody's War" is repeated in "Home Protection," and illustrates the greater sense of purpose contained in the latter. Willard's opening story in "Everybody's War" finished with the temperance speaker raising her eyes heavenward and asking, "How long, O God, how long?" In that speech, Willard leaves the answer ambiguous. She neither answers it herself, nor is the answer clearly defined for the audience to supply. Instead, the speech moves quickly to condemning the need to ask such a question. The question is more definitively answered in "Home Protection," and the speech uses the Bible itself to do so. Indeed, the question and its answer supply the climax to Willard's peroration: "Friends, there is always a way out for humanity. Evermore in earth's affairs God works by means. To-day he hurls back upon us our complaining cry: 'How long? O Lord! how long?' Even as he answered faint-hearted Israel, so he replies to us: *What can I do for this people that I have not done? 'Speak unto the children of Israel that they go forward.'*'

Willard's use of maxims also illustrates her improved style. In "Home Protection" she still uses maxims effectively as introductions to new sections of argument. "As God has provided in Nature an antidote to every poison," so women are the antidote to liquor. "Human heads and hearts are much alike," so, then, must the temperance movement labor to influence both. As with metaphors and synecdoche, however, her use of maxims has greater texture and a surer sense of purpose in this later address. For example, her first use of a maxim in this speech occurs in the first sentence, when she rejects a truism commonly believed by the audience. Americans are not a free people, she declares, although the ruler she later names—King Majority—is actually grounded in the same value system as the rejected adage. Willard also displays a capacity to use maxims ironically and with some humor. Sir Sapient's remark, Willard notes in passing, "furnishes a striking illustration of the power of the human mind to resist knowledge." In each case, Willard's ability to employ maxims with some facility and irony enhances the ethos-building effect of the device. As noted, maxims connote acquired wisdom and knowledge. To use maxims with dexterity as well as ease reinforces that connotation, in this case with some validity. Willard *has* acquired greater oratorical knowledge, and her style demonstrates her experience.

In "Home Protection" Willard again displays her ability to directly address her audience, but this time without the condescension apparent in her earlier effort. Early in the speech she weaves a complex dialogue from "I," "you," and "we," at times joining herself with her audience, while at other times confronting their doubts and opinions. "'But,' pursues our doubting friend, 'Maine is a peculiar state, in this: it has few foreigners, with their traditions of whisky and of beer.' I grant you, there we are at a disadvantage. But go with me to the

Cunard wharves." Willard judiciously uses imperatives—"enter yonder saloon"—to give added texture to the dialogue.

In directly addressing her audience, Willard is disclosive, but always with a purpose. To reveal that Mr. Readyright, the ex-senator denied reelection because he voted for prohibition, is in real life "a Democrat" reminds the audience that many supposed temperance men—usually registered Republican—vote the party ticket rather than for temperance candidates of either party. Therefore, the vote of temperance women, whose commitment to prohibition is instinctually stronger, will be needed. After citing women's instinct for self-protection as one reason they will overwhelmingly vote for prohibition, Willard makes the transition to a second instinct, that of the compassion, care, and love "instinctual" to women. "Then there is a second instinct, so much higher and more sacred that I would not speak of it too near the first." Disclosing her reluctance to move directly to the second instinct indeed allows her to do so. Additionally, it gently indicates her estimation of the argument's relative importance, assigns in greater proportion to the second instinct any credibility the first might have acquired, and further bonds Willard to her audience by sharing with them her own thoughts about her speech.

When confronting the audience directly, Willard avoids the condescension that marred "Everybody's War." At times, she avoids it by depersonalizing her disagreement, implicitly claiming superior knowledge with greater humility, though still being direct. "I don't suppose everybody who is listening to me knows" contrasts sharply with "Kind friends, I am not theorizing. I speak that I do know and testify what I have seen." In another instance, Willard uses a humorous maxim to soften the implicit message that she possesses truths her audience does not while simultaneously communicating the impression that she is addressing the audience directly. "But after all, 'seeing' is a large part of 'believing' with this square-headed Yankee nation; so let us seek the testimony of experience."

In addition to her improved use of style, Willard's arguments in "Home Protection" are also better developed. Her arrangement is sharper, her argumentation is more sophisticated, and her evidence is more extensive. Willard's organization of "Home Protection" obviously benefits from her clearer sense of purpose. Her introduction is more clearly demarcated from the body of her speech, yet effectively establishes the framework of the speech. Her conclusion, too, is more clearly delineated and, in this later effort, contains but a single focus. Its climactic structure is similar to "Everybody's War," but this time the climax echoes the speech, rather than generally charging the audience to "be good."

Where the introduction and conclusion are somewhat clearer and more productively used, the arrangement of the body is markedly improved. The speech parses neatly into four primary arguments in support of its general proposition that only the Home Protection ballot will bring the benefits of prohibition. Willard argues first that prohibition will work, second that giving women the vote would ensure its adoption, third that the common objections to women's suffrage are misplaced, and fourth that prohibition will never be adopted until women are given the vote.

The organization is not only clear, but logically patterned to develop each proposition in the most useful order. Her audience is already predisposed toward temperance; therefore, her speech assumes the problematic nature of alcohol. After arguing that women would indeed vote for prohibition, Willard immediately moves to answering the usual objections to suffrage. Saving for last the argument that prohibition will never be adopted without women's votes is logical. This final argument, that failure is assured until the Home Protection ballot is achieved, gives urgency to her appeal and allows her to move naturally into the peroration.

Even within this organization, Willard further organizes. The proposition that women will indeed "vote dry" is first evidenced by three examples, and then by a discussion of "the nature of things," that is, the two "instinctual characteristics" of women. The proposition that objections to women's suffrage are ill-founded is divided topically into the four objections commonly raised. Even the arrangement of the objections is purposeful. Willard begins with the one objection most damaging to her cause among temperance workers, that women should restrict themselves to educating their boys. This is also her second longest response. Each response after that grows shorter until the last. This sets a pattern climaxed in the third response regarding women's right to vote, of which Willard says "I shall say nothing." She does, of course, say something, but the tone and length of her response is dismissive—"all persons of intelligence . . . have been convinced already." The last objection—women do not care to vote—then provides the context for her story of Mrs. Pellucid. The story not only answers the objection but naturally segues into the fourth section of the speech: prohibition will never occur until women get the Home Protection ballot.

"Home Protection" is not only better organized than "Everybody's War," but its arrangement betrays a habit of thought common to Willard's oratory from this period through to her death. It is worth noting that, in a variety of rhetorical forms, Willard makes extensive use of contrast. The story of Mrs. Pellucid is representative. Where other orators might use enumeration, describing legislator after legislator as having similar reasons for voting against prohibition, Willard contrasts the stories of four—two who voted for prohibition and two who would not. Each has a slightly different story to tell, but in this instance their contrasting tales yield a single moral.

Willard often draws contrasts through her use of parallel structures which juxtapose one idea with another, mistaken beliefs with correct ones, alcohol with temperance, evil with good. For example, she uses parallel structure to contrast the reasons women will work for suffrage under the banner "Home Protection" where before, in the name of "Equal Rights," they would not. "Not rights, but duties; not her need alone, but that of her children and her country; not the 'woman,' but the 'human' question is stirring women's hearts and breaking down their prejudice [against suffrage] today."

This habit of thought generates many of Willard's rhetorical figures, which then combine with parallel structure to draw contrasts and comparisons. Her uses of polyptoton and antithesis discussed above are both examples of rhetorical figures used to communicate contrasting ideas. Similarly, Willard uses the synecdochic imagery of "hands" to compare drinkers' votes with those of women.

Hands which have just put aside the beer mug, the decanter, and the greasy pack of cards are casting ballots which undermine our Sabbaths, license social crimes that shall be nameless, and open 250,000 dram-shops in the shadow of the church and public school. I solemnly call upon my countrymen to release those other hands, familiar with the pages of the Book of God, busied with sacred duties of the home and gracious deeds of charity, that they may drop in those whiter ballots, which, as God lives, alone can save the state!

Finally, the drive to compare and contrast underlies much of Willard's organization and fuels her use of transitions. Her opening story concludes with the contradiction upon which the speech is founded: King Majority is at once the "bewildering danger and the ineffable hope of the Republic." With women's votes, he can be turned to good; without them, he is the dupe of King Alcohol. The speech is replete with sections or paragraphs which contrast each other: the Woman's Crusade with the WCTU (its "sober second thought"), Maine before prohibition with Maine afterwards, women's interests as a class with those of men, Mrs. Pellucid before her lobbying experiences with Mrs. Pellucid after. Routinely, Willard strategically acknowledges conditions as they are or as they are perceived, and then supplies her rebuttal. "The most conservative states are Connecticut, New Jersey, Pennsylvania, and New York, *but* in each of these there are many brave women, who *but* bide their time for this same declaration [for Home Protection.]"[28]

Inevitably, Willard's transitions reveal contrast as an habitual form of her thought. "But" is frequently used to introduce new sections or start new sentences: "But you say," "But I insist," "But the convictions which supply me," "But, as gallant Neal Dow hath it." Other transitions yield similar juxtapositions of thought: "Yet a few men and women," "By parity of reasoning," "Then there is a second instinct, so much mightier and more sacred."

Willard's improved uses of arrangement, contrasting thought, and direct address to her audience all suggest a better sense of the speaker's role as arguer and persuader. Her tactics of argumentation and use of evidence reinforce that conclusion.

To contrast others' perceptions with her own rebuttals is one typical argumentation device Willard employs. Other argumentative devices are plentiful. For example, Willard twice uses the device of the *reluctant witness*, that is, the testimony of the opponent against him or herself. She cites the president of the National Brewers' Convention, arguing that 'surely, this gentleman should be considered as good [an] authority on this subject as a convict is of the strength of his prison bars!" Similarly, the industry's feverish work against women's suffrage is the best evidence that suffrage would bring prohibition. "[By their work against the Home Protection ballot], they display their confidence in womankind. . . . The woman's vote is the way out of our misery and shame, 'our enemies themselves being judges.'"

Willard uses other devices of argumentation as well. *Reductio ad absurdum* is used to dismiss opponents' arguments that since women do not fight they should not vote. "Pray tell us when the law was promulgated that we must analyze the vote at an election, and throw out the ballots of all men aged and decrepit, halt and blind?" Willard employs reification in order to specify the results that would follow the Home Protection ballot.

Let the city council know that women have the ballot, and will not vote for them if they license saloons, and they will soon come out for prohibition. Let the sheriff, marshal, and constable know that tenure in office depends on their success in executing the law thus secured, and their faithfulness will leave nothing to be desired. Let the shuffling justices and truckling judge know that a severe interpretation of the law will brighten their chances of promotion, and you will behold rigors of penalty which Neal Dow himself would wince to see.

She uses enumeration to list portions of the population that supported the Illinois petition: Catholic priests, Irish women, saloon-keepers' wives, Scandinavians, and even some Germans.

Willard's increased sophistication of argument is best illustrated in her ability to use her opponents' arguments and premises against them. For example, many who supported prohibition but opposed the Home Protection ballot argued that the woman's role was to train her sons to vote correctly. Such an argument implicitly confirmed the critical importance of voting dry, a premise Willard then turned against them. "But if she [the mother] could go along with him, and thus make one vote two, should we then have a superfluous majority in a struggle intense as this one is to be?"

At another juncture of her speech, Willard acknowledges that, according to some, prohibition works in Maine because so few foreigners populate that state. Willard attempts to finesse the argument by noting that, among foreign immigrants, men outnumber women some three times to one. Only by granting the vote to women—a class of citizens where "native Americans" far outnumber immigrants—can foreign influence be minimized. Significantly, Willard is avoiding the thrust of her opponents' argument here. Their point is that, because of Maine's population, its prohibitory law is uniquely enforceable. Willard shifts the argument from a question of enforcement to one of adoption by focusing on the one term common to both questions: the foreign population.

Willard does not, I would argue, make this shift because of ignorance of her own argument. The move is, instead, an indication of her argumentative sophistication. The government's inability to enforce prohibition, and its resulting lack of effect, are the two strongest objections to the law's adoption. Willard attempts several answers to the objection, as her use of the millstones metaphor indicates. At this point of the speech she hopes to use the foreign objection to good use; to defend her position by attacking. Indeed, this is an argument she will use again in later speeches. It is hard to believe that she is never aware that the argument's strength lay in its ability to shift ground from a weaker to a stronger position. Willard uses the argument, I would suggest, not because she is ignorant of its logical flaws, but because she is also aware of its rhetorical effect.

In support of her arguments, Willard makes greater use of formal evidence in "Home Protection" than she did in "Everybody's War." Statistical evidence is used more often, and without the vacillation which marked the earlier speech: Twenty-three states have organized unions; of 54,000 papers published in the United States, 8000 print temperance facts; Maine formerly produced 10,000 barrels of beer, annual production under prohibition is seven; fifteen times as much money goes to saloons as to churches; Belleville voted against the Home Protection ballot because it has a population of 10,000 Germans and 3,000 "Americans."

Examples are also plentifully used, often in combination with statistical evidence. Polling Des Moines, 800 women said they were against saloons and twelve said they were for saloons. In Newton, 394 women voted against saloons, with one voting in favor. For a straw vote in Kirkville, ten voted for, twenty declined to answer, and 500 declared themselves against licensing saloons. Other examples are anecdotal: the chivalric German, Mrs. Pellucid, the Home Protection petitions of Illinois, Indiana, Minnesota, and Iowa.

Finally, formal use of testimony is more prevalent in "Home Protection." Regarding prohibition's effects on Maine, Willard paraphrases the testimony of four state officials. Regarding pre-prohibition times, she directly quotes Neal Dow. She uses testimony from Mr. Reuter, of the National Brewers' Convention, to certify the almost negligible beer production under Maine's prohibitory law. She includes quotes from Joseph Cook and Richard S. Storrs in support of the argument that women's suffrage would produce many positive effects.

In sum, "Home Protection" shows persuasive and argumentative polish not displayed in "Everybody's War." Willard makes better use of rhetorical figures, arrangement, argument, and evidence. Others noted her development as well. Writing from Boston to the editor of the *Chicago Tribune*, one Chicagoan commented in 1877 that "Miss Willard has improved in direct and favorable presentation of truth and in simplicity of style since she began her labors in Boston."[29] With its sharp sense of purpose, "direct presentation" and "simplicity of style" accurately describe the "Home Protection" address as well. In combination with her accumulated speaking experience, this sense of purpose probably accounts for Willard's noticeably improved eloquence.

Regardless of the cause of her improved eloquence, contemporary observers agreed with the conclusion that "Home Protection" was an eloquent speech. Listening to this speech, one reporter esteemed her a "gifted, logical, and eloquent speaker."[30] Another wrote that, "even if unconvinced by the logic of her arguments," the hearer would be impressed by Willard's "persuasive eloquence."[31] Her ability to bring new perspectives to old questions was also noted. "Her argument," wrote one, "was ingenious."[32] The audience, according to newspaper accounts, agreed with the reporters. "The lecture was listened to throughout with profound attention, and the many good points the lady made were heartily applauded."[33]

CONCLUSION

For five years, from 1874 to 1879, Frances Willard's work prepared her to become president of the National WCTU. She occupied a variety of local, state, and national offices within the organization. She toured the Northern and Midwestern states, making the acquaintance of many reformers, outside as well as inside the WCTU. When some delegates attempted to nominate her for the office of president in 1874, Willard declined, demurring that she was not experienced enough in the union's work to take on that leadership role. In 1879, despite Wittenmeyer's renomination for the office, Willard felt ready and inclined to allow her own nomination. During these five years, her oratorical ability, as well as her leadership and organizational skills, had grown to fit the office.

Frances Willard began her oratorical career with a solid foundation. She had an imposing command of English, a good sense of argument, a proclivity to engage her audience directly rather than orate at them, and a knowledge of and appreciation for the use of rhetorical figures. "Everybody's War" evidences those strengths, as well as her rhetorical deficiencies. In contrast, "Home Protection" illustrates Willard's maturation as an orator. She still used an impressive vocabulary and an array of rhetorical figures, but they were used in better measure and to better effect. She still addressed her audience in a fashion that made each think she was talking directly to them, but without her former condescension. Her arrangement was clearer, her arguments more sophisticated, her use of evidence more thorough. While her content would evolve throughout her career as president of the National WCTU, by 1879 Frances Willard had achieved her essential oratorical style, as well as established the two reforms which would remain the cornerstones of her career: temperance and suffrage.

NOTES

1. Frances E. Willard, *Glimpses of Fifty Years: An Autobiography* (Chicago: Woman's Christian Temperance, 1889) 336.

2. Ibid.

3. Ibid.

4. Respectively, see Mary Earhart, *Frances Willard: From Prayers to Politics* (Chicago: University of Chicago Press, 1944) 63; and Ruth Bordin, *Frances Willard* (Chapel Hill: University of North Carolina Press, 1986) 71.

5. The manuscript of this speech is in the "Woman's Christian Temperance Series," *Temperance and Prohibition Papers,* microfilm ed. (hereafter designated WCTU Series), folder 112, reel 26. The marginalia claims that this is Frances Willard's first speech, delivered at Clark Church, April 7, 1874. It probably is not. In her autobiography, Willard says she cannot remember what she said at that first speech, an unlikely claim if she had retained possession of the manuscript. Contemporary accounts and her autobiography itself indicate that she made thorough use of her journals and scrapbooks while writing the book.

Several references in the speech are significant for dating it. Because she never refers to the Woman's Christian Temperance Union, it is unlikely that the speech postdates the first National WCTU convention in November of 1874. "Secretary Bristow" refers to Benjamin Bristow, President Ulysses S. Grant's second secretary of the treasury. He was not appointed to that position until July 3, 1874. This reference makes the April 7, 1874, date impossible, and also calls into question either the chronology Willard gives regarding her second temperance speech, or, more likely, her recollection that she never gave another speech from manuscript. Two other significant points for dating the text are Willard's past tense reference to Chicago's nominating caucuses and primaries and her future tense reference to the coming election of aldermen. Political parties in Chicago held their nominating caucuses and primaries in early to mid-October of 1874. The general election was held on November 3, 1874. "Everybody's War" was probably delivered sometime during that interval.

The marginalia labeling this as Willard's first speech is probably based on Willard's reference to "Everybody's War" at the end of her description of the April 7th speech, as quoted at the head of this chapter. However, "everybody's war" was a phrase Willard frequently used to characterize the temperance movement. By 1888, when she was writing the autobiography, it had become a standard part of her lexicon. For example, see *The Des Moines (IA) Daily Leader*, 24 Jan. 1880: np, WCTU Series, Scrapbook 14, reel 32.

6. By and large, Willard probably abandoned manuscript delivery early in her speaking career, except for her presidential addresses. For example, in 1881, the *Washington Star* reported that "Miss Willard read her annual address, a reading which occupied an hour." *Washington Star* 26 Oct. 1881: 4. Her 1884 presidential address includes the notation "[Miss Willard here digressed from her manuscript to say] . . . ," and the *Cleveland Plain Dealer* reported that pamphlets of her address were distributed at the convention. "Address of the President," *Minutes of the National Woman's Christian Temperance Union*, 1884 convention, WCTU Series, 71; and *Cleveland Plain Dealer* 17 Nov. 1894: 6. It is clear that Willard read all of her presidential addresses except in 1896. In that address she apologizes several times for its extemporaneous nature.

7. Willard, *Glimpses of Fifty Years*, 336.

8. For purposes of comparison, see Francis Murphy, "Speech at Columbus, Ohio," reprinted in J. Samuel Vandersloot, *The True Path: Or, Gospel Temperance* (Cincinnati, OH: W. S. Forshee, 1878) 221-232; John Tennyson, "Address," reprinted in Vandersloot, *The True Path*, 200-201; and John Gough, "Apostrophe to Cold Water," reprinted in Frank H. Fenno, *The Science and Art of Elocution* (New York: Hinds, Noble and Eldredge, 1878) 159-160.

9. The use of the male pronoun here is purposeful. Most temperance lecturers of the day assumed that drunkards were male. While there was a tacit admission that women, too, could become alcoholic, few lecturers or speakers in the 1870s explicitly addressed that problem.

10. Richard W. Leeman, "Believing and Make-Believing: Metaphors of Christianity in the Rhetoric For and Against Prohibition," *Metaphors and Symbolic Activity* 4 (1989): 19-37.

11. Joseph Gusfield, *The Symbolic Crusade: Status, Politics, and the American Temperance Movement* (Urbana: University of Illinois Press, 1966).

12. Ruth Bordin, *Woman and Temperance* (Philadelphia: Temple University Press, 1981) xv.

13. Anthimeria is the "substitution of one part of speech for another." Edward P. J. Corbett, *Classical Rhetoric for the Modern Student* (New York: Oxford University Press, 1971) 484.

14. Antanaclasis is the "repetition of a word in two different senses." Corbett, *Classical Rhetoric,* 482.

15. Synecdoche is a figure of speech in which the part stands for the whole. Corbett, *Classical Rhetoric,* 480. A synecdochic phrase could be a slogan, summative sentence, or a short phrase such as "home protection ballot." In each case, the word, phrase, or sentence summarizes and recalls for the audience a larger argument. In "Everybody's War," "Hamburg" is an instance of synecdoche, standing for "cities of Germany"; "decanter" is synecdochic for "any container of alcohol." For a good discussion of synecdoche and its rhetorical use, see Kathleen Hall Jamieson, *Eloquence in an Electronic Age* (New York: Oxford University Press, 1988) 90-117.

16. "A white life for two" called for the elimination of sexual double standards. It campaigned against the social acceptability of young men "sowing their wild oats" and against prosecuting the prostitute but not the prostitute's customer.

17. An enthymeme is an argument in which a significant part of the argument is supplied by the audience.

18. By "maxim" I do not simply mean well-known adages or sayings. Any generalization which is immediately acceptable to an audience--for example, "in America ballots are bayonets"--can be used rhetorically as a maxim in the fashion described by Aristotle. See *The Rhetoric of Aristotle*, trans. W. Rhys Roberts (New York: The Modern Library, 1954) 135-139 (1394a-1395b), 212 (1418a), and 215 (1418b).

19. Willard was still calling her basic lecture "Everybody's War" as late as January 1876. See the *New York Times* 30 Jan. 1876: 7.

20. Willard, *Glimpses of Fifty Years,* 452-459.

21. For a larger discussion of the doctrine of the spheres, see Barbara Lee Epstein, *The Politics of Domesticity: Women, Evangelism, and Temperance in Nineteenth Century America* (Middletown, CN:

Wesleyan University Press: 1981); Barbara Welter, "The Cult of True Womanhood, 1820-1860," *American Quarterly* 18 (1966): 151-174; and Ruth Bordin, *Frances Willard*, 246. For additional discussion of the doctrine and Frances Willard's use of it, see Bordin, *Frances Willard*, 134; and Karlyn Kohrs Campbell, *Man Cannot Speak For Her*, vol. 1 (New York: Praeger, 1989) 125-126, 128.

22. The first reported version of the speech is the Woodstock, Connecticut, version reprinted here. On a spring, 1880, tour of Northern and Midwestern states, however, Willard is reported to have spoken specifically on "home protection." Substantive, detailed accounts of her speeches on this tour are scarce. However, some of the reports mention stories or arguments which are clearly included in the Woodstock version, for example, Mrs. Pellucid's story, God provides an antidote to every poison, and the general organization. These accounts also mention elements of the speech which are different. See, for example, Sarah K. Bolton, "Joseph Cook's Symposium on Temperance," *The (New York) Independent* 18 Mar. 1880: 5; and *The (Chicago) InterOcean*, 14 Oct. 1879: np, WCTU Series, Scrapbook 14, reel 32.

23. Polyptoton is the "repetition of words derived from the same root." Corbett, *Classical Rhetoric*, 478.

24. Emphases mine.

25. Emphases mine.

26. Emphases mine.

27. Emphases mine.

28. Emphases mine.

29. "To the Editor," *Chicago Tribune* 27 May 1877, WCTU Series, Scrapbook 7, reel 30.

30. Untitled Des Moines newspaper, 24 Jan. 1880: np, WCTU Series, Scrapbook 14, reel 32.

31. *Adrian (Michigan) Times and Expositor*, 9 Feb. 1880: np, WCTU Series, Scrapbook 14, reel 32.

32. *Henry Republican*, 29 Jan. 1880: np, WCTU Series, Scrapbook 14, reel 32.

33. Unnamed Des Moines newspaper, 24 Jan. 1880: np, WCTU Series, Scrapbook 14, reel 32. See also *The (Chicago) InterOcean*, 14 Oct. 1879: np, WCTU Series, Scrapbook 14, reel 32.

3
Gospel Politics

Across eighteen presidential addresses, averaging forty-five pages apiece, Frances Willard detailed her vision of what she called "Gospel Politics." For Willard as for many nineteenth-century reformers, politics and the law were the answers to many of society's ills. Laws were, after all, supposed to be the codification of society's moral norms, and politics was the vehicle whereby laws were enacted. Murder was morally wrong, therefore murder had been outlawed. Stealing was morally wrong, so stealing was outlawed. In Willard's view, as well as the WCTU generally, temperance was fundamentally a question of morality. Drinking caused immoral behavior, and was, therefore, wrong. Just as society prohibited murder, so, too, should it prohibit drinking.

Woman suffrage, too, was a question rooted in one's morals. As Willard had so clearly announced in her First Home Protection Address, she entertained no doubts regarding women's moral *right* to vote. Additionally, women's ballots would be necessary in order to secure prohibition and other palliative reform legislation. Woman suffrage was thus both a moral good unto itself and a means by which moral improvement could be attained. However, suffrage could only be acquired through legislation, and, once acquired, legislation would be the mechanism by which suffrage brought moral improvement.

In short, for Willard and the WCTU, morality and the law were intimately intertwined. From 1876 until 1881 Willard campaigned to have the National WCTU endorse the Home Protection ballot, so that women's votes could be secured on behalf of moral laws. In 1881 she successfully secured that endorsement. Characteristically, however, even before the convention's approval was official, Willard used her Annual Address to redirect attention to a different question of politics.

Whereas prohibition and the Home Protection ballot were specific laws sought by the WCTU, Willard also wanted the organization to "lend its influence" to a single political party.

ELECTION POLITICS: THE PROHIBITION PARTY

In 1881, the WCTU already favored the legal prohibition of alcohol. Indeed, the decision in 1874 to create the WCTU was due in large part to the organizers' belief that voluntary prohibition—shutting down saloons via the "praying bands"—would not succeed in the long run.[1] While initially the organization focused on educational and benevolent work, by 1878 the legal prohibition of alcohol had become a central tenet, and was strongly endorsed at both the state and national levels.[2] Frances Willard did not have to prove that the WCTU and the Prohibition party had a common agenda in order to secure the former's endorsement of the latter.

However, two prevalent attitudes among the members caused most of them to refrain from electioneering on behalf of the Prohibition party in 1880. First, many felt that electioneering itself was inappropriate for women, and that the work of temperance should be kept separate from partisan politics. Women could petition the legislature for prohibition, but ought not dirty themselves in the mire of campaign politics. Second, most of those who were inclined toward partisan activity were deeply committed to one of the two established parties. Reconstruction had barely concluded at this time, and sectionalism still ran high. Northerners, who constituted the majority of the Union's membership, were generally devoted to the Republican party, which had in fact made some conciliatory gestures toward temperance. For Southern women, loyalty to the Democratic party was similarly strong. If Frances Willard wanted to obtain the WCTU's endorsement of the Prohibition party, she would have to surmount these two common obstacles. For some members of the WCTU, she would first have to persuade them that partisan activity was essential for the movement. Then, for all but the most radical members, she would have to convince her audience that neither the Republicans nor the Democrats presented an acceptable partisan alternative.

Willard's initial plea for endorsement of the Prohibition party came in the fifth section of her 1881 address.[3] Characteristically, she couched her call for the new in a slogan laden with previously accepted symbols, and titled the section "The Home Protection Party." However, while the title summarized the argument in terms of Home Protection, the address itself focused on the need for partisan politics and the inadequacy of the two existing parties.

Willard begins her call with two foundation-laying points. First, she reminds her audience that she has been a devoted Republican, as evidenced by her support of Garfield for president in 1880 rather than Neal Dow, that "brave father of the Maine [Prohibitory] Law." She recalls her Republican credentials so that subsequently she appears the reluctant convert to the Prohibition party, diverted from her upbringing by the logic of events.

After recalling her Republicanism, Willard testifies to the reconstructed attitude of the South. She had traveled the South throughout 1881 on a speaking tour which promoted temperance, prohibition, and the organization of local WCTUs. Her National WCTU audience, still heavily Northern, needed reassurance that the South could be trusted and that it should again become a full member of the national family. Willard's testimonial also reminds the audience of the tangible success of her Southern speaking tour. The 1881 convention is the first to have Southern delegates in attendance.

Willard then makes a stylish transition to the substance of her argument, declaring that a "re-United States" needs a truly national party. It is hardly her strongest argument, but it allows her to move naturally from the necessary testimonial regarding the South's reconstruction to the central argument at hand: abandon the Republicans and endorse the Prohibitionists. From this transition forward, Willard's two primary arguments become entwined, forming two parts of a syllogism which in turn fashions an argument of residues. The major premise of the syllogism postulates that, in order for prohibition to be adopted, the WCTU must work through the good offices of a political party. The minor premise contends, however, that neither the Republican nor the Democratic party will endorse or actively promote prohibition. The syllogism's conclusion, or the argument's residue, is clear: the WCTU must work through the auspices of a different, third party. Given its obvious agenda, the Prohibition party is the natural choice.

Willard initially argues that neither the Republican nor Democratic party will "do" because both are sectional parties. The Republican party is the party of the North, the Democrats, the party of the South. She does not linger on this geographic argument, instead moving quickly to the point that, regarding the issue of Prohibition, both parties are divided. Willard names names, of Democrats for prohibition, Democrats against, Republicans for, and Republicans against. Neither party, she concludes, can be counted upon to wholeheartedly support prohibition at the national level.

Willard returns to this argument at various junctures of the speech, but moves next to discuss the major premise of her syllogism: Should a temperance organization actively support a political party? In her initial response to the question, Willard justifies an answer in the affirmative by using an argument of equivalency. "Since Beer is already in the political arena shaking its fists, Temperance must go forth to the encounter." It is the liquor industry's partisan politics which necessitates a like response from the WCTU. In colloquial terms, fire must be fought with fire.

In the description which ensues, Willard has two reasons for focusing on the liquor industry's "control" of the Republican party. First, as noted above, the WCTU membership is most heavily Republican, and it is from that affiliation that Willard must dislodge the majority of delegates. Second, among most voters and women, it is the Republican party that was usually identified with temperance. It is Republican First Lady Lucy Hayes who, in 1877, bans the use of alcohol at White House social functions. In 1884, it is the Republican presidential candidate James G. Blaine who calls Democrats the party of "*Rum*, Romanism, and Rebellion." As Willard herself put it in 1889, "The Democratic party pleads guilty and no proof is needed; but the Republican party denies its guilt and thus compels us to furnish proof."[4] Throughout her campaign for partisan "Gospel Politics," Willard would have to disabuse her audience of this "mistaken" belief that the Republican party favored the temperance movement.

Yet Willard's primary point in this passage is not that the Republican party must be abandoned, but that partisan politics is necessary and acceptable for the temperance movement. That the passage works toward both purposes is an indication of the symbiotic relationship between the two halves of her syllogism.

That symbiosis is again clear as Willard makes the transition to the next section. She begins by cogently summarizing her previous discussion: "Parties are the moulds into which God pours principles." Principles such as temperance and prohibition, Willard implies, can be actualized in society only through political parties. Her argument here speaks to the first premise of her syllogism. However, Willard then posits an organic view of politics: Parties form and coalesce around certain principles, enact them into law, and then wither away. Both of the established parties have reached that third stage, outlived their usefulness, and "sadly need interment." Temperance workers should abandon those parties and coalesce around one "committed to the proposition, '*The saloon must go[!].*'" She thus moves easily from the first premise of her syllogism to the second.

In addition to containing both parts of her basic syllogism, this paragraph of the speech introduces a major argument, used frequently by Willard, on behalf of women's involvement in partisan politics. She couches her argument in an activity already acceptable to the membership: "Our Temperance women have long been petitioning Legislatures." However, these "Temperance women" have "grown tired" of petitioning "companies of soldiers"—that is, senators and representatives—elected "for no other purpose than to defeat [our] measures." Logic leads these women to an obvious conclusion: Before petitions will be enacted, political leaders who support those petitions must be elected to office. Just as protection of the home legitimated woman suffrage, so petitioning legislatures makes electioneering acceptable. Once again, Willard justifies the new by planting the roots of her argument in the old.

Willard concludes her argumentation with several testimonials. First, she reiterates her dual argument by citing two sets of resolutions, one passed by the Lake Bluff Temperance Convocation and the other formulated by the Illinois WCTU convention.[5] The former summarizes the first premise of her syllogism: "A political party, whose platform is based on constitutional and statutory prohibition . . . is a necessity." The latter summarizes the second: "We have patiently appealed to existing parties, only to find our appeals disregarded." Both resolutions also include the conclusion of the syllogism, as they call for the endorsement of the "Home Protection party"—that is, the Prohibition party.[6]

Willard's final use of testimonial recalls her earlier argument for equivalency. "Beer" is in the political arena, she had argued, therefore "Temperance" must go forth and also campaign. Now she quotes from the Liquor League's own resolution. "[The League must] make a vigorous fight against all such candidates for the General Assembly, no matter what political party they may belong to, who cannot be fully relied upon to vote in favor of personal liberty and an equal protection of ours with all other legitimate business interests." If the equivalency argument is accepted, that the WCTU must fight fire with fire, then Willard's use of the Liquor League's resolution constitutes a strong rallying cry. It justifies a vigorous fight, against *all* such candidates, no matter their party. The Liquor League's use of the word "protection" is fortuitous, as it allows Willard to make the equivalency argument succinctly: "They want protection, too! and they know the Legislature alone can give it."

The remainder of Willard's "Home Protection party" appeal details the action which she calls on the convention to undertake. Several elements of her formulation are characteristic of her treatment of Gospel Politics. First, she allows room for differences. Her "Second" and "Third" proposals are the clearest statements in this regard. For example, the Iowa state WCTU was staunchly Republican, partly because in that state the Republican party actively supported prohibition. Willard's second proposal accommodates the Iowa position. Also, during this period Southern women were typically either anti-suffragist or reluctant to commit themselves publicly to woman suffrage, even under the guise of Home Protection. Proposal three accommodates those differences.

Second, although she provides room for accommodation, Willard attempts to rally as many activists as possible to her cause. While her syllogism lays the rational foundation for her position, her peroration uses the appeal of praise: Those women and men who endorse the "Home Protection Party" exhibit the bravery of Martin Luther, saying

as he did, "Here I stand. I can do no other. God help me. Amen!";
Ohio men "*dared* to break away from party leadership"; the "*best*
elements" of the old parties will gravitate to this new one.[7]

There is an inherent tension, however, when one allows diversity
but categorically praises only one course of action. That tension is
revealed most clearly in Willard's motto "Falter who must, follow who
dare!" Diversity is allowed, but those who side with Willard "dare,"
while those who do not, "falter." Time and again in her presidential
tenure, Willard invested the membership with the responsibility and
power to determine their own course of action. Willard's preferences,
however, and her impatience at the sometimes glacial pace of change,
were also clearly enunciated.

Third, Willard gives the peroration a sense of movement. She
evokes the imagery of a resistless tide of progress, an evolution of
reform. Maine, New Hampshire, and Delaware "have wheeled into
line beside us." Vermont, Pennsylvania, and Michigan have sent
"hearty greetings." Implicitly, active endorsement will undoubtedly
follow. In New York, Massachusetts, and Vermont, women have been
given the vote on school issues, surely the Home Protection ballot will
be next. Soon, this "new party of great moral ideas will hold the
balance of power." At first, it will hold power locally, then at the state
level, and eventually, "by the inevitable sequence of party evolution,"
nationally. Like many reformers, Willard uses the imagery of progress
and evolution to rally followers to 'take the first step.' As discussed
in Chapter 4, however, progress and evolution come to occupy an
increasingly central place in Willard's lexicon.

In sum, Willard is an astute, persuasive arguer in this speech.
First, she sets forth a fundamental syllogism which logically endorses
the Prohibition party. It is a syllogism she will repeat often, both
before and after the National WCTU passes a resolution of endorsement in 1884. Second, despite her occasionally obvious chafing,
Willard permits diversity, both structural and individual. Even when
the Prohibition party is endorsed by the National WCTU, she does not
insist that state Unions fall into line. Individuals, too, are free to
choose whichever party they please. "The Good Templars, *as
individuals*, may [or may not] be component members of the [Prohibi-
tion] party, but, as societies, they lend their influence, their good will,
good word—and, if any society shall so choose, their good work—to
help advance its fortunes. We do the same—no less, no more."[8]
Willard does not gain the convention's endorsement in 1881, but, by
sanctioning diversity, she strategically allows herself some maneuvering
room for temporary failure. Tolerance is a two-edged sword. Just as
it allows the more conservative unions to lag behind, it permits those
like Illinois to work actively on behalf of the Prohibitionists. The
progressive, partisan activity of some then breaks ground for others to
follow, even if more slowly than Willard would prefer. Indeed, in her

presidential address of 1896 Willard revealed that a similar strategy was used on behalf of Home Protection.

> When some of us in the early days wanted woman suffrage put into the W.C.T.U. platform and our sisters would not do it and used to debate the subject by the day; we who kept up this "stirring among dry bones," as we thought them, then said to one another, "Let us get up a strong resolution out and out for woman's ballot, let the bravest present it, at least the one who is the most convinced; then have another resolution ready that is milder and coach it along with that strong resolution, and the women who do not want the strong resolution will take the one that is less strong."[9]

Eventually, this strategy of "some ahead of the rest" was successful, and electioneering was added to petitioning as an acceptable and desirable part of Gospel Politics. As exemplified in her 1881 address, Willard had provided her membership with both the rationale and the exhortation to move farther along the path of reform.

PETITION POLITICS: WOMAN AGAINST EVIL

In *The Politics of Domesticity*, Barbara Epstein argues that, during colonial and early American history, women's role in society evolved into one in which they were seen as arbiters of public morality.[10] Originally grounded in their religious lives, the one public sphere in which women could participate, their role as the conservators of morality accompanied their transition into public politics.

Frances Willard's advocacy of reform legislation is a singular instance of the politics of domesticity, and Willard's presidential address of 1889 is representative of her discourse.[11] First, the proemium of her speech develops a rationale for reform that embodies the central tenets of Willard's politics of domesticity.[12] Evil is prevalent in the world, Willard argues, and can only be reversed through the active application of Christianity, a task for which women are uniquely prepared. Then, later sections of the speech apply the rationale to specific elements of the reform agenda, some political, some social. Early in its history, the WCTU had elected to campaign for the legal prohibition of alcohol as well as for social education against the custom. Willard applied that dual approach to her entire reform agenda.

Rationale

Throughout the proemium of her speech, Willard weaves the logic of her rationale justifying women's reform efforts. Over the first several pages, she begins by presenting a series of maxims, which, taken together, suggest that women form the vanguard of Christian reform.

Willard begins with the principle that the kingdom of God will be accomplished only through human endeavor: "Immortal things have God for architect. And men are but the granite He lays down." In this passage, "men" is used in its generic sense meaning people, but she quickly details women's unique ability to be God's "granite": "Woman's simplicity and sufferings have made her, more than man, receptive of the will of God." Willard then expends several paragraphs reiterating the moral dictum of being "receptive of the will of God." In a categorical manner typical of her style, Willard concludes that "the disintegration of our wills, that God's may take their place, is slowly dawning on us as life's one beatitude."

At this point, Willard makes a significant shift as she redirects her focus from the principle of embodying God's will to defining what God's will is. The fact of this shift is not significant—it is a typical oratorical turn—but the direction and content are. Willard paraphrases a passage, written by an unnamed "spirit of our age," which calls upon the hearer to "sacrifice to the mob, . . . to that disinherited, vanquished, vagabond, shoeless, famished, repudiated, despairing mob." The idea of the mob here is interesting in its ambiguity. The passage is at once New Testament in its imagery, echoing Christ's command to "sell all ye have and follow me," yet it is simultaneously pejorative, with its use of the term "mob." The mob is "the great victory of darkness," it will "hunt" and "exile" the reformer, and it is implicitly the cause of Christ going to Calvary. There is an evil in the "mob" which is not communicated in the benign imagery of, say, "Blessed are the poor." It does, however, appropriately foreshadow the second half of Willard's proemium.

The remainder of these opening paragraphs are devoted to summarizing the purpose of reform. Through poetry and metaphor Willard argues that the WCTU should be led by the "Star of Bethlehem," that is, it should bring Christ's kingdom to earth. "As Christian women, we should set before our minds the ideal toward which we move in individual life, social custom and national law, nothing less than an agreement as complete between the Bible and them all, as is the agreement between a healthy eye and the light of a June day." In Willard's view, reform begins at home, in "individual life." From that domestic sphere, the "natural domain" of women, it extends naturally into voluntary work (i.e., social custom) and politics (i.e., national law). Significantly, each area of this triumvirate is equally important. The reformer should strive for "nothing less" than complete accord between each area of reform and the teachings of the Bible. With a reference back to the "Star of Bethlehem," Willard concludes this opening section: "Beloved comrades, we are here to guide the old white-ribbon ship by that one star!"

Willard's opening discussion establishes for the audience the broad purpose of Christian reform. Once the direction of reform is ascertained, however, Willard identifies the motivation which impels the audience to move along the path at all. She makes the transition by briefly discussing patriotism, a subject naturally related to the opening paragraphs because "patriotism has always been part and parcel of my religion." This union of religion and patriotism is but briefly asserted, however, because it only serves as a bridge to the next major portion of the proemium, a description of the scene.[13]

In any oratory, the description of the scene can act as a powerful motivating force. As Kenneth Burke writes, "From the motivational point of view, there is implicit in the quality of a scene the quality of the action that is to take place within it."[14] Willard's opening scenic description performs precisely that service for her speech. America's ills, as pictured in her proemium, contain within themselves the motivation for and direction of Willard's reform agenda.

America, in Willard's description, is in desperate straits because it has become "the dumping ground of European cities." The population has "deteriorated" in quality at the same time that it has grown in quantity. Foreign-born anarchists have an "army" of "drilled soldiers" with "many a concealed red flag" and "many a hidden bomb." Business leaders exacerbate the problem, with their "enormous accumulations of capital" and the "octopus grip" of their "Trusts." America is "asleep on the edge of a volcano," in great need of reform. Foreign immigration will not abate, however, and in the course of describing its voluminous nature, Willard summarizes the dilemma that faces the reformer. "A million feet yearly sound the signal of an ominous invasion on our wharves as these strange people come. Whether this swift tattoo shall prove to be the reveille of hope or the requiem of despair for America, doth not yet appear, and depends decisively upon the amount of Christian endeavor that is put forth in the next quarter century." Willard continues with her statistical description of the foreign "invasion," but begins to detail the elements of the scene which foreshadow the reforms necessitated by the "invasion."[15] For example, foreign neighborhoods have few churches, while saloons are plentiful: "All who wish sittings in the *saloon* can be accommodated."[16] Because the foreign-born population is less church-going than the "native" American, Sunday closing laws must be strictly enforced in order to increase church attendance as much as possible. Or again, young males are less likely to go to church, more likely to patronize saloons, and Willard correlates them as a class with the increased death rate and growth of crime. Obscene plays and literature tempt the young male toward immorality. Impure art must therefore be controlled.

From church, crime, and young men, Willard makes a somewhat abrupt jump to describing poverty. There is some "temptation to crime," she says, because of low wages, although the wages she singles out are those of seamstresses, while most of the criminals are male. Still, she laments, "Alas that gold should be so dear and flesh and blood so cheap!" The paragraph breaks the continuity of the proemium, but allows Willard later in the speech to propose wage reform. Also, given her audience, the attention to *female* workers who are poorly paid for sewing *women's* clothing is a natural appeal, to both their empathy and their guilt.

Willard does not stray far from the topic of the foreign invasion. She quickly moves to a traveler's description of poverty in England, reputedly the "best" of the European countries. By implication, unless Christian reform prevails, the horrific society Willard describes in this paragraph will, with foreign immigration, inevitably come to America. It is here that Willard unites her purpose of reform with the motivating force to undertake reform *now*.

> There is one remedy—one only—and that is Christianity in action; not fashionable church-membership, but actual Christian living and Christlike reaction on the work around us. But so long as religion is kept like canned fruit bottled up at a fixed price of pew rent or other contribution, so long will the crime list continue to increase. God be thanked that the womanhood of Christendom begins to go out into the highway and hedge, shaking into the laps of the people the rich ripe fruit of the gospel trees without money and without price.

Willard begins the conclusion of her proemium with two paragraphs describing voluntary reform efforts being undertaken in Chicago, the site of the 1889 convention. Her introduction, however, has equally established the logic and rationale for compulsory reform legislation. She finishes, appropriately, with a paean to the politics of domesticity: "Some are born mothers, some achieve motherhood, some have it thrust upon them. Blessed beyond all the rest is she who has carried a motherly heart in her breast since ever that heart began to beat, and in these gospel days her holiest work will be to play the part of mother to the thousands worse than motherless to whom she goes with Bible in her hand and Christ enshrined in body and soul."

In her proemium, Willard's attack on foreigners is obvious. Through numbers and description she plays to nativist fears, and, given her description of anarchists, she probably experienced those fears herself. Interestingly, her extended description of the "foreign invasion" is a notable break from other presidential addresses, however. The nativist theme is never far removed in those speeches, but the 1889 address is singular in its clear enunciation. Here is a proemium meant to energize Willard's audience to action. She is reminding them of what they already "know," but, with almost overwhelming statistics, she attempts to impress upon them the desperation of the moment.

However, Willard's attack is vitiated in some significant respect, as her description and numbers lack the latent hostility evidenced in "Everybody's War." Few references are made here to strange cultures and customs, no nicknames are used, and no quotations given in which a foreign accent is imitated. Willard even weakens her case, including statistical evidence which demonstrates that, despite an increase in percentage of foreign-born population, the percentage of foreign-born *prison* population has remained the same. There is a sense here in which Willard has to utilize the immigration argument in order to motivate her audience, but does so with some ambivalence. Later, in the 1890s, she will develop a more comfortable group of villains, barely mentioned in this proemium: capitalists.

In addition to establishing a rationale and motive for action, Willard's proemium serves a second purpose of providing a unified perspective for her reform agenda. During her life as well as after it, she would be criticized for sending the WCTU in too many different directions. Her speeches routinely defended her position, and this proemium serves as one defense. Prohibition was, clearly, the central reform sought by the WCTU, and it is mentioned several times in this introduction. All reform, however, served the single purpose of bringing Christianity to everyone. All her reforms, Willard says, are missionary work. Like many missionaries before and after her, Willard felt that people's lives needed to attain a certain quality before God's word could effectively take root. The reformer needed to change people's lives—in outer ways as well as inner—and not all the changes required could be effected through voluntary means.[17]

Legislative Reform

In two decades of delivering presidential addresses, Frances Willard advocated numerous legislative reforms, including kindergarten, a minimum wage law, a higher age for consent laws, required temperance instruction in public schools, and the forty-hour week, in addition to prohibitory law and woman suffrage. Four legislative reforms are discussed in the excerpts from her 1889 presidential address and are reprinted in this volume: Sunday closing laws, theater/advertising restrictions, institutional reform, and boards of public health. Willard's discourse here is representative in several ways. First, the excerpts suggest the breadth of her reform interests. Second, all are grounded in the logic of reform established in her proemium. Third, voluntary reform efforts are intermixed freely with these legislative proposals.

In the first section of the speech following the proemium, Willard calls upon the WCTU to lobby for strict enforcement of Sunday closing laws as well as for prohibition generally. Sunday closing laws had

been promulgated in order to enforce the third Mosaic command-
ment—to keep holy the Sabbath—and in this section of the speech
religion acts as the primary vehicle by which Willard argues the
legitimacy of her position. To lobby against "Sunday saloons and
gambling dens" is "proof that God is not yet dead, [and] neither is the
devil crowned." To vote for prohibition "consecrates" one's vote.
Summarizing her argument, Willard suggests a religious motto for the
movement: "The Lord hath not given me the spirit of fear, but of
power and of love and of a sound mind."

Sunday closing laws are further justified, however, because their
roots can be traced to the Women's Crusade of 1874. Recalling in one
story the movement's early drama and heroines, Willard brings to her
political activism the Crusade's mantle of legitimacy. Later in the
section she recites the words of a "veteran Crusader . . . now a white-
ribboner of fifteen years' standing." The quoted passage is revealing
in that it summarizes in a single sentence the movement's transformed
focus. The passage begins with a recollection of kneeling in saloons
and praying to God for deliverance from "this awful curse" and ends
with a prayer for prohibition votes.

Willard's argument makes an interesting distribution of responsibility in this passage, one which illustrates the impetus of her reforms and
reinforces the need for political action. The wageworkers are not to
blame for the de facto elimination of the Sunday closing laws. True,
Willard acknowledges, they are the primary customers of the Sunday
saloons and gambling houses. However, they are simply victims of the
"saloon-keepers and ward sneak-thieves," the "bosses of politics" who
form a "pitiful minority" which "holds our people by the throat" and
manipulates the vote. Even the saloonkeepers are somewhat excused,
as they are the "political chattel" of the brewer and the political boss.
Just as it legitimated support for the Prohibition party, the evil
conspiracy of brewer and boss justifies the use of reform legislation.

Finally, Willard's Sunday closing argument reiterates the theme
that brave women will form the political vanguard. Using the
metaphor of war, Willard notes that the well-known phrase "bringing
the regiment up to the colors" implies that the standard-bearers—those
carrying the colors—have gone ahead of the regiment. Just as she had
subtly condemned those who had to "falter," here she casually
dismisses the "conservatives," who will "come along slowly enough *at
best*."[18] If Christian reformers are to be "true to their light"—that is,
to do God's will rather than their own—then they must occupy their
place at the "front of the army." Here Willard subtly relies upon and
extends the rationale established in her proemium.

While distinctions of gender are relatively submerged in Willard's
discussion of Sunday closing laws, her attack on public obscenity is
securely grounded in the theory of women's unique moral role.
Willard begins the discussion in much the same fashion as she started

the speech. In her introduction, she had cited Ruskin: What woman wills will be accomplished. In this later section she argues that, if the "aggregate self-respect of women" could only be brought to bear on the problem of public obscenity, such "exhibitions" would be eliminated in "a twelvemonth." Further, these "public atrocities" are easily identified. They are "abominations [that] strike *her* eye," a "public insult to all virtuous *women*."[19] It is also significant that, while telling one story, Willard notes that such exhibitions were "for men only."

In that story, Willard also brings gender to the forefront by making Ada H. Kepley the heroine. In some regards, the story is typical temperance fare. Offended women from the community form a prayer group, from which four go forth to tear down the obscene theatrical advertisements. Except that the story's scene is now a post office rather than a saloon, it echoes the Crusade stories told and retold within the WCTU. One feature of the story is significantly different, however. Early on, Willard pointedly notes that Kepley is a lawyer, and that, when arrested for tearing down theatrical posters, defended herself in court. Like the quoted passage from the veteran Crusader, this story, too, summarizes the evolution of the movement. Women still act out of moral conviction, grounded in prayer, protesting immorality as best they can. Now, however, they are willing and able to utilize the law against those who promote such irreligious behavior.

Willard's attack on public obscenity is also representative in the attitude it displays regarding legal proscriptions. As noted at the beginning of this chapter, for Willard as well as the WCTU, law contained within itself the potential to operate as the benign enforcer of public morality. It is "in the interest of public decency" that Willard urges her audience to "go before the municipal authorities." There, women will be "asking for protection" from "this leprosy," that is, these "wholesale demoralizers of the young." It is for just such protection that the Illinois WCTU secured "our helpful new law on this subject." In the hands of the political boss, the law is a tool of immorality. When wielded by women, the natural custodians of the common weal, law becomes the weapon of the righteous.

Lastly, Willard's discussion of public obscenity moves easily from the legal to the social sphere. Her discourse here parallels the beginning of the section, by commenting specifically on women and morality. "We can not forget that some women sin against public modesty so woefully . . . I mean the women who parade what ought to be the mysteries of the dressing-room before the public gaze of men." Coupled with the "dance-delirium," these women's "fashion-idolatry" works evil upon their "tempted brothers." No legal proscriptions are urged, however. Willard simply condemns the immoral behavior.

Interestingly, Willard excludes three categories of women from personal condemnation. Two of the categories—the very young and the very giddy—provide sardonic, additional condemnation. The implicit message in both is that dancing and immodest dress are acts of immaturity, about which sensible women should know better. Willard's third category of exclusion exhibits some genuine compassion, however, as she excuses those women "bound in the toils of half-barbarous social usage." While euphemisms for prostitution were common to the period, Willard's language is purposeful in its connotated meaning. Prostitutes are victims, "bound" in their toils and "used" by the prevailing customs of society. Their actions are immoral, but such behavior is caused by the spiritual deterioration of which Willard's proemium speaks. Both voluntary and legal reform are needed in order to train people away from spiritual danger: obscene art, immodest dress, and all other such public displays of immorality.

The politics of domesticity also provides the backdrop for the next section, "Home for Incapables." Prohibition is necessary in order to protect the home from the ravages of alcohol. Likewise, legally established institutions are necessary in order to protect the home from the kleptomaniac, the libertine, the gambler, the drunkard, and the mentally incapable. More than in any other section of the speech, society here is portrayed as the only force capable of providing "protection." "Homes deserve protection," Willard argues, and so, too, "those victims of an abnormal make-up . . . deserve protection from themselves." The state—that is, the legal manifestation of society's moral character—thus becomes the potential agent of cure. "The state is not yet awakened, on behalf of the home," Willard asserts, and "[impoverished children] can never be educated unless the state founds for them industrial schools." Finally, "[juvenile offenders] should be strictly secluded [by the state] from the company of old offenders and helped to learn a trade." Mothers cannot prevent the evil of society from crossing home's threshold and there violating "home's sacred walls." Mothers must, therefore, venture into politics in order to force society to police itself.

Willard finishes the section by inoculating the audience against critics' complaints that such reforms would prove too costly. She returns to the theme developed earlier, in this speech as well as others, that the legal system is controlled by the political boss. The question should not be whether the public is willing to pay for such reforms. After all, she points out, "the people are sure to be taxed." The question is whether tax monies will be spent on institutions which protect the home, or on the "political sugar plums" mentioned previously, when Sunday closings were the topic of discussion. Willard's choice of verbs is purposeful when she concludes, "Let us then *crusade* the public treasury."[20]

Health and Hygiene are Willard's final topics which include legislative reform proposals. In "Physical Culture," she proposes first that school curricula teach the "rules of hygiene." "Let children learn the structure and functions of their own bodies," she analogizes, "as openly and plainly as they learn their problems in mathematics." Next, Willard advocates that each state establish a board of health, which should include "well-educated women physicians" as members. Once more the politics of domesticity is implicit in Willard's argument: "for as sanitarians they are unexcelled if not unrivalled." Finally, she moves again from legal to voluntary reform, as she addresses the problem of "woman's everlastingly befrilled, bedizened and bedraggled style of dress."

Religion is little found in this section, as either a reason for action or a standard by which to judge the public good. Instead, secular arguments are prevalent, and at many junctures Willard presages many a reformer of the twentieth century: "We see starvation in the midst of plenty—sickness, misery and death in a world where there should be perfect health, happiness and life, and we no longer rest satisfied with the assurance that as an enlightened people we are in no way responsible. Surely these evils are no law of nature. There must be a cause, and we can not shirk the responsibility. Reason tells us we are directly responsible, and the cause must be found." Once found, of course, the logic of reform demands the eradication of that cause.

Perhaps the most interesting feature of this section, however, is its contradiction of the proemium's logic. Although Willard's proposals are consonant with her proemium's conclusion—that the WCTU must work for Christian reform—her discussion of evidence negates her opening indictment of the "foreign invasion." In this part of the speech, the incidence of insanity functions as an index of America's deterioration, the proemium's scenic description. In marked contrast to the introduction's condemnation of Europe, Willard now argues that the United States suffers a much greater incidence of insanity than England, France, and Germany. If insanity is an index of alcoholism and poverty, and it occurs with far greater frequency here than abroad, then how can Willard claim poverty and alcoholism are worse in Europe than in America?

The answer probably lies in the myriad reforms Willard advocates. When speaking generally, the "foreign invasion" is the root of America's ills. When addressing the Sunday closing problem, the brewer and political boss are to blame. Obscene public art is caused by the alcoholized brain, and the lack of adequate penal institutions by special interests' greed. Poor health, bad hygiene, and insanity are caused by a lack of education and proper state regulation. At this point in her career as orator and reformer, Willard has moved beyond the search for a common cause of society's ills. She provides one in the proemium because it motivates her audience to act. The true focus of her speech, however, is not what causes society's problems, but how to identify the targets of reform, and in that regard Willard's proemium is illustrative. The reformer is meant to do *God's* will, not Willard's or any other person's. Those things which prevent the creation of God's kingdom on earth—Sunday saloons, impure art, increased disease and insanity—are *ipso facto* society's ills. They must therefore be changed, re-formed in the literal sense of the word, whether by legal or by voluntary means. The particular cause of the problem—Willard's proemium notwithstanding—is of lesser importance than the effects the reformer should seek.

CONCLUSION

Throughout the 1880s and early 1890s, Willard's Gospel Politics would be a two-sided activity. She would combine her call for electoral work with continued petitioning on behalf of specific legislation. In that regard, the presidential addresses examined above represent Willard's twofold, complementary approach to politics. Neither asks the audience to engage in every reform activity sanctioned by the terms Do Everything and Gospel Politics. Instead, Willard urges her audience to bear witness in the political arena wherever one has both the talent and the opportunity to do so.

However, Frances Willard's attempt to wed politics and the union were not always well received. In 1881, Annie Wittenmeyer, former president of the WCTU, and some dozen other members withdrew from the union in protest of its endorsement of woman's suffrage.[21] In 1889, staunch Republican J. Ellen Foster led a similar breakaway group and formed the Non-Partisan Woman's Christian Temperance Union. Foster and many other Republican members were disgruntled with Willard's fierce promotion of and loyalty to the Prohibition party.[22] Willard was attacked from outside the union as well, particularly by Republicans. Immediately following the 1889 convention the *Chicago Tribune* lambasted her for wanting to ruin the Republican party in order to replace it with one in which she could become a "boss": "Women [who] joined [the WCTU] for high moral and Christian reasons have been gradually lured by fanatics. . . . [Once the Republican Party is destroyed] Miss Willard et. al. will be ready to run for office and capture the spoils in the name of charity, reform, Christianity and temperance."[23] There were, of course, many conservatives—men and women—who felt that women had no place in politics at all, whether partisan or nonpartisan.[24]

But for all those who remained unconvinced, there were many others who were persuaded. The *Washington Post* reported that Willard's 1881 address "secured the close attention of the large audience which, from time to time, loudly applauded the views of the gifted lady. It was a masterly effort."[25] Although that address failed to wean her audience from the Republican party, it laid important groundwork for change. Again, the *Post* was complimentary: "Miss Willard discussed at length, and in a very sensible manner, the political aspect of the prohibition cause."[26] Willard's efforts in this and other annual addresses bore fruit in 1884 and 1888, when the WCTU endorsed the Prohibition party's candidate for president. In 1889, with the question of partisanship at its height, Willard was greeted by the convention with a "tremendous burst of applause which lasted several minutes."[27] Ellen Foster, in contrast, was audibly hissed when she attacked the convention's partisanship.[28]

Other political efforts of the WCTU actively reflected Willard's charge to Do Everything. Petitions, circulars, and lobbying abounded in state and local unions as well as the national. Much was accomplished legislatively by the WCTU, and even more was attempted. Among other actions, the WCTU lobbied for federal aid to public elementary schools, public kindergarten schools, police matrons in women's prisons, and better regulated working conditions for women industrial laborers.[29] As Ruth Bordin points out, the evolution of departments in the WCTU reveals the growth of its political interests. In 1882, of the twenty departments, only three were primarily nontemperance in purpose—Franchise, Prisons and Jails, and Juvenile Affairs. In 1896, that number had changed to twenty-five out of the thirty-nine departments.[30] Under Frances Willard's leadership, and persuaded in no small part by her oratory, the WCTU had become not simply the largest organization of women of its time, but an active vehicle for lobbying municipal councils, state legislatures, and the U.S. Congress. It was, indeed, a *political* organization of women.

NOTES

1. Jack S. Blocker, Jr., *"Give to the Winds Thy Fears"* (Westport, CT: Greenwood, 1985) 227-230.

2. Ruth Bordin, *Woman and Temperance* (Philadelphia: Temple University Press, 1981) 55.

3. The other sections were: I. Work of the Superintendents; II. Suggestions for 1881; III. General; IV. Hygiene; VI. Mutual Criticism; and VII. True Greatness.

4. Frances E. Willard, "President's Annual Address (1889)," *Minutes of the National Woman's Christian Temperance Union* (hereafter cited *Minutes*), 1889 convention, 104. The *Minutes* may be found in the "Woman's Christian Temperance Union Series," *Temper-*

ance and Prohibition Papers, microfilm ed. (hereafter cited as WCTU Series), reels 1-5.

5. As noted in the speech, the Lake Bluff Temperance Convocation was an informal meeting of temperance leaders, held in August 1881.

6. Willard, a moving force behind both the resolutions she cites, was strategic in her use of the title "Home Protection Party." No such party existed in 1881, but its logical counterpart was the Prohibition party. Endorsement of the Prohibition party in spirit but not in name allowed her to maneuver a name change the following summer at the Prohibition party convention. There the party officially renamed itself the "Prohibition Home Protection Party," thus making woman suffrage an inherent part of its political message.

7. Emphases mine.

8. Frances E. Willard, "Address of the President," *Minutes*, 1884 convention, 69. Emphasis hers.

9. Frances E. Willard, "President's Annual Address," *Minutes*, 1896 convention, 70. Willard was rarely so candid in discussing backroom politics. She was probably more self-disclosive in this speech because her 1896 address was the only presidential address which she did not deliver from a manuscript. Ostensibly, her delivery was extemporaneous because she had been deeply involved in working with the Armenian refugees in Marseilles. See pp. 67, 73, 76.

10. Barbara Leslie Epstein, *The Politics of Domesticity* (Middletown, CT: Wesleyan University Press, 1981).

11. In fact, this is a central argument in Epstein's volume. Ibid, 108-148.

12. I am using the Greek term "proemium" rather than its synonym, "the introduction," because the former connotes a longer prelude to the speech. Willard's proemium can be aptly called the "overture," as it establishes the mood for and foreshadows the action of the speech. "Proemium," literally, "before the song," is a particularly appropriate term for this section of Willard's address. See Edward P. J. Corbett, *Classical Rhetoric for the Modern Student* (New York: Oxford University Press, 1971) 303-304.

13. It may also have been briefly asserted because it was taken as a truism by Willard and her audience.

14. Kenneth Burke, *Grammar of Motives* (Berkeley: University of California Press, 1969) 6-7.

15. Significantly, one notable element of the "scene" is absent from this statistical description: the higher incidence of drinking among the foreign-born. This oversight is undoubtedly because such a conclusion was thoroughly assumed by both speaker and audience.

16. Emphasis hers.

17. Despite her protestations to the contrary, Willard had, by 1889, changed her emphasis from Woman's Christian *Temperance* Union to Woman's *Christian* Temperance Union.

18. Emphasis mine.

19. Emphasis mine.

20. Emphasis mine.

21. Bordin, *Woman and Temperance*, 119.

22. For reports of the rancor that attended the 1889 convention, see *New York Times* 10 Nov. 1889: 1; 14 Nov. 1889: 3; 21 Dec. 1889: 2; and *Chicago Tribune* 14 Nov. 1889: 1. Nor was this the first time leaders of the WCTU had resigned or been "fired" because they could not accept Willard's partisanship in support of the Prohibition party. See, for example, *New York Times* 15 Aug. 1885: 2.

23. *Chicago Tribune* 14 Nov. 1889: 4.

24. See, for example, Kate Field's essay "An Enemy in the Field," *Chicago Tribune* 9 Nov. 1889: 16. Originally published in the *New York Herald*, the essay gained national attention with its vituperative attack on the "fanatical women" of the WCTU who engaged in political activity.

25. *Washington Post* 27 Oct. 1881: 1.

26. Ibid.

27. *Chicago Tribune* 9 Nov. 1889: 3.

28. *Washington Post* 13 Nov. 1889:1.

29. Bordin, *Woman and Temperance* 105, 103, 99-100, and 112.

30. Ibid, 97-98.

4
Christian Socialism

In 1880, Frances Willard had instructed the WCTU to "Do Everything." As long as she continued to speak primarily about temperance and prohibition, her reform agenda could maintain some central focus despite the centrifugal force of her motto. As "Do Everything for Temperance Reform" became transformed into "Do Everything for Reform," Willard began searching rhetorically for a single raison d'etre. That search was complicated when she abandoned her active political campaigning, because until that time her emphasis on a single method—that is, the Prohibition party—had substituted for a unified philosophical vision. Throughout the 1880s, Willard's view of reform had been rather like Justice Potter Stewart's conception of pornography: she knew a good reform when she saw it.

Rhetorically, Willard's shotgun approach to reform was a liability. Despite her eloquent defense of the Do Everything policy, her continued attempts to give voice to a philosophy of reform indicated that she understood the strategic weakness of her oratory.[1] Without a central rationale for reform, Willard's tactical gains could be reversed with a single change of strategic direction. Even more, by the 1890s Willard seemed to have set a larger task for herself. Always able to skillfully portray the immediate problems and available solutions her audience faced, in her later years Willard aspired to paint a vision of the future which could guide reform for years to come. "Do Everything" could not be that guide. Willard wanted to answer the question, do everything *for what* purpose? Ultimately, Christian Socialism supplied that purpose.

A WHITE LIFE FOR TWO

One of Willard's early attempts at describing a cohesive program of reform began in 1885, when she supported the formation of a Department for Suppression of the Social Evil. As described in her 1885 Annual Address, the purpose of this department was initially limited in scope. Using euphemisms common to the times, Willard proposed three specific goals: study the relationship of alcohol and sexual crimes, create halfway houses for prostitutes, and lobby for stronger penalties against rapists.

The special aim . . . will be to trace the relation between the drink habit and the nameless practices, outrages and crimes which disgrace so-called modern 'civilization'; . . . provid[e] a temporary home for the women whom our police matrons rescue from the clutch of penalties whose usual accompaniments often render them still more familiar with sin . . . [and] we could be instrumental in the passage of such laws as would punish the outrage of defenceless girls and women by making the repetition of such outrage an impossibility.[2]

It was only in passing that Willard, in this 1885 speech, alluded to larger changes of social behavior, namely, what came to be called "social purity" or "a white life for two." "It is rather by holding men to the same standard of morality which, happily for us, they long ago prescribed for the physically weaker, that society shall rise to higher levels."[3]

By the following year, however, the limited sense of stamping out social evil had been supplemented by a broader purpose, as reflected in the name "Department for Promoting Social Purity." In addition to the goals enunciated the previous year, Willard proposed the equal division of estates between husbands and wives, improved education and training for women, woman's suffrage, and a woman's "pledge for purity."[4] The purity pledge began with a vow "to uphold the law of purity as equally binding upon men and women."[5] By her presidential address of 1887, the transformation from narrow concerns to fundamental social reform was complete. No mention is made in the 1887 address of harsher penalties for rape, work among prostitutes, or lobbying for changes in law, even though work in those areas still continued. It was broad-based change, not a few scattered laws, which would ultimately allow the realization of social purity, and so Willard discussed the nature of marriage, the relationship of men and women, and the work of "reconstructing the ideal of womanhood."[6]

Significantly, Willard incorporated most of this portion of her 1887 address in "A White Life For Two," a speech she reprinted in her 1890 book of the same name.[7] In that book, the speech presented a rationale for and discussion of the WCTU's work in social purity. There, Willard began assembling her vision for society, a vision she could bequeath to later generations of reformers.

Karlyn Kohrs Campbell has argued that "A White Life for Two" is a "rhetorical touchstone" of Frances Willard's rhetoric, and that, as such, it "embodie[s] the paradox of 'feminine feminism.'"[8] In tone and value it is a romantic, idealistic, and traditional speech, while in its specific proposals, such as woman's control over procreation, it is "a collection of positions ostensibly more suited to Elizabeth Cady Stanton."[9] However, because Willard grounded her somewhat radical reforms in traditional values, Campbell argues that her rhetoric "precluded both analysis of the barriers to full equality and reform efforts to remove such obstacles."[10] Thus, according to Campbell, speeches such as "A White Life for Two" were endorsements of the status quo rather than clarion calls for change: "[Willard] consistently appealed to traditional religious and patriotic values linked to the cult of true womanhood, and . . . refused to disturb her listeners' prior beliefs by taking controversial positions. . . . Willard's rhetorical alchemy involved relabeling and reframing proposals in ways that transformed them from demands for social change into reaffirmations of traditional arrangements and values."[11]

In support of these general claims, Campbell advances several specific charges. For example, when Willard proposes equal physical education and manual training for girls, the purpose is to promote "healthier motherhood and more efficient domestic labor . . . [rather than] female self-actualization and entry into the professions."[12] In the matter of sexual crimes, Campbell argues that "the problem of rape was reduced to the problem of statutory rape, which was legally defined in terms of the age of consent."[13] Further, regarding these sexual crimes, Willard "held men and women equally culpable for the problem, to avoid any suggestion that males were particularly blameworthy."[14]

Campbell is particularly critical of Willard's rhetorical treatment of men. "No blame was attached to males; even when discussing legislators she presented their intentions in the most positive light."[15] According to Campbell, men did not need to alter their fundamental beliefs or behaviors in order to accept Willard's worldview. They could accept Willard's reforms with absolutely "no social cost" to themselves.[16]

In all regards, as to the fundamental roles of men and women, Campbell sees Willard as reinforcing the status quo: "In her extraordinary efforts to be persuasive and to adapt to her audiences, she ended up generating discourse which was suited only to reinforce existing beliefs. By entirely avoiding confrontation, by refusing to challenge, much less to blame men, even for the rape of children, she chose rhetorical strategies at odds with the major reforms she herself espoused."[17] In Campbell's view, Willard's rhetoric exuded concession and compromise, rather than possess the "intensity" which marked

the discourse of Lucretia Coffin Mott, Elizabeth Cady Stanton, or
Susan B. Anthony, among others.

It is true that Willard grounded her appeals in traditional values.
"A White Life For Two," especially, develops itself around Willard's
vision of "true manhood" and "true womanhood." A question arises,
however, whether her affirmation of traditional values translates
directly into a reaffirmation of the status quo, or whether "A White
Life for Two" is indeed an early example of Willard's attempt to define
a radically transformed society.

There is no doubt that "A White Life for Two" contains many
"traditional" allusions. It is, for example, quite romantic in tone.
Marriage is the union which "alone renders possible a pure society."
True, monogamous love is one of the "proofs of a beneficent Creator"
and "the fairest, sweetest Rose of Time, whose petals and whose
perfume expand so far that we are all inclosed and sheltered in their
tenderness and beauty." Marriage is "the sum of earthly weal or woe
to both [men and women]."

In Willard's view of romance, men are as much the creatures of
love as women. Early in the speech she details the "heart histories" of
men such as composer John Howard Payne and poet Barnard Taylor,
and, among others, mentions those of Dante, Petrarch, Michelangelo,
and Washington Irving. Again, the romantic attractions of marriage
are such that man "still chooses home freely and royally for her sake
who is to him the world's supreme attraction." Pure love, according
to Willard, is neither solely nor primarily the domain of women.

Willard does, however, endorse the view that men and women are
different, and in that difference affirms the "traditional" view of
women. With their traditional interests in morality, religion, and
sentiment, women will "bless and brighten every place she enters."
The new woman will not "cling" to men, but will still remain "every
bit as tender and sweet as if she did." This division of spheres is,
according to Willard, by nature, not tradition. Thus, for example, "the
mother's custody of children will constructively be preferred in law to
that of the father, on the ground that it is surer and more consonant
with natural laws." Whereas women have "instincts of self-protection
and home protection," males, in contrast, suffer an "inherited appetite"
which leads to sexual temptation.

Home, of course, is the major symbol of tradition in "A White
Life for Two." As with the Home Protection ballot, to which she
explicitly refers at the very beginning of the speech, Willard justifies
women's interest in social purity in their traditional sphere of the
home. She lays out the logic of her argument almost immediately in
the introduction. Marriage, which requires social purity, is the "one
relationship" which "makes [home] possible." As Willard concludes
her rationale, "For the faithfulness of two, each to the other, alone
makes possible the true home, the pure church, the righteous Nation,

the great, kind brotherhood of man." The pursuit of social purity is simply another part of the "sacred cause of protection for the home."

Traditional values, however, even when they include traditional views of "true men" and "true women," do not necessarily endorse the status quo. Just as Martin Luther King could fashion his dream of the future around the "promissory note" of the Declaration of Independence, Frances Willard recognized that status quo actions and behaviors did not always embody the traditional values Americans espoused. The true woman, Willard argued, was financially and emotionally independent—but few "status quo" women were. The true man endorsed equal rights—something few "status quo" men did. True monogamous love required an equal standard of purity for both sexes—a standard not usually reflected in the mores of the time.

The "true woman" in "A White Life for Two" is the equal of man, and as such is intended by God to be an independent co-partner in the sacrament of marriage. True, Willard holds to the traditional view that women by nature are different in temperament and physical attributes. The latter difference, however, has been rendered insignificant by the age of invention: "Meanwhile, the conquest, through invention, of matter by mind, lifts woman from the unnatural subjugation of the age of force. In the presence of a Corliss engine, which she could guide as well as he, men and women learn that they are fast equalizing on the plane of matter, as a prediction of their confessed equalization upon the planes of mind and morality." Temperament, and by nature different spheres or interests, are similarly irrelevant, "as God sets male and female everywhere side by side throughout His realm of law, and has declared them one throughout His realm of grace."

Willard envisions a world in which wives would be the legal and physical—as well as spiritual—equals of their husbands. Willard calls for equal property rights, coeducation, and woman suffrage, in order that there should be "one undivided half of the world for wife and husband equally." She states her demand for women's equality unequivocally: "In that [better] day the wife shall surrender at marriage no right not equally surrendered by the husband, not even her own name."

Willard's defense of coeducation is not, as Campbell interprets it, a plea for "better motherhood and more efficient domestic labor." Certainly, neither term appears in "A White Life for Two." Willard argues that coeducation is necessary so that women do not have to marry out of financial necessity.

I have long believed that . . . [the] greatest of all questions, the question of a life companionship, . . . [should] be decided on its merits, pure and simple, and not complicated with other questions, "Did she get a good home?" "Is he a generous provider?" "Will she have plenty of money?" . . . I would make women so independent of marriage that men who, by bad habits and niggardly estate, whether physical, mental or moral, . . . should find the facility with which they enter its hallowed precincts reduced to the lower minimum.

Although Willard only mentions the possibility of women's "self-actualizing" in a passing reference to travel or "a career," her challenge to the status quo should not be understated. This is a speech about social purity; hence, it naturally focuses on the relationship between men and women, rather than on the self-actualization of women. Within those limitations, however, Willard justifies education for women because it will make them equals in their relationship with men, not because it will make them better mothers or improve their domestic labor.

Moreover, although Willard's justification for change is indeed limited to "true marriage," traditionally a part of women's "sphere," the change Willard calls for is to break away from the physical limitations of that sphere. The status quo, in its current customs and laws, is a "snare and a danger." Not only should women become financially independent of marriage; Willard would free them from the "[social] reproach or oddity" of choosing a career instead of marriage. She has, perhaps, envisioned change for the "wrong reasons," but it is a radical change of social customs, mores, and beliefs that she describes. She is indeed proposing, as she phrases it, "reconstructing the ideal of womanhood," and not the simple reaffirmation of the present construction. She has not been "trapped" into simply ratifying the status quo.

For Willard, the status quo is similarly deficient in its production of true men. Contrary to Campbell's claim, Willard in fact perceived fault in many men. Indeed, that there are any true men at all is evidence to Willard of the inherent good character of some, not the acceptability of the status quo. "The magnificent possibilities of manly character are best prophesied from the fact that under such a system [of only men making laws] so many men are good and gracious." For every instance in which she exclaims "how grandly men are growing," there is opposite passage about the "awful deeds" done by men in Alaska, the "daily calendar of crimes against women," or the "brutal relations of our soldiery to the Indian women of the plains."

Men's sins are not restricted to sexual atrocities, however, despite the centrality of those crimes to the stated purpose of her speech. Willard sees the discrimination of men against women in everyday behavior and everyday life. Man, because he controls the legislature in toto, "legislated first for himself and afterward for the physically weaker one within 'his' home." Man, because he controls the literature on hygiene and medicine, makes birth control the responsibility of women: "My library groans under the accumulations of books written by men to teach women the immeasurable iniquity of arrested development in the genesis of a new life, but not one of these volumes contains the remotest suggestion that this responsibility should be equally divided between husband and wife." Current laws and customs, which by prejudice favor the interests of men, must give way to a different, more fairly ordered society: "It will not do to give the husband of the modern woman power to whip his wife, "provided the stick he uses is not larger than his finger"; to give him the right to will away her unborn child; to have control over her property; to make all the laws under which she is to live; adjudicate all her penalties; try her before juries of men; conduct her to prison under the care of men; cast the ballot for her, and in general, to hold her in the estate of a perpetual minor." The true, or ideal, man, according to Willard, supports such reform, but it was unnecessary to state that most *actual* men did not.

Willard does blame men for the status quo, as the foregoing passages make clear. Willard does not avoid the problem of rape, either. Although she uses the euphemisms of the day, to her audience the meaning of those euphemisms is clear. Willard does more than just attack statutory rape by addressing the "age of consent," she also condemns "the outragers of *women*, whose unutterable abomination crowd the criminal columns of our newspapers each day."[18] She returns to this issue again in the speech, as she directly confronts those who would remain silent out of some notion of decorum: "Womanhood's loyalty to woman has overleaped the silence and reserve of centuries and Christendom rings with her protest to-day. It is now the deliberate purpose of as capable and trusty women as live, that the *laissez-faire* method of dealing with these crimes against nature, shall cease." Just as Willard had advanced the cause of Gospel Politics by praising the "courageous," so too she urges her audience to help fashion a better world, by following the lead of "capable" and "trusty" women.

All these changes in the status quo would not come, as Campbell has it, with "no social cost" to the men in her audience. They would lose absolute fiscal and legal control over their families, the relative weight of their ballot would be cut in half, and traditions of all sorts—such as higher education for men only or the use of husband's surnames—would be changed. Rhetorically, of course, Willard labels the cost a benefit. Men will lose an "incumbrance" and a "toy," but gain a "companion" and a "counsellor." It is clear in her speech, however, that she is advocating the reform of deep-seated beliefs and customs, and that such reform would incur significant changes in the lives of men—including those sitting in her audience.

In the name of true love and perfect union—traditional values, to be sure—Willard creates a vision of a very different world than the one which she addressed. At times she does indeed seem to be praising the status quo—it is a "gentle age," an "age of peace," one of "immense advances" which is "moving forward rapidly." Such congratulatory passages, however, can only be fully appreciated in the context of Willard's idea of evolution. The present is indeed better than the past, which was an "age of force," "primeval," "medieval," and "barbarous." Although better, however, contemporary society is, for Willard, only a "transition age," one still cloaked in "darkness." The present age still suffers the "heritage of a less developed past" and wreaks "anguish and injustice upon woman." It is not the status quo but the future which will be utopian. "The time will come," Willard prophesies, and "better days are dawning." There is a "constant evolution," as the world "rolls onward toward some far-off perfection, bathed in the sunshine of our Father's Omnipotent Love."

To reach this perfection, the present must continue to evolve into the future. Part of that evolution is the adoption—through custom and law—of a "white life for two." True love between true women and true men may be a romantic ideal grounded in the values of the status quo. However, based on those values, Willard envisions a society with mutual respect and equality between genders, a vision hardly embodied by American society in 1890. "A White Life for Two" is not a simple reaffirmation of the beliefs and values already held by Willard's audience. It is, instead, an early instance of her Christian Socialist philosophy of reform, a philosophy she continued to construct throughout the remainder of the decade.

A CHRISTIAN SOCIALIST

Throughout the 1890s Willard fashioned her vision of reform around what she called "Christian Socialism." In 1894, for example, she announced that, contrary to previous WCTU doctrine, poverty was as much a cause of intemperance as intemperance was a cause of poverty. In various annual addresses of the decade, Willard called for the nationalization of the utilities, railroads, and newspapers. Increasingly, Willard saw morality as grounded in economic conditions, and wanted government to play the lead role in creating an economic—and therefore moral—utopia. To be sure, Willard understood that paradise could not be attained in an instant. Christian Socialism was a philosophy of reform not only, or even primarily, for the nineteenth century, but for the twentieth, twenty-first, twenty-second, and beyond. It was a philosophy avidly pursued by the woman who once wrote that she wished she had been born in the twenty-fifth century, in order to have lived in a more just and equal society.

Frances Willard's last Annual Address, delivered in 1897 about three months before her death, provided a final defense of her Christian Socialist beliefs. Two sections of Frances Willard's 1897 presidential address are particularly pertinent: her discussion of labor and her peroration. In the former, Willard sets forth a defense of Christian Socialism that includes specific appeals for legislative and voluntary reforms. In the latter, her last public communication with the WCTU,

Willard issues an eloquent appeal for the adoption of Christian Socialism by the women's temperance movement.

Four themes emerge from Willard's defense of Christian Socialism. First, by 1897 Frances Willard has in fact adopted an identifiably socialist position. Second, she legitimates her socialism by grounding it in Christian doctrine. Third, her union of economic socialism with Christian millennialism naturally invites the imagery of scientific, evolutionary progress. Finally, out of practical necessity, she attempts to locate her entire defense of Christian socialism within the temperance movement.

Socialism

Frances Willard clearly enunciates a socialist position in her 1897 address. She urges legislation creating the eight-hour day and the forty-hour week. She praises Germany's plan of universal compensation, which provides for the injured and the sick, its retirement insurance program, and Denmark's adoption of a similar plan for public pension. In her peroration, she extols the Employers' Liability Bill, the Fabians, the trade unions, and "corporate ownership by the great firm of the people." Indeed, it is in this 1897 presidential address that she most clearly defines her position as a Christian Socialist: "I would take, not by force, but by the slow process of lawful acquisition through better legislation . . . the entire plant that we call civilization . . . and make it the common property of all the people, requiring all to work enough with their hands to give them the finest physical development, but not to become burdensome in any case, and permitting all to share alike the advantages of education and refinement." In her peroration, Willard summarizes Christian Socialism as the "law of Co-operative Commonwealth."

While "better legislation" dominates Willard's vision of Christian Socialism, she still recommends voluntary reform as well. She proposes, for example, that the WCTU add rescue work—i.e., efforts to persuade alcoholics away from drink—to its general classification of "methods." Also, she urges the organization to assist the Salvation Army in its efforts to relocate the "unemployed industrial population" of New York to the farmland of the Southwest. However, each detour praising voluntary reform soon returns to the dominant theme of Christian Socialism. Willard follows her discussion of rescue work with a proposal that each state should establish industrial schools for those arrested on charges of public drinking. Similarly, her complimentary remarks toward the Salvation Army segue naturally into a general paean to Christian Socialism.

Frances Willard's conversion to reform socialism is apparent in her enunciation of philosophy as well as her endorsement of socialist proposals. On the one hand, Willard defends socialistic proposals because they stimulate reform. "These [reform] laws are intended 'to check the socialists,' and they show the good that the socialistic movement has already accomplished, and predict the infinitely greater good that is to come." Such reform legislation in response to socialism does not constitute that movement's ultimate good, however. Willard predicts that all this "dyke-building" will not keep back the "rising tide of social democracy." "[Reform legislation] is no anodyne, but a good sized 'entering wedge' toward corporate ownership by the great firm of the people."

Throughout this address, Willard's moralizing expounds and illustrates the philosophy of reform socialism. For example, she says early on that "I do not wish to know what the country does for the rich, they can take care of themselves; but what it does for the poor determines the decency, not to say the civilization, of a government." Significantly, in this passage Willard singles out government specifically, not society generally, as the responsible agent. She has separated legislative from voluntary reform in a fashion not seen in her addresses of the 1880s.

Similarly, Willard would not have the treatment of employees left to the vagaries of the market. "The fate of so many persons ought not to be dependent in anywise on the peculiarities of those who employ them. Servants should organize as other working people are organized." Government thus becomes the institution that manages the economy. For example, the eight-hour day is now supported not simply because it is humane, "but for the reason that if eight hours were the fixed period a great many more wage-workers would be employed."

As Willard has now framed the argument, when government fails to regulate the economy for the benefit of the poor and the wage-worker, it is in political as well as moral default. When government actively persecutes the worker, it is a force for evil. Willard joins labor unrest with images of patriotism, comparing the police shootings of coal miners to the British attack at Concord and Lexington. "The firing of Sheriff Martin and his deputies on unarmed miners at Hazelton, Pennsylvania, is likely to prove one of the 'shots heard around the world.'" Capitalism—the exploitation of the worker—is now a "species of tyranny."

In this speech Willard seems to have redirected her attention, deemphasizing the "micro-reform" perspective which marked her command to Do Everything. Instead, she takes a larger view, one which could be termed "macro-economic," and discovers there the path of reform. Lessons in economics replace the earlier ones on temperance and politics.

There is a commodity in the market which has the magic power of creating more than it costs to produce it. This is the labor power of the human being, of a free wage-worker. He sells it for a certain amount of money, which competition reduces to the average necessaries of life to produce it; to so much food, clothing and shelter, which are absolutely necessary to recuperate his lost powers on the next morning, and to reproduce a new generation of wage-workers after this one is gone. Almost all above this goes to the employing class, and is called "the surplus value."

Later in her speech, Willard again instructs her audience in the workings of the economy. "Look about you," says Willard, "the products of labor are on every hand," and she proceeds to detail the "unyielding, unwritten law of caste": "Labor is under foot, money is on top; idleness is a token of refinement; pleasure is the mark of birth and breeding; whoever devotes his time to useful pursuits belongs to a tabooed class, and you cannot be in Society unless you do the things that are of no mortal use to anybody and become the sort of person whose death would be no loss to the community, but oftentimes a gain." So taken is Willard with economic philosophy, that it supplies her peroration with the material for an extended analogy. Manufacturing becomes a metaphor for life: One must not judge the product while it is still undergoing production. Similarly, the reformer must work each stage of production as best she can, holding in abeyance her final judgment until the manufacturing is completed.

Willard's preoccupation with economics does not signal an abandonment of either her earlier reform agenda or her commitment to "do everything." Indeed, other sections of her 1897 address discuss "micro-reforms" in some detail. However, where Do Everything as a policy of reform lacked a cogent, coherent philosophy beyond the admonition to "do good," by 1897 Willard had found in social democracy her philosophic center. Macro-economics provided the pragmatic justification for that philosophy, while Christian millennialism supplied its moral imperative.

Christianity

In spite of her open admiration for socialism, Willard did not abandon traditional values. Ever the pragmatic reformer, she couched her call for socialism in patriotism, Christianity, and accepted practices. Her soliloquy, which came to her on a walk through the New England countryside, justifies social democracy because of its American common sense. The country simply needs to "set at work" in order to abolish poverty in "this great generous land." Municipalities own and operate electric companies, why not railroads, street cars, telegraph and telephone, gas works, and the like? "Why do we not,"

Willard asks, "make the money basis of the country . . . the country itself with 'I promise to pay' gleaming across its breast from Mt. Katahdin to Mt. Shasta?" However, while patriotism, common sense, and hard work are some of the traditional values Willard uses to render socialism palatable, Christianity is a far more prevalent theme. In many regards, Christianity provides the same justification as other traditional values, but it also lends social democracy its moral imperative.

Willard frequently yokes Christianity to socialism, arguing that each espouses a similar moral philosophy. "All for each and each for all" is introduced in her address as the motto of Christian Socialism, and Willard repeats the slogan in her peroration: "We shall never climb to heaven by making it our life long business to save ourselves. The process is too selfish; the motto of the true Christian is coming to be, 'All for each and each for all.'" Christianity thus justifies socialistic reforms. Servant laws should be enacted in order that a "Christian standard" be achieved. The "law" of supply and demand is a "pagan political economy," and "it is infidel for anyone to say that [it] is as changeless as the law of gravitation."

In addition to bestowing on socialism its imprimatur, Christianity also legitimates the audience's confusion, and converts that confusion into implicit evidence of the very proposition which creates the confusion. WCTU members are not, by and large, socialistic reformers, but, rather, middle and upper middle class women. Their values are indeed traditional ones, whereas, in 1897, socialism, communism, and anarchy are synonyms for anti-American labor agitation. The audience's respect for Willard is apparent, but in these later years their president is asking them to abandon many of the values, beliefs, and attitudes formed throughout a lifetime.

Willard understands their predicament, and in her peroration likens the mysteries of faith to those of life. The nineteenth century—almost the twentieth—is a confusing time, she tells the audience, a "Babel century." No belief expressed by "fallible human beings" can be a "final formulation of truth." One must, instead, seek the "white light of God's truth," and say, as the Bible commands, "What Thou wouldst have me believe, Son of Man who are the Son of God, that I believe." God's heavenly words are "oftentimes too great" for human understanding. If the audience is confused as to the logic or acceptability of socialism, it is simply one more instance of a common theological pattern. Indeed, the apparent contradiction between socialism and the audience's traditional beliefs becomes evidence of God's great and sometimes unfathomable purpose.

Willard does not, however, carry that logic too far. Instead, she puts greater rhetorical emphasis on the common purpose of socialism and Christianity, rather than upon any apparent contradiction: "We Christians must not sit by and let the fires of intemperance burn on; we must not permit poverty to shiver and squalor to send forth its stench and disease to fester in the heart of great populations. All this must be stopped, and we are the Christ-men and Christ-women to stop it, or else we are pitiable dreamers and deluded professors of what we don't believe." Hypocrisy is a critical moral error in any age and among any family of beliefs. To implicitly call her audience hypocritical—if they are not willing to work for economic justice as well as temperance, they are not Christian—bestows to socialism a strong moral charge. Christianity not only legitimates socialism, but creates a moral imperative for the reformer to act.

It is not enough, however, to simply note that Willard allied Christianity with the philosophy of socialism. Willard went further, sounding the theme of millennialism and making socialism a precondition for the Second Coming of Christ. "The resurrection of Christ is the need of our day," Willard tells her audience. "The Christ is being reincarnated before our eyes and we know it not." We *can* know it, she argues, for it is present in the socialist principles which her audience has generally rejected: "[W]hat the socialist desires is that the corporation of humanity should control all products. Beloved comrades, this is the frictionless way, it is the higher law, it eliminates the motives of a selfish life, it enacts into our every-day living the ethics of Christ's Gospel; nothing else will do it, nothing else can bring the glad day of universal brotherhood." Willard has drawn clearly here the line of her argument. *Nothing* will bring the Second Coming of Christ except a total commitment to his teachings, which in turn are enacted by the economics of socialism.

The importance of Christian millennialism to Willard's argument is apparent in her use of biblical verse. Where earlier speeches were dominated by Old Testament references—Genesis, Deuteronomy, and especially Psalms—it is the New Testament—Matthew, Mark, Luke, John, and Acts—which is quoted here. It is obeying the two commandments of Christ—"love to God and love to man"—which "makes men free from sin."

Evolution, Science, and Christian Socialism

For Willard, as for many late nineteenth century millennialists, the signs of a "new day" were all around her. Science and invention were growth industries in the Gilded Age, and their magic and mystery permeated the oratory of the day. For speakers like Willard, scientific advances such as the theory of evolution did not threaten their religious beliefs; they proved them. The march of progress was the march toward Christ's Second Coming.

Willard places great faith in the ability of science and invention to improve the human condition. New sources of energy, for example, can solve the problem of the factory. "It looks as if electricity would bring back those better times when men did their work in their own homes, instead of flocking to the factory to make machines of themselves as they do now." In Willard's discourse, therefore, metaphors of science are common because science "improves" upon the "old ways" just as reforms improve society. Socialism is thus the "frictionless way," enhancing the quality of life in the same manner that the frictionless engine refined the quality of the machine.

What science generally, and the theory of evolution specifically, gives Willard's discourse is a sense of movement, an imagery of human society progressing toward the Second Coming. It is science and human ingenuity which empower Willard to proclaim that "there is no limit to the forces that man's thoughts will yet start into motion." Other forces, also the products of science and progress, are already at work in society: "Nothing proves the growing solidarity of people more than the fact that since the succession of the Queen the number of letters passed through the mails in Great Britain has grown from 80 to 2,000 millions in a year, and that before her reign shall close it is probable that the earth can be circumnavigated in a little over thirty days when the Siberian and Alaska railroads shall be in operation." This growing solidarity, when people from around the globe can "freely communicate their thoughts," makes human progress inevitable.

This "human progress" in turn becomes evolutionary in its conception, as Willard transforms the evolution of science into the evolution of human society, or "civilization." "The evolution of man is brought about by the same influences that create a sun in the heavens." That science can prove the existence of astronomical influences thus "proves" the evolution of society. Once human evolution is accepted as fact, Willard can superimpose Christian millennialism upon that structure. "An age is hustling to the front . . . and that is the age of the carpenter's Son."

Willard's conception of moral evolution creates for her speech a well-defined hierarchy of terms. Ideas are easily evaluated by their location within the hierarchy. The Second Coming of Christ is the god term, literally and figuratively, which occupies the highest position. For example, Willard's metaphor of direction is revealing and purposeful: "[Christian socialism] is the *higher* law, it eliminates the motives of a selfish life, it enacts into our every-day living the ethics of Christ's Gospel."[19] The lower regions of the hierarchy are similarly clear. "I believe [Christian socialism] to be perfectly practicable, indeed that *any other method* is simply a relic of barbarism."[20] Barbarism, of course, is a term which indicates human society before its evolution to its present civilized state, itself just another stage in the march toward the millennia.

Willard's theory of moral evolution also allows her to argue that certain changes must be endured if we are to reach the "higher levels." In this worldview, the life of a species, like the life of a planet, occurs in well-defined stages, and one stage simply builds upon the other. Willard's extended analogy of the coral zoophytes is representative. Millions of tiny organisms labor and die over thousands of years, thus forming a coral reef. Winds bring dust and birds bring seeds, until an island is created with the variety of flora needed to sustain human life. The "next stage" in any evolutionary pattern is possible only because of the previous one and, in Willard's view, scientific discovery plays a critical role in the transformation of stages. For example, it is science that allows global communication, which will in turn impel people the world over to "seek to improve their condition." Their search, Willard predicts, will lead them to Christian Socialism. Similarly, "science is killing out superstition as disinfectants kill microbes." When superstition is removed, true religion—namely, Christianity—can triumph, and the millennia can commence.

Thus, instead of threatening religious tenets, science provides evidence for Christian beliefs. The discovery that solid materials like iron may be heated until gaseous—"invisible" but still present—is proof that "the invisible [is] the most real thing in the material world." God, like the roentgen rays but vastly more so, is invisible to the senses but great in power. "There is nothing in the universe but matter and force, force being the most recent name given by scientists to Him whose constant presence moulds and fashions all that we see." For Willard, Louis Pasteur and Herbert Spencer, studying, respectively, the infinitesimal and the infinite, provide testimonials to the existence of God.

Temperance and Christian Socialism

Throughout her 1897 address, Willard weaves the themes of socialism, Christianity, and science. Occasionally, she attempts to relate her message back to the issue of temperance and the roots of her organization: "And what has this to do with the temperance reform and all the others grouped around it? Much every way. . . . The renaissance is here; the 'revival of religion' has taken new form. The Christ is being reincarnated before our eyes and we know it not." Temperance, Willard is telling her audience, aims to bring a clear mind and a pure heart to the message of Christ. Clear minds and pure hearts will ultimately realize that Christian Socialism is the enactment and embodiment of that gospel.

Willard constructs contradictory scenarios, however, for the role temperance will play in achieving this higher evolution of humanity. At times, it is the evolution to a higher, holier plane of existence which will achieve temperance: "[It] is Christian Socialism, 'all for each and each for all'; the utilization of the utmost force of this earth for the corporate benefit of Man; the cherishing of his labor as the holiest thing alive, and the development of individual gifts of brain, heart and hand under the inspiration of that universal sense of brotherhood which will be, as I believe, the perpetual tonic that will some day render all coarser stimulants distasteful." At other times, it is temperance which must precede universal brotherhood. "Alcoholic drinks introduce added friction into the machinery of body and mind; by their use the individual is handicapped in the race toward a higher and more perfect individuality, and what hinders one in this race hinders us all."

If Willard's true view of the relationship of temperance and Christian Socialism can be stated, it is perhaps discerned in the closing paragraph of her peroration. There, she talks of the day "long after the triumph of the temperance reform," and long after the triumph of Christian Socialism as well. Although both society and the individual will have evolved into greater and finer things than can be conceived, still, "people will group themselves in separate camps even as they do to-day." Within this ongoing evolutionary struggle, working toward the kingdom of God, Willard firmly places her audience and herself. "And it is not improbable that the chief value of the little work that we have tried to do on this small planet, lies in the fact that we have been to some extent attempered by it, we have become inured to contradiction, and we may be useful either in coming invisibly to the help of those who toil in the reforms of the future, or we may be waging battles for God upon some other star."

CONCLUSION

Although historian Susan Lee argues that "Frances Willard continued throughout life to search for a principle," Willard's oratory of the 1890s indicates otherwise.[21] In Christian Socialism, Frances Willard found her unified vision of reform which could extend long past her death. It did not, however. While Willard could persuade the National WCTU to endorse specific planks of her agenda, she could not move the members to adopt her philosophy. Writes biographer Ida Tetreault Miller, "[Willard's influence was weakest in the area of labor and economic reform. . . . Without her spirit to guide it, the WCTU was not able to maintain the breadth of vision and scope of activity that she had created in it."[22] Ruth Bordin concurs, arguing that "[Gospel Socialism] propounded a political doctrine, unlike home protection, woman suffrage, and party allegiance, that she could not sell to the membership."[23]

The reasons for Willard's failure to move her organization in the desired direction are difficult to establish. Her oratory of the 1890s is no less persuasive, no less grounded in traditional values than her earlier rhetoric. Her early attempts at promoting fundamental social change, such as "A White Life for Two," were themselves successful.

Perhaps time is one answer. It took Willard five years to secure the national organization's endorsement of total suffrage, and even longer to sway many of the rank and file. Perhaps her frequent absences and extended illness provide the answer. Willard was barely able to maintain the organization's commitment to the Temple project during this time, a cause far less controversial than socialism. Or perhaps the membership was just unpersuadable in this instance. Perhaps this time Frances Willard had not simply "gone ahead" of the WCTU, but had taken a philosophy the WCTU could never accept.

Yet, to say that Willard failed to move the National WCTU is not the same as establishing that hers was a failed rhetoric. Willard's audience was always larger than the WCTU, just as her rhetoric was really always larger than just Home Protection, Do Everything, A White Life for Two, or Christian Socialism. Her rhetoric was rich with nuance and detailed in its observations on American society. Her concerns were not bound by gender, age, geography, or chronology, and neither should our evaluation of her oratory.

NOTES

1. See, for example, Frances E. Willard, "Annual Address (1893)," *Minutes of the National Woman's Christian Temperance Union* (hereafter cited *Minutes*), 1893 convention, 104-105. The *Minutes* may be found in the "Woman's Christian Temperance Series," *Temperance and Prohibition Papers,* microfilm ed., (hereafter cited as WCTU Series), reels 1-5.

2. Frances E. Willard, "President's Annual Address (1885)," *Minutes*, 1885 convention, 73-74.

3. Ibid, 74.

4. Frances E. Willard, "President's Annual Address (1886)," *Minutes*, 1886 convention, 75-78.

5. Ibid, 76.

6. Frances E. Willard, "President's Annual Address (1887)," *Minutes*, 1887 convention, 88-91.

7. Frances E. Willard, *A White Life For Two* (Chicago: Woman's Temperance Publishing Association, 1890).

8. Karlyn Kohrs Campbell, *Man Cannot Speak For Her*, vol. 1 (New York: Praeger, 1989) 123.

9. Ibid.

10. Ibid, 122.

11. Ibid, 124, 126. See also Susan Earls Dye Lee, "Evangelical Domesticity: The Origins of the Woman's National Christian Temperance Union Under Frances E. Willard," diss., Northwestern University, 1980, 362-363.

12. Ibid, 126.

13. Ibid, 127.

14. Ibid, 127. Lee also concludes that Willard "did not concentrate her energies on reforming men's behavior nearly as much as she cared about changing women's." "Evangelical Domesticity," 363.

15. Ibid, 127-128.

16. Ibid, 128.

17. Ibid, 129.

18. Emphasis mine.

19. Emphasis mine.

20. Emphasis mine.

21. Lee, "Evangelical Domesticity," 372. Lee provides no substantiation for her claim. The major explanation for Lee's misunderstanding is that her study focuses primarily on the periond of Willard's ascendancy, 1874-1879.

22. Ida Tetreault Miller, "Frances Elizabeth Willard: Religious Leader and Social Reformer," diss., Boston University, 1978, 170-171.

23. Ruth Bordin, *Woman and Temperance* (Philadelphia: Temple University Press, 1981) 138.

5
Legacy

It would be easy enough to call Frances Willard "eloquent" and leave it at that. Certainly her audiences thought her eloquent, as evidenced by their attendance, their applause, and their support. The report of one Arkansas newspaper was typical. "[Willard] held her audience in close attention for more than an hour."[1] Other newspapers contained similar stories. "By the hour appointed the house was filled to overflowing, many standing and a large number went away because they could not get in the house. A more respectful and attentive audience for such a number was never assembled in any city. . . . The very silence of the audience and the expression of satisfaction on every face was evidence that they had been highly entertained and edified."[2] "Clear, logical, and eloquent," reported Sarah Bolton to the *New York Independent*, "she held the closest attention of everyone present."[3]

While some newspaper accounts were more restrained in their general estimation of her oratory—"*at times* [she] grew quite eloquent"[4]—most were wholeheartedly positive in their assessment. Wrote the *Hot Springs (AR) Evening Star*, "We must join in the general expression that hers was the most powerful appeal to which it has ever been our pleasure to listen."[5] Dr. A. G. Howard of Emory University concurred. "Modest, self-poised, with masterful use of her resources, she gave us the best address I have heard on the subject of temperance."[6]

Indeed, so obvious was Willard's oratorical excellence that her eulogists and obituaries invariably made reference to her eloquence. "She was . . . an orator of the first order," observed the *Review of Reviews*.[7] "She was [prohibition's] most eloquent advocate" commented *The Outlook* magazine.[8] As with so many talented speakers, her oratorical ability seemed more inherited than acquired. Commented

Dr. Charles Little in *Chatauquan* magazine, "Frances Willard had the gift of eloquence."[9]

Scholars since have similarly pronounced her "eloquent." Ruth Bordin called her a "platform spellbinder."[10] Ida Tetreault Miller termed her "a magnificent platform speaker."[11] "As an orator," wrote biographer Mary Earhart, "Frances Willard had no peer among women and few among men of her generation. Anna Shaw wrote that she never knew a woman who could grip an audience and carry it with her as she could."[12] Regardless of whether such hyperbole was precisely accurate, during her career as a temperance leader Frances Willard had clearly proved herself an eloquent and popular speaker.[13]

Willard herself, however, like most great orators, understood that she achieved eloquence only in the service of a greater purpose. While Willard had many goals—and public adulation may have been one—she especially sought to make women equal players in the world's affairs, such that, in Willard's words, "[woman] will enter fully upon her heritage, as an equal, independent citizen of the world."[14] More broadly, Willard wanted everyone to "make direct, honest, hard work to help [people] in the daily business of life."[15] In the final analysis, Willard's eloquence can only be fairly appraised when seen within the larger context of her purpose.

A credible argument can be made that Willard's impact on the world around her was limited, in spite of the success she enjoyed in recruiting women to the WCTU and in some of her lobbying efforts. Karlyn Kohrs Campbell lists several such successes, for example, raising the age of consent laws, requiring scientific temperance instruction in schools, and the adoption of partial suffrage in some states on liquor, education, and municipal issues.[16] Similarly, the WCTU was influential in gaining the appointment of police matrons to women's prisons.[17] But many scholars, like Campbell, judge Willard's impact primarily by the WCTU's change of policy in the years following her death and by the eventual failure of prohibition as a national policy. "The aftermath of [Willard's] death demonstrated how transient her impact was, even on the women in her own organization. Between 1897 and 1910 no gains of any sort were made for woman suffrage; anti-suffrage activism was at its height. Moreover, the WCTU underwent a startling transformation. . . . Other factors contributed to this narrowing of concerns, but Willard's rhetoric played a key role. Willard had not converted the WCTU membership to the broad range of reforms that she had espoused."[18]

Ruth Bordin lends some support for Campbell's position when she writes that, upon Willard's death, "the change in emphasis [in the WCTU] was immediate, abrupt, and dramatic."[19] Abandoning the broad spectrum of reform, the organization began focusing more and more heavily on temperance alone. It continued support for suffrage and social purity, but fewer and fewer of the other issues such as labor reform were actively pursued.[20]

If Frances Willard's impact was in fact transient, history's relative silence on her might be partially explained. Few general histories mention her contributions, and even specialized studies which focus on reform give her but passing notice. Most historians, such as Robert Walker, suggest that Willard's major accomplishment was her ability to create a mass organization of women. "The example of Frances Willard—her patience, her organizational skills, her wise reliance on education as the principal means for making long term gains—created a model for such groups of lasting influence as the League of Women Voters."[21] Aside from the fact that it helped her to organize the WCTU, however, Frances Willard's oratory seems to have left little of its own legacy. Woman's suffrage did not arrive for another twenty-two years. Prohibition came about the same time, and died fourteen years later an ignominious death. The WCTU turned away from supporting prison reform, labor reform, the living wage, and the host of other reforms Frances Willard had advocated. For all its eloquence, what had her oratory accomplished?

Ruth Bordin, in her history of the WCTU and her biography of Frances Willard, argues that Frances Willard did make an important contribution to the reform movement in America. "Prohibition" has, even today, such negative connotations attached to it that we tend to stereotype prohibitionists as narrow-minded, anti-enjoy-life kinds of people. Temperance, however, and its pursuit of prohibition, was a genuine search for reform during an age troubled by alcoholism.[22] While one can debate the wisdom of prohibiting alcohol, it was no more irrational or irresponsible than the prohibition of narcotic drugs. Frances Willard spoke about a very real problem in American society, and prohibition was not the only solution she promoted. She helped change a society's view of alcohol—from a substitute foodstuff to a dangerous drug.

Bordin also contends that Willard and the WCTU, as "pragmatic feminists," "played a major role in heightening women's awareness."[23] Writes Bordin, "Through the Union women learned of their legal and social disabilities, gained confidence in their strengths and talents, and became certain of their political power as a group and as individuals."[24] Significantly, Bordin argues that it was Willard's ability to link radical change to traditional values through her oratory which drew thousands of women to suffrage and reform work, when they would not otherwise have been attracted.[25]

Still, from a rhetorical point of view, it seems possible to claim a larger legacy than simply "heightening awareness." Contemporary accounts of her oratory, even after adjusting for their eulogistic exaggeration, are far more commendatory of her oratory. From them, one understands that Frances Willard not only "woke people up," but also moved them to act. Part of her rhetorical legacy can be found in what she moved them to do.

One place to start is with the WCTU itself. Willard's inability to convert the WCTU to Christian Socialism and a continued commitment to "do everything" seems to be a singular indicator of her failure. Writes Bordin, "The public image of the WCTU was changing—from the best, most respected, most forward-looking women in town to narrow-minded antilibertarians riding a hobbyhorse."[26] Campbell places great weight on the fact that "Willard had not converted the WCTU membership to the broad range of reforms that she had espoused."[27] Bordin, too, argues that "in the 1890s [Willard] was unable to carry the Union with her."[28] However, it seems unlikely that the "best, most respected, most forward-looking women" *suddenly* reverted to being "narrow-minded antilibertarians." It is much more probable that, over time, the member*ship* changed, not that 250,000 members abruptly changed their points of view.

The leadership of the WCTU had always been upper- and upper middle-class women, although the membership in general covered the broad spectrum of economic and social status.[29] Many of the officers, such as the new president, were far more conservative than Frances Willard had been, and there is much to support the belief that the organization's change was top-down rather than bottom-up.[30] In fact, no small controversy accompanied the leaders' abandonment of the Do Everything policy, as the pages of the *Union Signal* suggest.[31] And, although conservative, even the officers could not immediately walk away from Willard's legacy. In her first presidential address, Lillian Stevens addressed a range of issues beyond temperance and prohibition: social purity, woman suffrage, peace, polygamy, prison reform, living wages, curfews, lynchings, and vivisection. Thus, while Bordin does indeed argue that the change in emphasis was abrupt, she also notes that the overall change was "gradual, and certainly not complete until the late 1920s."[32]

But what happened to the "best, most respected, most forward-looking women"? It is more than hypothesis to say that Frances Willard influenced many men and women who would later be part of the Progressive movement of the early twentieth century. Knowledgeable contemporary observers, such as B. O. Flower, editor of *The Arena*, a leading reform magazine of the 1890s, understood that Willard's rhetoric reached beyond the WCTU, and could not be judged solely by the later performance of that organization.

These movements [temperance, suffrage, labor reform] that seem to have arisen so suddenly and spontaneously, are the natural and inevitable results of the patient, determined work of a number of women, and some men, who were in a very real sense the sowers of virile thought-seeds throughout the land, chief among whom was Frances E. Willard. . . . Miss Willard went North and South, East and West, and wherever she went she fired the hearts of men and women, some of whom, remaining true to the vision, set to work in every community to advance the great movements to which she had devoted her life.[33]

Frances Willard did not simply assemble a mass organization of women. For all her eloquence, she did not merely charm women into "joining up" and paying dues. She spoke of ideas, to men and women, and many of them were changed by her vision. There is where we should measure her rhetorical legacy.

Woman's suffrage is a case in point. Willard's argument of expediency—that suffrage would bring prohibition—converted many members of the WCTU to the cause of suffrage. In 1881, when the convention adopted Willard's resolution endorsing full suffrage, one delegate told the *Washington Post* that fewer than one in six delegates—herself included—supported the franchise on the basis of natural rights theory. The majority were swayed, she reported, by the expediency argument. "We are not anxious to vote, but if by wielding the ballot we can better accomplish our aims, then welcome the female franchise."[34]

The case can be made that Willard's ability to mobilize the WCTU's membership on behalf of woman's suffrage was instrumental to its ultimate adoption. The suffrage movement counted heavily on WCTU support in many of the Western states, where suffrage was more easily gained, such as South Dakota and Minnesota.[35] Illinois's first suffrage bill—allowing women to vote in certain educational elections—had been drafted by that state's WCTU.[36] By 1900, four states had adopted full franchise laws, while twenty-one other states allowed partial franchise.[37]

It is true that many woman suffragists were ambivalent or hostile to the WCTU's "help" because linking suffrage with prohibition alienated many male voters.[38] Susan B. Anthony, for example, pleaded with Willard to keep the WCTU out of the California campaign, a request Willard tried to keep. It was hard, however, to impose full central control on the independent locals, and Anthony blamed the WCTU for the loss in California.[39] Yet Anthony also had Willard provide the closing address in testimony before the Senate Committee on Woman Suffrage in the spring of 1888, and in *History of Woman Suffrage* Anthony and Ida Husted Harper called it a "touching address."[40] In 1923, Carrie Chapman Catt, former president of the National American Woman Suffrage Association wrote that "[Frances Willard] captivated her audiences, disarmed their prejudices and enrolled them in her cause," of which woman suffrage was one of the most important.[41]

Anthony and Catt understood Willard's importance to the cause because they understood that she brought more than just her organizational skills to the struggle. Willard's arguments—persuasive to conservative, traditional-minded women—attracted many women to the cause of suffrage. John Guinther notes that "the suffragist message was spread throughout the nation by the prohibitionists to working-class women whom the upper-class suffragists, on their own, might have found difficult to reach."[42]   Conservative-minded men were also persuaded. Wrote one observer of the WCTU's 1887 convention to the *Nashville Banner,* "These women are more intelligent than any body of men I ever saw. They are one hundred per cent better orators than men, and display, on average, more intelligence. . . . We need such women to do our voting."[43] Even in the ultra-conservative South, the WCTU helped change minds and "aroused considerable enthusiasm."[44] Significantly, Aileen Kraditor argues that it was the argument of expediency which eventually brought ratification of the Nineteenth Amendment.   "The new era saw a change from the emphasis by suffragists on the ways in which women were the same as men and therefore had the *right* to vote, to a stress on the ways in which they differed from men, and therefore had the *duty* to contribute their special skills and experience to government."[45] This, of course, was very much the argument Frances Willard had advanced two decades earlier. In fact, Kraditor links the suffragists' expediency argument to "the rise of the social gospel," for which Frances Willard had been one of the earliest, and most persuasive, of advocates.[46]

Some scholars, though, argue that appeals to expediency—that is, social feminism—rather than natural rights proved ultimately counterproductive, as it prevented the arrival of complete equal rights.[47] Yet Frances Willard never abandoned the natural rights argument, nor did she ever limit the activities women could or should engage in on behalf of "the home." She simply yoked those arguments to ones which also said that woman would bring a unique perspective to the political sphere, a perspective long ignored but belonging to one-half the country's population. She did not use one argument to the exclusion of the other, even as she emphasized one more than the other. To say women were different from men was not to say they were less than men, nor that they had fewer natural rights than men. Frances Willard simply accepted, and employed, the belief that some differences inherently existed.[48]

Like equality for women, Willard's influence regarding Christian Socialism merits closer examination. She was heavily criticized at the time for adopting the philosophy. Those newspapers which did not ignore her arguments, condemned them.[49] For example, The *Detroit Evening News* chided her for "abandoning" prohibition and emphasizing "personal" change.[50] *The Chicago Inter-Ocean's* criticism was even more to the point: "[Miss Willard's philosophy is] a curious piece of patchwork . . . . it [has] branched out into general politics in a grotesque way. Socialism supplies the material for a large patch of this quilt. The truth is Miss Willard is the victim of a radically wrong theory of reform."[51]   In an editorial responding to her 1894 president's address, the *Cleveland Plain Dealer* was similarly condemnatory. "The Socialistic idea rests largely upon the shallow delusion that under the present order the rich and poor are permanently divided as distinct classes."[52]

If Willard was, however, scorned by the press and abandoned by the leadership of her own organization, Mari Jo Buhle argues that, once again, Willard gained an audience for her rhetoric outside the WCTU. "[Frances Willard] continued to provide inspiration for thousands of [Socialist] party members and sympathizers and reigned as the definitive proof that Socialism was neither immoral nor unAmerican. . . . Even Elizabeth Cady Stanton, champion of women's rights also known for socialistic leanings, paled in reputation next to Willard. One of the most popular propaganda leaflets [of the American socialists] . . . was an excerpt from Willard's 1897 address to the National WCTU."[53] Although Christian Socialism, as a term, never gained much currency in the United States, much of its agenda, renamed the Social Gospel, did become popular with the Progressive movement. Frances Willard wanted the eight-hour day, child labor laws, minimum wage laws, better working conditions for women, the recognition of labor unions, government ownership or regulation of utilities, worker's compensation, and government-sponsored health and retirement plans. All these have been adopted in the twentieth century, even as America continues to reject "socialism" as a label.

While much of Willard's oratory seems dated by its language, many of her ideas sound remarkably modern. Her sense that government was in some large measure responsible for the world in which we live is a twentieth-century political theory. The strength and pervasiveness of that idea, that government can and must play a vital role in creating a kind of "utopia," explains why a modern conservative like Ronald Reagan felt compelled to reassure the nation that he was not removing the "safety net" from under the poor, that he could not overtly dismantle the entitlement programs, and that he was forced to add departments to his cabinet rather than remove them. Willard also sought to redistribute income, although the term was not then current. She not only asked, "Why do one-eighth of the people in the United States own seven-eighths of the property?"; she also suggested that this immense wealth "could be shared with those who are in poverty, not as the outcome of spasmodic individual action, but by steady gravitation of social and governmental laws."[54] By the end of her career she thought poverty was a prime cause of alcohol abuse, and government inaction a prime cause of poverty. To see America turn to the federal government for a "war on drugs" is to see Frances Willard's philosophy in action, but now applied to narcotic and hallucinogenic drugs instead of alcohol. Specific planks of her agenda may have been rejected over time, but Frances Willard's idea of government and society—the essence of her rhetoric—is still with us. Hers was not the only voice raised to propose and defend those ideas, but hers was a loud, and persuasive, one. Hers was an eloquence which influenced a nation then, and now.[55]

However, to gauge Frances Willard's rhetorical legacy only by the content of her discourse is to appreciate but half of her oratory. Her discourse was not only influential, but "eloquent." With what rhetorical style did Willard achieve her influence and eloquence? To what measure were her style, influence, and eloquence joined? To what degree did they, perhaps, work at cross purposes?

Rhetorical critic Karlyn Kohrs Campbell describes Willard's rhetoric as one of "feminine feminism." "Both in content and in style," argues Campbell, "Willard was wholly feminine, utterly ladylike."[56] Regarding content, Willard "fuse[d] traditional values to proposals for social change," and "framed her demands for change so that they appeared to reinforce traditional gender roles."[57] As discussed in Chapter 4, this "traditional perspective" viewed the home as the focal point of women's unique interests, portrayed women as the guardians of family and public virtue, and "appealed to men in terms of their traditional role as protectors of women."[58] As for style, Campbell argues that Willard used "flowery statements," "preferr[ed] vague, undetailed references whose content would be determined by her audiences rather than herself," and her "dresses were ladylike and fashionable."[59]

Many contemporary observers agreed with Campbell's assessment. At a reception for the Reverend Joseph Cook, at which Willard was a featured speaker, the master of ceremonies noted publicly that "Miss Willard proves that a woman can speak logically, earnestly, eloquently, and yet be womanly."[60] A Cheyenne (Wyoming) paper noted similarly, that "in coming before the public she has preserved her womanly gentleness, and endeavors to persuade rather than to convince by argument," and another observer commented on her "womanly voice and manner."[61] Bishop John Heyl Vincent, the founder of Chatauqua, wrote to Willard asking, "[A]re you not an exception? Are you not womanly and yet are you not determined to talk?"[62] Commented Willard on the back of that letter, "I am so glad he thinks me womanly for he said once I couldn't stay so and speak in public."[63]

While the question of content and traditional values has been discussed both in this chapter and in Chapter 4, the matter of style remains. That Frances Willard made some use of a "feminine" style seems correct. For example, in spite of advocating dress reform for women, as a speaker Willard dressed and presented herself in a traditionally feminine manner.[64] As the speeches reprinted in this volume demonstrate, her language was relatively florid.[65] However, Willard also employed significant elements of a masculine style, elements which paradoxically opened new ground for women orators while reassuring her audience that the changes she advocated were rooted in the established order.

In *Eloquence in an Electronic Age*, Kathleen Hall Jamieson contrasts the masculine and feminine styles of speaking. Masculine discourse, writes Jamieson, is impersonal, unemotional, and competitive. It is the discourse of science: tough, rigorous, and rational. In contrast, the feminine style is delicate, emotional, noncompetitive, and nurturing. Where the masculine style tends toward reasoned, evidenced argument, the feminine style is intuitive, relying heavily on personal examples to buttress the speaker's claims.[66] In fact, two of Willard's earliest speeches, "Woman's Lesser Duties" (1863) and "Everybody's War" (1874), could serve as exemplars of what Jamieson calls the feminine style. Significantly, however, Willard's style evolved to include masculine elements as well (e.g., deductive organization, statistical and expert evidence, and an assertive style of attack).

While Willard's speeches were hardly organized as tightly as twentieth-century norms might require, her speeches generally flowed smoothly from proposition to proposition, each tested in turn, each in service of a larger proposition which thematically controlled the speech.[67] Her "Home Protection" address, delivered in 1879, is representative. The speech developed a single, general proposition: that the liquor trade was perverting the democratic process and that only by enlarging the process to include women—by nature opposed to the liquor trade—could the perversion be eliminated. In support of this general proposition Willard formulated four subpoints: that prohibition would work, that giving women the vote would ensure its adoption, that the common objections to woman's suffrage were misplaced, and that prohibition would never be adopted until women were given the vote. As discussed in Chapter 2, Willard organized this speech with a construction and logic conspicuously designed for maximum effect. Indeed, only the last section of the speech was organized in narrative form, but even then the narrative was deductively structured. The story related the experience of Willard and several other women temperance leaders going to the state capital to lobby for prohibition. They met several legislators, all of whom reinforced one message: Because women had no votes, the liquor interests retained a majority of the voters. Without a majority, the temperance movement had no influence to gain prohibition. Each legislator encountered in the story illustrated the point from a different angle. One senator was antiprohibition because his district always voted wet; another wanted to vote prohibition but feared for his reelection; an ex-senator had voted his conscience and lost his reelection; and a fourth legislator did vote dry but only because *his* district was for prohibition.

Within her deductively organized speeches, Willard enfolded arguments and evidence typical of the masculine style. For example, she evidenced many of her claims rigorously. As evidence that prohibition was working in Maine, she included a direct quotation from the president of the National Brewers' Convention lamenting that fact. In support of the proposition that women would indeed vote for prohibition, she cited elections and straw votes from three towns. "In Des Moines, Iowa, . . . as a test of popular opinion, the women voted on the license question: twelve declaring in favor of saloons and eight hundred against them. In Newton, Iowa, at an election ordered by the council, 172 men voted for license to 319 against—not two to one against it; while the women's vote stood one in favor to 394 against licensing saloons. In Kirkville, Mo., ten women favored the liquor traffic, twenty declined to declare themselves, and five hundred wanted 'no license.'"[68]

Similar use of evidence may be found in other speeches as well. For example, her 1885 Annual Address refuted the charge that she had inappropriately linked the nonpartisan WCTU with the Prohibition party. For evidence she noted that she herself had spoken under the auspices of the Prohibition party "less than half a dozen times in my whole life," that the treasurer's report revealed "not a penny" paid for any political purpose, and that other committee reports showed great work done for "philanthropy," but none for partisan politics.[69] Her 1889 Annual Address was awash in the use of statistical evidence. Willard cited the percentage of foreign-born U.S. citizens, the percentage of Americans who attend church, and compared the amount of money spent on alcohol versus the amount spent on education. More exotic figures included the number of steamships landing in New York each month, the number of foreign language newspapers in the United States, and the number of men who patronized a saloon in Cincinnati in the space of a single hour.[70]

Along with her use of statistics, Willard quoted authorities and, in a device typical of the age, unnamed common persons. In "The Coming Brotherhood," she cited Helen Campbell's "The Prisoners of Poverty," a personal interview with Laurence Gronlund, a professor at Harvard, Edward Bellamy's "Looking Backward," and closed with a quote from sociologist John Ruskin.[71] In that speech, too, was an example typical of her use of the unnamed common person. Documenting the terrible conditions existing in the textile sweatshops of the city, Willard began with some statistical evidence regarding the wages made by the women and girls employed in such labor. She then quoted one of the workers, a young girl: "We have six children at home; I give all my money to mother. Father is a builder, and is laid off for the best part of the year, and I don't have a cent for myself; I give it for meat and groceries. My sister is younger than I. She works on neckties. Fun? You ask me if I have fun? I've no time for it."[72]

Finally, Willard's style was also masculine in its willingness to attack those whom she opposed. Although it is true that Willard typically favored compromise over confrontation, she did not usually seek common ground at the expense of principle. Willard repeatedly challenged the liquor interests, the legislators who opposed prohibition, and the business trusts. She was, for example, rather harsh in her denunciation of legislators as she related the lobbying story discussed above. Her speeches often attacked the "foreign element," who disproportionately favored and patronized the saloons. Even the Republican party, typically favored by much of the WCTU membership, was attacked for its general lethargy in regard to prohibition and woman suffrage.[73]

Finally, as noted in Chapter 4, Willard was also quite willing to criticize men. While she praised the "best men" for supporting temperance, suffrage, and labor reform, she was quick to point out that "in short, there are men—and men."[74] There were, for example, "good but unenlightened men" who opposed woman's suffrage.[75] There were also selfish men, who wanted power kept in their hands. "'We want the earth,' is the world-old motto of men. They have had their desire, and we behold the white male dynasty reigning undisputed until our own day, lording it over every heritage."[76] But whether those men opposed to her were devious or naive, Willard recognized and identified—repeatedly—the inherent injustice of a system based on inequality. "Already much has been done in the way of having a police matron at every police station. Before this, women were arrested by whom? By men. Tried by whom? By men. Sentenced by whom? By juries of men. And taken to the Bridewell by whom? By men. They never saw anybody but men."[77] Clearly, Willard's was an oratorical style that did not avoid all confrontation. Willard knew how to blame and attack, and she did so throughout her oratorical career.

In sum, Willard used significant elements of a masculine style throughout her rhetoric. She organized her speeches deductively, she evidenced her carefully reasoned arguments well, and, when she thought it appropriate, attacked her opposition. An editorial in the *Toronto Citizen*, which began by acknowledging a general distaste for speeches by women, commented approvingly that Willard's "style of address is sharp, incisive and convincing," adjectives typically applied to tightly reasoned speeches.[78] Many other commentators similarly noted the deductively logical quality of her speeches. "She is both an eloquent and scholarly speaker, and presents her cause in a manner calculated to elicit the attention, as well as to convince the judgment and touch the heart. . . . Her consideration of the 'personal liberty' argument was logical and strong."[79] It was not simply "sentiment" or "pathos" which Willard elicited from her audience. "[Willard's speeches] will take the hearer somewhat out of the beaten track and send you home with ideas."[80]

A question remains, however, as to why a masculine style, used by a woman orator, might *reassure* rather than *threaten* her audience. Even in the conservative South, Willard's style of address was so overwhelmingly acceptable that it provided a mantle of legitimacy for other women orators. A contemporary observer in Louisiana noted that "women advocates are springing up in the South and are tolerated since Miss Willard's tour."[81] Three reasons help explain the acceptability and reassuring nature of Frances Willard's style: the traditional values the style embodied and espoused, the well-developed ethos of the orator herself, and her metaphors of change.

As discussed above, Willard indeed grounded her arguments in those values traditional of the time. Woman's special place, for example, was the home. Their involvement in the WCTU, in temperance lobbying, in the suffrage movement, child-labor laws, or other reform issues was ultimately based on women's roles as the "necessary and tender guardians of the home."[82] Willard said, "I solemnly call upon my countrymen to release those other hands [i.e., women's], familiar with the pages of the Book of God, busied with sacred duties of the home and gracious deeds of charity, that they may drop in those whiter ballots, which, as God lives, alone can save the state!"[83] Christianity, too, served as a fundamental value upon which Willard based her call for change. Reform was the method by which Christians could "prepare the way" for the Second Coming of Christ. "Note the orderliness of God's method of gradualism and how all tends to good. The evil shows itself and is then tackled by the strong arm of reforms because it can be endured no longer. . . . Little by little, we improve, until finally perfection, which is no trifle, will be the outcome."[84] A host of lesser traditional values were similarly employed: the value of hard work, American values of independence and liberty, the importance of fair play.

Significantly, Willard's style complemented her appeal to traditional values. For example, Willard's use of deductive structure helped clarify the relationship of traditional values to her proposed reforms. At various times woman's suffrage was logically linked to woman's sphere of the home; a "white life for two" to Christian ethics; peace and arbitration to the traditional qualities associated with women.

Willard's mixed-gender style of address was, paradoxically, similarly reassuring. The more obvious indicators of femininity—dress, vocal inflections, general demeanor—suggested the feminine style of address Campbell claims Willard projected, and observers seemed to have seen. The linguistic elements of style, however, were predominantly masculine. By using the traditional linguistic style of public discourse in concert with dominant social values, Willard implied that the changes were ones of degree, not kind, even when calling for total equality for women and for socialist government.

The masculine elements of Willard's style were also reassuring because, by the 1890s, they were an integral part of her platform ethos. Frances Willard began her career preaching only for temperance and Christianity. When in the 1870s she began speaking for suffrage, initially she only advocated the ballot on questions of licensing saloons. She then broadened her appeal to include suffrage for all elections. In the 1880s and 1890s her reform proposals slowly expanded to include other elements of the women's rights and labor movements. By the time Willard was speaking overtly of Christian Socialism, her ethos was well established. As her reform agenda radicalized, she could use her earlier developed ethos—which included significant elements of a masculine style of discourse—as a means of signifying her emphasis on evolution rather than revolution. Frances Willard's style had not changed, the enthymeme would go, therefore, the reassuring, tradition-minded speaker herself had not changed either. Indeed, to have changed to a purely feminine style of address in her later speeches would, rather than reassuring the audience, have likely unsettled them.

Finally, Willard's metaphors and analogies were another element of her style which reinforced the message that her seemingly radical changes were in fact consonant with her audience's traditional value structure. It is important to remember that metaphors are not simply adornment, but epistemic and argumentative. Once accepted by the hearer, they impose a perspective which in turn invites the hearer to arrive at beliefs which are consistent with that perspective. Each of Willard's three dominant metaphorical clusters—Christianity, nature, and science—asked the audience to see change as a natural process, grounded in time-honored laws, through which a Christian utopia could evolve.

Many of Willard's metaphors and analogies were biblical in nature, thus reinforcing the *Christian* in the Woman's Christian Temperance Union. For example, when contrasting towns with saloons against towns with prohibition, Willard argued that "One was the Wilderness, the other is the Promised Land."[85] Amidst the controversy of whether the WCTU should or should not support the Prohibition party, Willard declared that "we love our WCTU too much to cast the first stone."[86] In yet another speech, she called upon her audience to sacrifice themselves to the cause "like Elijah to Horeb, like Isaiah to Exiongeber, like Christ to Calvary!"[87] Grounded in the dominant religion of the time, Christian and biblical metaphors and analogies strengthened Willard's assertion that her changes were rooted in traditional, not radical, values.

Nature was the second metaphorical theme Willard sounded in order to emphasize change within the established order. "A mother's love," for example, "is sure and resistless as the tides of the sea."[88] "Vice," she argued in a different passage, "is the tiger, with keen eyes, alert ears, and cat-like tread, while virtue is the slow-paced, compla-

cent, easy-going elephant."[89]   The latter was the stronger, but the
former more actively sought out its prey. Willard developed a similar,
extended analogy comparing "legitimate" business with that of the
liquor industry. "Legitimate traffic is like the oak tree; in its branches
the birds gather and make their pleasant music; under its shade the
weary herds and flocks find rest and shelter.   There is scarcely
anything living that cannot get good out of the oak tree. It is like
legitimate industry; every other industry is benefitted and helped by it.
But the liquor traffic is like the upas tree, forsaken by every living
thing, because it is the deadly foe of every living thing and drips not
dew, but poison."[90]   As a metaphorical theme, nature suggested a
permanent order to things, even amid change. It implied the presence
of principles that guided all life, principles which were, implicitly, the
traditional values that the audience held and that Willard reinforced.

A third family of metaphors employed by Willard were those of
science and invention. Like Nature, the use of science as metaphor
implied first an established order which could not be denied.[91] For
example, liquor was "impelling to ruin the youth of our day with a
force strong as gravitation."[92] Science was also the means of discov-
ering useful facts within these first principles: "Egyptian astronomers
caused a slanting shaft of stone to be cut through one of their great
pyramids. It pointed to a star near the pole. . . . If we could look
through that stone spyglass of the pyramid to-night, the star that shone
there once would no longer be visible, so greatly has the earth's axis
changed its place. It is so with the human soul; its axis changes, and
stars once bright before the telescope of aspiration pass everlastingly
from view."[93]

Science was also the language of invention. Together, science and
invention indicated the progress which was so honored in the late
nineteenth century. Temperance was advanced as scientific, as part of
the evolutionary progress of civilization toward the eventual millennia.[94] Lobbying efforts to have temperance taught in schools came
under the department of "Scientific Temperance Instruction." For
these reasons, metaphors of invention were common in Willard's
discourse. They indicated the modernity of the temperance cause.
"Battery," for example, was a favorite metaphor indicating the great
energy needed for advancing reform.[95]   Other modern inventions
caught Willard's oratorical eye as well. "The person who would win
must follow a chosen path, as the engine does the track, or the
telegraph message the wire."[96]

The rapid pace of inventions was part of the status quo in the late
nineteenth century. It was change, but change which reassured the
public that progress was indeed at hand. Furthermore, it was change
which reinforced certain traditional American values: hard work,
industry, and "Yankee know-how." Metaphors of invention suggested

that temperance, too, was change, but change which was part of humanity's upward evolution.

These three dominant metaphors in Willard's discourse—of Christianity, nature, and science—were stylistically used to situate her proposed changes within her audience's traditional values. Together with traditional values embedded in a masculine style and her well-developed ethos, these metaphors reassured her audience that the changes she proposed were evolutionary rather than revolutionary. Willard's language was indeed, as Campbell writes, "florid," but it contained flowers with an epistemic purpose.

CONCLUSION

Longinus, in his book *On the Sublime*, commented upon the symbiotic nature of Thought and Diction, also called content and style. They often explain each other, he wrote, for "beautiful words are the light of Thought." In classical rhetorical theory, true eloquence was the unity of great Thought and Diction, each matched perfectly to the other.[97] Many contemporary rhetorical theorists formulate eloquence similarly. "Eloquence," writes Kenneth Burke, "is a frequency of Symbolic and formal effects. One work is more eloquent than another if it contains Symbolic and formal charges"—that is, great thought and powerful diction—"in greater profusion."[98]

If Longinus, Burke, and like-minded theorists are correct, then perhaps it *is* enough to say that Frances Willard was eloquent. She was an astute, broad-minded thinker, and her oratory displayed a talent at uniting thoughts with diction. She blended those values that she found in her audience with her own vision for the future, and she gave voice to both in a style uniquely appropriate to them. Her rhetorical legacy is that of an orator pursuing excellence, often attaining it, sometimes falling short, but always in pursuit of ideas, of which some seeds found fertile ground in America and the world. Certainly she erred at times in her oratory, but her errors were those which result from human fallibility. Her beliefs were, perhaps, not always correct in some philosophical or ontological sense, but we ought not ask of our orators that which we do not ourselves own: possession of absolute Truth. Frances Willard pursued truth to her fullest ability, and she gave that truth, as she saw it, a commanding voice in the public dialogue. Eloquence is neither more, nor less, than that.

NOTES

1. Fort Smith (AR) Daily Herald, 31 Jan. 1882: np, Scrapbook 7, *"Woman's Christian Temperance Union Series,"* Temperance and Prohibition Papers, microfilm ed. (hereafter cited as WCTU Series), reel 30.

2. *Marshall (TX) Tri-Weekly Herald*, 7 Feb. 1882: np, Scrapbook 7, WCTU Series, reel 30.

3. Sarah K. Bolton, "Joseph Cook's Symposium on Temperance," *New York Independent* 18 Mar. 1880: 5.

4. *Freeport Daily Bulletin,* 1 Feb. 1881: np, Scrapbook 14, WCTU Series, reel 32. Emphasis mine.

5. *Hot Springs (AR) Evening Star*, 2 May 1881: np, Scrapbook 14, WCTU Series, reel 32.

6. As quoted in Mary Earhart, *Frances Willard: From Prayers to Politics* (Chicago: University of Chicago Press, 1944) 180.

7. *Review of Reviews* 17 (April 1897): 407.

8. *The Outlook* 26 Feb. 1898: 514. Additionally, see *Washington Post* 21 Feb. 1898: 7; *Chicago Tribune* 19 Feb. 1898: 12; *New York Times* 21 Feb. 1898: 10; and *New York Times* 28 Feb. 1898: 5.

9. Charles J. Little, "Frances E. Willard," *Chatauquan* 27 (1897): 75. Similarly, the *New York Times* wrote that Willard's "gift of language was great." 18 Feb. 1898: 1.

10. Ruth Bordin, *Frances Willard: A Biography* (Chapel Hill: University of North Carolina Press, 1986) 92.

11. Ida Tetreault Miller, "Frances Elizabeth Willard: Religious Leader and Social Reformer," diss., Boston University, 1978, 63.

12. Earhart, *Frances Willard*, 382-383. For the original quote, see Anna Howard Shaw, *The Story of a Pioneer* (New York: Klaus, 1970) 155-156. Originally published in 1915.

13. It should be noted, however, that some eulogists, while generally laudatory, were condemnatory in part. For example, the *Chicago Tribune* noted that it disagreed with Willard on suffrage, third-party politics, and the possibility of universally reforming society, but still acknowledged her "world-reaching influence" and "a power . . . for love, and fellowship, and brotherhood." (19 Feb. 1898: 12)

14. Frances E. Willard, "President's Address (1894)," *Minutes of the National Woman's Christian Temperance Union* (hereafter cited as *Minutes*), 1894 convention, 119. The *Minutes* may be found in the WCTU Series, reels 1-5.

15. Frances E. Willard, "President's Address (1897)," *Minutes*, 1897 convention, 145.

16. Karlyn Kohrs Campbell, *Man Cannot Speak for Her,* vol. 1 (New York: Praeger, 1989) 131.

17. For example, see Sara M. Algeo, *The Story of a Sub-Pioneer* (Providence, RI: Snow and Farnham, 1925) 89-90.

18. Campbell, *Man Cannot Speak For Her*, vol. 1, 131. See also Susan Earls Dye Lee, "Evangelical Domesticity: The Origins of the Woman's National Christian Temperance Union under Frances E. Willard," diss., Northwestern University, 1980, 366-372.

19. Ruth Bordin, *Woman and Temperance* (Philadelphia: Temple University Press, 1981) 154.

20. Ibid, 153-154.

21. Robert H. Walker, *The Reform Spirit in America* (New York: G. Putnam's Sons, 1976) 209-210, 476.

22. Bordin, *Woman and Temperance*, 5-8.

23. Ibid, 9, 157.

24. Ibid, 157.

25. Ibid, 158-160; and Bordin, *Frances Willard*, 9-13.

26. Bordin, *Woman and Temperance,* 155.

27. Campbell, *Man Cannot speak for Her,* vol. 1, 131.

28. Bordin, *Woman and Temperance,* 154.

29. Ibid, 159-160.

30. See Earhart, *Frances Willard*, 373-378. One of the more intriguing questions revolves around the role of Willard's longtime companion, secretary, and organist, Anna Gordon. Later the president of the WCTU, Gordon oversaw much of the organization's transformation. Indeed, Earhart reports that at the 1898 convention Gordon gave a speech in which she claimed Willard had resolved to abandon the Temple project--a highly unlikely occurrence. That speech turned the tide against the project, and the WCTU sold the building. Ibid, 379.

31. Bordin, *Woman and Temperance,* 149-150.

32. Ibid, 155.

33. B. O. Flower, *Progressive Men, Women, and Movements of the Past Twenty-Five Years* (Boston, MA: The New Arena, 1914) 269, 273.

34. *Washington Post*, 28 Oct. 1881: 1.

35. Ibid, 201; and Elizabeth Cady Stanton, Susan B. Anthony, and Matilda Jocelyn Gage, *History of Woman Suffrage*, vol. 3 (New York: Fowler and Wells, 1902) 660.

36. Steven M. Buechler, *The Transformation of the Woman Suffrage Movement: The Case of Illinois, 1850-1920* (New Brunswick, NJ: Rutgers University Press, 1986) 149.

37. Earhart, *Frances Willard*, 209.

38. See, for example, Abigail Scott Duniway, *Path-Breaking: An Autobiographical History of the Equal Suffrage Movement in Pacific*

Coast States, 2d ed. (New York: Klaus, 1971) 187-208. Originally printed in 1914.

39. Rheta Childe Dorr, *Susan B. Anthony* (New York: Frederick A. Stokes, 1928) 316-318.

40. Susan B. Anthony and Ida Husted Harper, *History of Woman Suffrage,* vol. 4, (New York: Fowler and Wells, 1902) 142.

41. Carrie Chapman Catt and Nettie Rogers Shuler, *Woman Suffrage and Politics* (New York: Charles Scribner's Sons, 1923) 134.

42. John Guinther, *Moralists and Managers* (Garden City, NY: Anchor, 1976) 150.

43. Letter to the *Nashville Banner* 19 Nov. 1887, as quoted in A. Elizabeth Taylor, *The Woman Suffrage Movement in Tennessee* (New York: Bookman, 1957) 16.

44. Anthony and Harper, *History of Woman Suffrage,* vol. 4, 874. See also Taylor, *The Woman Suffrage Movement in Tennessee,* 16, 34; and A. Elizabeth Taylor, *Citizens at Last: The Woman Suffrage Movement in Texas* (Austin, TX: Ellen C. Temple, 1987) 79-84.

45. Aileen S. Kraditor, *The Ideas of the Woman Suffrage Movement, 1890-1920* (New York: Columbia University Press, 1965) 66. See also Buechler, 201-202.

46. Ibid. Regarding Willard's role in the Social Gospel movement, see Miller, "Frances Elizabeth Willard," 174-192.

47. Campbell, *Man Cannot Speak for Her,* vol. 1, 121-122, 129; Bonnie J. Dow, "The 'Womanhood' Rationale in the Woman Suffrage Rhetoric of Frances E. Willard," *The Southern Communication Journal* 56 (1991): 305-6; William L. O'Neill, *Everyone Was Brave: A History of Feminism in America* (New York: Quadrangle/New York Times, 1971) 352-353; and Lee, "Evangelical Domesticity," 363-366.

48. For one of her clearest expositions of natural rights versus expediency, see Frances Willard's "President's Address (1894)," 123-124.

49. See, for example, reports on her 1897 Annual Address in the *Buffalo Commercial* 29 Oct. 1897: 8, 11; and *Buffalo Evening News* 29 Oct. 1897: 1. Both papers ignore her section on Labor, although she probably delivered it. (The *Evening News* reports her two-paragraph introduction to the section. It is hard to believe she delivered the introduction but did not follow with the section itself.) The *Commercial* did note, in an oblique comment, that the speech was "wide in scope."

50. As quoted in Earhart, *Frances Willard,* 358.

51. *Chicago Inter-Ocean,* 20 Oct. 1895: np, as quoted in Earhart, *Frances Willard,* 335. Previously, *The Inter-Ocean* had often reported favorably about Willard's work. Many clippings from the paper are included in Willard's scrapbooks.

52. *Cleveland Plain Dealer* 17 Nov. 1894: 8.

53. Mari Jo Buhle, *Women and American Socialism, 1870-1920* (Urbana: University of Illinois Press, 1981) 108.

54. Willard, "President's Address (1894)," 115, 120.

55. Willard was not always "ahead of the curve," however, and a case in point is the controversy about lynching. In 1893, as lynchings in the South were increasing dramatically, the National WCTU passed a resolution condemning lynching as unlawful, but, in a move designed to mollify Southern members, also condemned the "underlying causes" of the lynchings– namely, black rape of white women. Willard and the union came under strong, vocal attack from Ida Tarbell and other reformers who perceived the compromising nature of the resolution. Willard denied any equivocation, but in subsequent resolutions removed the offending codicil. (Bordin, *Frances Willard*, 216-218, 221-222.) Significantly, by 1899 their anti-lynching position was so strong that it was one of the issues which continued to be mentioned in Lillian M. Stevens presidential address. (Lillian M. Stevens, "President's Annual Address," *Minutes*, 1899 convention, 116.) It is worth noting, too, that Willard frequently spoke to black and integrated audiences, and that she shared the platform with black speakers at least as early as 1874. (See Bordin, *Frances Willard*, 113, 222-223; and *Chicago Tribune* 18 Oct. 1874: 4.)

56. Campbell, *Man Cannot Speak for Her*, vol. 1, 129.

57. Ibid, 123.

58. Ibid, 128.

59. Ibid, 129.

60. Dr. Bartol, as quoted in *Our Union*, nd.: np, Scrapbook 14, WCTU Series, reel 32, frame 337.

61. Respectively: untitled newspaper clipping, 23 Apr. 1880: np, Scrapbook 14, WCTU Series, reel 32; and untitled newspaper clippings, June 1875, Scrapbook 4, WCTU series, reel 30, as quoted in Bordin, *Woman and Temperance*, 68.

62. John Heyl Vincent to Willard, 7 Jan. 1877, WCTU Series, reel 30, as quoted in Bordin, *Frances Willard*, 254.

63. As a note to Mary Bannister Willard, 4 Nov. 1884, WCTU Series, reel 13, folder 22, as quoted in Miller, "Frances Elizabeth Willard," 63.

64. Bordin, *Frances Willard*, 122-123. Willard did, however, reject styles and "fads" that she thought unhealthy and impractical.

65. See also Campbell, *Man Cannot Speak for Her*, vol 1, 129; and Bordin, *Frances Willard*, 109.

66. Kathleen Hall Jamieson, *Eloquence in an Electronic Age* (New York: Oxford University Press, 1988) 67-89.

67. As Bordin notes, this is less true of Willard's presidential messages to the WCTU. Like State of the Union messages, however, those addresses were alternately designed to energize the audience and to report on the organization's yearly activities. Those contrary demands disrupted Willard's usual adherence to deductive structure regarding the entire speech. Within sections, however, Willard's use of organization was consistently masculine in style. Bordin, *Frances Willard*, 126-127.

68. Frances E. Willard, "Home Protection," *Home Protection Manual* (New York: The "Independent" Office, 1879) 9.

69. Frances E. Willard, "President's Annual Address (1885)," *Minutes*, 1885 convention, 89.

70. Frances E. Willard, "Tenth Annual Address (1889)," *Minutes*, 1889 convention, 94-97.

71. Frances E. Willard, "The Coming Brotherhood," *Arena* 46 (1892): 321, 324.

72. Ibid, 319.

73. Willard, "President's Annual Address (1885)," 89.

74. Frances E. Willard, *Woman in the Pulpit* (Chicago: Woman's Temperance Publishing Association, 1888) 61.

75. Frances E. Willard, "President's Address (1897)," 133.

76. Willard, *Woman in the Pulpit*, 45.

77. Willard, "The Coming Brotherhood" 321.

78. As quoted in Bordin, *Frances Willard*, 109.

79. *Williamsport (PA) Daily Sun and Banner*, 9 Oct. 1882: np, Scrapbook 7, WCTU Series, reel 30.

80. *Waterbury (CN) Evening American*, 26 Aug. 1878: np, Scrapbook 9, WCTU Series, reel 30.

81. Dr. Davis, as quoted in Earhart, *Frances Willard*, 180.

82. Willard, "Home Protection," 7.

83. Ibid.

84. Frances Willard, "President's Address (1891)," 87.

85. Willard, "First Home Protection Address," *Woman and Temperance* (Hartford, CN: Park, 1883) 455.

86. Willard, "President's Annual Address (1885)," 88.

87. Willard, "Annual Address (1889)," 93.

88. Willard, "First Home Protection Address," 453.

89. Ibid, 452.

90. Willard, "The Coming Brotherhood," 318.

91. Significantly, "science" is also one of the attributes of a masculine style of address. See Jamieson, *Eloquence in an Electronic Age,* 78.

92. Frances E. Willard, *A White Life for Two* (Chicago: Woman's Temperance Publishing Association, 1890) 11.

93. Willard, "Annual Address (1889)," 93.

94. This is a common theme of Willard's speeches. See, for example, Frances E. Willard, "Annual Address (1887)," *Minutes*, 1887 convention, 71-75; and Willard, "The Coming Brotherhood."

95. Frances E. Willard, *What Frances Willard Said*, ed. Anna Gordon (Chicago: F. H. Revell, 1905) 162.

96. Frances E. Willard, "Annual Address (1888)," *Minutes*, 1888 convention, 27.

97. Longinus, *On the Sublime,* trans. W. Hamilton Fyfe (London: Loeb, 1932) 30, 40.

98. Kenneth Burke, *Counter-Statement* (Berkeley and Los Angeles: University of California Press, 1968) 165.

II
COLLECTED SPEECHES

HV5132.W5.A33
HV5232.W5.A25

2667

PF3116 Das Anfangs-buch. Oder, Einleitung zu
.A57   grösseren Schulbuchern, zum Gebrauch
            für kleine Kinder. -- Vermehrte,
IN: verbesserte und illustrirte Auflage. --
gets   Cleveland : Evangelischen Gemeinschaft,
            [1800]?
            64 p. : ill. ; 17 cm.

            1. German language--Readers.   I.
            Evangelische Gemeinschaft.

ABW8041 vbw   10/29/80 GE   Sgets

Everybody's War, 1874

At one of the meetings of the Woman's Temperance Union there was a poor fellow present, written all over from head to foot with evidence of a dissolute life. He came to the altar after the meeting and said to the speaker, "I want you to remain a few moments when the rest are gone for I have something I propose to show you."

Now boys and girls I want you to listen. What do you suppose it was? He took out of his pocket an old soiled package—he took off a paper and inside of that was another, a little cleaner. He took that off and inside was *another* and inside of that was a tissue paper, nice and white, and inside of all this was a photograph. The lady looked at the photograph. It represented a young man about eighteen years old, a pleasant, nice looking young fellow. She looked at this man who was standing there before her, so distressed an object in every way, and she said curiously, this photograph represents a friend of yours perhaps, and what do you suppose he answered her? "Well lady, I ain't showed myself much of a friend to him. That photograph is me, before I took to drinking whisky and I thought to show it to you for my mother's sake." She looked at the frank, open face of the photograph and at the bleared, sad, wrinkled face of the man; at the nice white collar and nice tie in the photograph, then at the thin collarless [undecipherable] of the man. Standing before her so weary and [undecipherable], lay in his happy boyhood days sleeping upon his mother's breast. She thought of the time when first his footsteps wandered beyond the shelter of the great happy home towards the sinful resorts that we legalize on either side along our street. Then she turned to the man and photograph, and turned her eyes to heaven with that old cry, "How long, Oh God, how long?"[1]

This sort of thing might do for others—for other lands, but it will not do for the land of the star spangled banner. It may have done for other times, but it will not do for the nineteenth century. It might do for other people, but it will not do for the descendants of the Pilgrim Fathers and William Penn.

I say there is a war about it in America. A war about that sort of thing which changes men so that their mothers after a few years would not know them, for though all mothers may not have their hearts broken—may have no sons—no boys who carried on to destruction, yet our Christian republic may not legalize the deadly traffic in that which they know by observation is likely in all cases to lead to that precise result.

Ladies of the north side, I am sad but frank to say it, there has not been so much interest shown in this quarter of the city as in others in the temperance movement by the women.

I want to ask you now, if you have not formed before in this work, hadn't you better in the name of these boys and girls sitting here. Hadn't you better? I came here to-day through blocks and blocks of saloons, and almost under the very shadow of great grinding distilleries. There are no insurance policies upon your homes. The rum shops have the free run of the whole place—the home of the American Eagle.

Remember it is simply a matter of fact that from the rum shops every year in America sixty thousand of our citizens reel out inebriated and taste a drunkard's death. There are half a million steady drinkers, behind this a million moderate drinkers, behind *them* two million occasional drinkers, behind them all little boys go tramp, tramp, tramp, to a drunkard's tomb. And remember these reinforcing ranks, for they are always full, you know, must be recruited from somebody's cradle, from somebody's fireside, perhaps your own, no matter how stately or proud your home may be. Some ladies say to me with all sobriety, saying at the same time, "I wish the best in the world for your good cause—I hope it will succeed, but then I have no boys." Perhaps you have daughters. If you have not, somebody has and somebody has boys. If you have daughters and not sons, try to fathom the unfathomable lessons of these words, *"a drunkard's wife."*

There is a war about this in America, a war of mothers and daughters, sisters and wives. There is another sort of war and I want to have the boys and girls follow me as I talk to them and I think I can make you understand me. There is a war between the rum shops and

---

[1] "How long, O God," is a frequent lament in the Old Testament, especially in Psalms. See, for example, Job 19:06, Psalms 13:01, 35:17, 74:10, 79:05, 119:84, and Isaiah 6:11.

religion. They stand against each other, insurmountable and unassailable foes. You know that the late William F. Seward wrote of our late war as our irrepressible conflict. We have an irrepressible conflict, a war to the knife and the knife to the hilt. Only one can win, the question is which one is it going to be. Now think about it. In this war with them, I take it we Christians of the church, we outnumber them.

Did you ever think of it, little people? There are in this city, for instance, a number of churches and for every church there are from twenty-five to thirty whisky shops. There are for every minister twenty-five or thirty barkeepers, and while the churches only meet and open their blessed doors once or twice, or at most four or five times a week, the whisky shops grind on their mill of destruction all the days of every week, all the weeks of every month, and all the months of every year.

We are outnumbered or are we not. We are outgeneraled by the people who keep the rum shops—we who keep the Sunday school and the church. They have a series of lessons, international if you please, with which ours of the Sunday school does not compare at all. They have their music of which I would not speak, their literature free by license of which I would not think. One of our reformed men was talking with me one day of a friend of his who had signed the pledge and broken it. He was discouraged. He had taken a binding pledge and broken it again and again. This is what the reformed man said to me. I said you don't understand this business, that is all. You are new in the business. You must not get discouraged. Don't give Tim up or anything of the sort! You remember he is a graduate in a seven years course in a saloon. It took him seven years to learn all that education in the saloon, now give him a year or two to unlearn it—the education of the saloon.

Then the man went on to say "do you know that, in the saloon, conscience is considered a fraud and a jest? Do you know that in the saloon the religion of Christ is considered just simply an old wife's fable? That Christ is an exploded myth, the Christ of whom you women like to talk about is only the fevered fancy of woman's dreams? I tell you my eyes have been opened with wonder to see things I didn't use[d] to see at all. I saw dear friends going up and down our streets. I saw things I liked to see. I saw [undecipherable] and homes on every side of the way. I saw churches which are suggestive of immortal hope. I saw bookstores at once honey hives of thought."

Do you know that until the Woman's Crusade came sweeping up over our prairies I never cared. I never saw a saloon—it was a question with which I had nothing to do. It was nothing to me. I hoped it would succeed but I did not see it the same as I do today. Let me tell you young people the way I seem to see it now. You just reflect. I go up and down the streets here in Chicago. I go up and down the streets of other towns and cities throughout the west on the errand I believe God sent me to go upon. If I did not believe it I would not go. I see on one corner church spires, both stately and pointing heavenward. I see over on another corner of the same street a schoolhouse with doors opening wide—and little boys and girls, youths and maidens drinking at the pure fountain of knowledge. And between these two are institutions called a saloon, equally guaranteed by our laws—equally fostered by our nation; and more than equally patronized by our people. There is no boy or girl so high that they don't know what I mean. It has a sanded floor, its curtains half way down. It has a screen across the front so you can't see what is going on inside. It has fumes and odors coming out that makes you wish you had passed on the other side. You know I mean the rum shop.

Let us go in with this man who was taught in our Sunday schools. When he was the least bit of a boy he sat on his father's knee, Sunday after Sunday, with an honorable and useful life stretching before him when the minister spoke of life, duty and destiny and another life coming on afterwards. Let us go in with him, with this boy who later was taught in our public schools until he knew something of the world.

But he got in the way of going in here. He did not go at first because he wanted to but because someone asked him to. He did only as often as young men did, and he thought it the proper thing to do, to be sociable. As the habit grew upon him, he failed in business, his friends deserted him, he lost those who were dearer to him than life, then he did not care. Let us go in with some friend and see this transaction. Behind the counter stands avarice, before the counter appetite, and between the two a transaction that puts a few dimes into the till of the proprietor and throws voluntary insanity into the brain of the patron. The man goes out, he goes to the primary meeting and election, he loiters away his time, he fritters away his earnings. He goes to the house where he is best beloved, to the best friends he has in the world, where they love *him* better than they do anybody else. Yet upon that wife that loves him so well and little children clinging about his neck he inflicts atrocities which imagination cannot picture and no tongue dare describe.

Now I am not telling you anything that does not happen in Chicago a hundred times a day. If it had happened away up among the Esquimaux [*sic*], if it had happened down among the South Sea Islanders, or on the prairies where the wild Indians live, we would say it is just what we should expect of such people. But these rum shops do exist and this rum traffic is going on by permission and apathy of well-born, well-bred and well-taught Americans. These rum shops exist in the shape of Juggernaut's old car. They stand in the shadow of the sacred wide arms of the cross of Christ, the Jesus Christ our Lord. That is why there is a war about it in America.

I shall not dwell long on that, but pass on to the taxpayers' revolt. We people don't see the effect of all this. You know, we used to say we must have this money to help pay the taxes, this liquor tax of seventy millions a year. But we have found out that the liquor traffic makes a cat's paw out of the taxpayers to rake in the hot chestnuts of ninety millions a year for extra paraphanalia [*sic*]. I want the boys particularly to remember this—that more than all the revenues derived from the whisky shops must go to build prisons, must go the hospital, the home for the friendless, police justices and police officers to take care of these people who go crazy on purpose and to pay all that so that it costs us yearly the difference between seventy and ninety millions of dollars. We have lost yearly on that old financial basis twenty millions a year. Twenty millions lost. I want you to think about that—that is the very thing we do.

Another thing—I don't suppose everybody who is listening to me knows what all these drinks are made out of. Out of nice clean grain that grows out of the ground, wheat, rye, barley, corn. We use in America forty millions of bushels of nice clean grain is [*sic*] turned over into alcoholic drinks every year. Now a good man has found out by mathematical calculation that we drink enough to pay for paving a good wide street all the way from Chicago to New York. The yearly drink bill in Illinois is forty-two millions of dollars and in the country six hundred millions. There is no use in stopping to dwell longer upon these statistics. These are facts and figures which we cannot deny. We have to take this money out of our pockets and pay it to the very last cent. This we find out from Secretary Bristow[2] in his last report—so it is plain enough.

There is another kind of war—it is the patriot's war. I do not believe there is one boy or girl here to-night that he or she does not revere the old flag, the red, white, and blue. I remember when I was a little girl, away up in Wisconsin, the 4th of July. I remember when we had our little procession and flag made from a pillow case with red calico stripes sewed on and gold stars pinned on the corner. I was going to talk about the harm the liquor traffic does to the country and the flag we love so well, for I tell you I always loved the flag.

Yes, it is a patriot's war because in our country we get up public opinion. Everybody thinks one man's vote is as good as another, even though he staggers up to the polls and drops in the ballot on election day. Our people are made to think you cannot change the habits and drinking customs they had across the sea where one man is not as good as another on election day, where they have such a different government altogether. We should I think remember what difference there is

---

[2] Benjamin Bristow was secretary of the treasury under Ulysses S. Grant. His appointment began on July 3, 1874.

between them and us. We are taught to pray, "Thy kingdom come, thy will be done" where? "On earth" we sing in the sacred hymn "bring forth the diadem and crown him Lord of all." We as people believe what this good book says when it plainly again and again declares that Christ is again going to rule on earth. How is he going to rule until we get all the rum shops out of the way?

Now let us take the contrast—there is Germany, let us take that. Germany is a country governed by a hereditary monarch. They know who is to be the next king. This king, he rules until he is relieved by death. Then his son rules and so on in the never ending formulae. They never ask who is going to be the next President, they know who is going to be the next king. In America, every man is King—King over whom? King over his own self. In Germany, they are ruled by two million bayonets. In America, ballots are bayonets. Every drunkard and every rumseller holds that in his hand, which may shake the very President in his chair. In America there are one million drunkards and rumsellers who stagger up to the polls and exercise that sacred right. They are in every ward, in every precinct and every election district. They stagger up to the polls and drop in their bleared ballots. What fruits can we expect but salary grabbers, credit rings, whisky rings, post tradership rings, and every sort of ring except the ring of the true metal.[3]

Going on at this rate no one needs to be a prophet to see what this thing will lead to. It is a patriot's war indeed, it is everybody's war, great and small, from the least to the greatest, and what a war it is. We must guard it as we would a foreign foe. I like the idea of marching along with men and women who have their eyes open. I like to go along keeping time to the same music, even singing that good old song, "I'm glad I'm in this army/I will battle for the cause." You think maybe the crusade is dead and its banner trailing in the dust. I tell you no. The women who marched with the crusade—don't you believe they are somewhere? The children of these men and women are being sworn at the home altars against this traffic as Hannibal was sworn against Rome. The method is changed, but the movement is just the same. If the world was asleep, you young people would understand that, but the world is awake; its heart is sad, its lips are apart, and its eyelids wide.

I am here tonight dear friends, an American woman forever grateful to the land that has been so good to me and whose path in life has been turned out of the expected channel by the crusade. I am here to ask you just this simple question. Is all this anything at all to you?

---

[3] "Credit rings" refers to the Credit Mobilier scandal. All references in this sentence are to corruption that occurred during the Grant administration.

How do you stand effected by it? How are you toward the temperance reform? How are you in the sentiments you cherish in your hearts, that is it. You know what Mrs. Stowe[4] said about it. If you can't say anything about it, you can feel right. How are you in the sentiments you express? How are you on election day, when aldermen are to be elected? How are you when a notice comes for a primary? How do you stand on the question of New Year's Day? How do you stand in the social sanctity? Let me tell you it makes all the difference in the world how you *stand*, though you never say one word or give one dollar toward our cause. If you only just care.

There is a noble fellow on the board of trade in this city who said to me the other day—I can't do much for the cause. I read about it and think about it but it has just come into my head what I could do. I often am asked when closing a bargain to go out and take a glass of beer or even something stronger. I always used to and used to say to them "I don't care" and thought it was the proper thing to do. I just stopped short off—I will not do it. When men ask me I will say I have joined the temperance ranks—I believe as the women do. That man is a walking temperance lecturer, better than nine-tenths of the temperance lecturers, for he *acts*.

I think we are all sympathetic on this subject. I don't believe there is any difference between us in the contest. We are moving on the enemy's track. I think if I were to ask any little boy or girl here the reason why these people carry on this business, the answer would be because there is money in it. That goes straight to the mark. That answer is just exactly right. There is this about it, there are large sums of money invested in this traffic. Ours is no light reform. There is seven hundred millions invested in this rum traffic this very day, and you know the way to get at these men is to touch them in their pocketbooks. Every man who is reformed by our efforts makes that much less revenue for them. This seven hundred millions ought to be taken out of this rum traffic and be invested in other branches of trade which would go toward making up our national life and prosperity.

I want to say a few words more before I close. I want to say just this one thing more on this subject. In a few days from now you will be called upon to go to the polls in as much as there are to be thirty-six or thirty-eight aldermen to be elected in the city of Chicago. It is a vital question to us what sort of men they are. Although the women cannot go to the polls to vote, let me urge upon their sons and husbands here. Will you remember, good sirs, that when you go to the election you represent more than you did once. You represent more

---

[4] Harriet Beecher Stowe (1811-1896) was a noted abolitionist and author of *Uncle Tom's Cabin*.

thoughts, more work, more prayers. Remember whom you want and whom you will have.

Let us work and pray for the good time coming when this city shall be redeemed. Although we are not voters, we are daughters of America as much as you are sons and patriots. We need money to carry on this war. We cannot like King Midas turn everything into gold. I know that times are hard. You have your office rents to pay and all your other expenses, but we need money to buy temperance literature and different things we have to have to carry on this war. And when you can give a dollar, remember that you cannot give it to a more worthy cause than ours.

Then I want the boys to remember that men are only boys grown tall. We count on you to help our cause. We should have the aid of the young men in the strength and vigor of their youth, in the glory of their manhood. And I want the young ladies to support them in their work. You who are sheltered at home must remember that they are tempted and tried. I want you to remember that your words and acts in the social circle have everything to do with the way in which young men stand affected by this temperance question.

And often to me nowadays comes the thought of something in my life very dear and distant—something which I do not hesitate to speak to you about. I want to speak to you about my sister, loved and lost. Many years ago away up in Wisconsin where we spent our girlhood days—that girl was my only playmate, and there upon a fallen tree trunk Little Lizzie, she would stand and make a temperance speech to me, little thing, and I in turn would make one to her just for play. And now I think as I go about this new and strange work that she knows about it, that I am not alone.

I am reminded of the sad, sweet message she left when she went away from us. It was on a bright June morning when she died and Father said to her, for he loved her, no one better than her, "My child, if I should tell you that God wanted you, how would you feel?" She turned to him almost reproachfully and said, "Father, I did not think I should die because you know I am so young. And yet if God should want me I would say take me home." She said—"it is Christ I want, I wish he would come nearer." Although I never had prayed before, Father and Mother and I knelt beside her dying and we prayed that she might feel the grasp of Father's hand, so kind and loving. I remember she smiled, and said "Sister, you need not pray now, he has come. It seems as if he is all my own." And then she laid [*sic*] her dying head upon the pillow and looked at me with that strange look in her eyes which were growing dim. She uttered these last words, "Sister, I want you to tell everybody to be good." Then she turned her face away and when I saw it next it had upon it that smile of God's eternal peace.

I say to-night I want to leave in your hearts these burning words. I do not think I shall ever forget her sweet dying message. I wish it might be remembered as she so greatly expressed it, "be good." Be good and help everybody to be good who needs help. God grant that each of us this night may have a clear formula of life which should be nothing more nor less than be *good*.

Home Protection, 1879

Once more will the time-honored declaration be made to-day, by a thousand Fourth of July orators, that "the Americans are a free people." But I insist that we are governed by the most powerful king whose iron rule ever determined the policy, molded the institutions, or controlled the destinies of a great nation.

So pervasive is his influence that it penetrates to the most obscure and distant hamlet with the same readiness, and there wields the same potency as in his empire's capital; nay (with reverence be it said), he is like Deity in that his actual presence is co-extensive with his vast domain. Our legislatures are his playthings, our congressmen his puppets, and our honored President the latest child of his adoption. We do not often call him by his name, this potentate of million hands and myriad voices; but, to my thinking, nothing is to-day so vital to America as that we become better acquainted with our ruler. Let me then present to your thought his Majestic Highness KING MAJORITY, Sovereign Ruler of these United States.

Let me now introduce a different character, who comes to the court of King Majority as chief ambassador from the empire of his Satanic Majesty. Behold! I show you the skeleton at our patriotic banquet. It has a skull with straightened forehead and sickening smile; but bedecked with wreaths of vine, clusters of grape, and heads of golden grain—King Alcohol, present at court in radiant disguise. With a foaming beer-mug at his lips, he drinks the health of King Majority; and, placing at his feet a chest of gold labeled "Internal Revenue," he desireth conditions of peace.

Behold in these two figures the bewildering danger and ineffable hope of the Republic! How can we rouse the stolid giant, King Majority? How light in those sleepy eyes the fires of a holy and relentless purpose? How nerve once more, with the resistless force that smote African slavery to death, the mighty sinews of the Republic's sleeping king?

How?   Only by "sweet reasonableness"; only by ceaseless persuasion; only by noble examples; only by hard work based upon fervent and effectual prayer.

Human heads and hearts are much alike. I remember that the great Temperance Crusade of 1874 found me with a beer keg in my cellar, a fatal haziness in my opinions, a blighting indifference to the temperance reform upon my will. But how did its intense pathos melt my heart; how did its mighty logic tune the lax cords of opinion to concert pitch; how did its miracle of prayer bring thousands to their knees, crying: "Lord, what wouldst thou have me to do?"[1]   For myself, I could never be the same after that. As a woman, a patriot, a Christian, my heart is fixed in deathless enmity to all that can intoxicate. The same influences which so transformed one brain and heart are steadily at work to-day in a thousand quiet ways.

The sober second thought of the Woman's Temperance Crusade was organization. The voice of God called to them from the lips of his prophet: "Make a chain, for the land is full of bloody crimes and the city is full of violence."[2]   And so in every town and village we are forming these chains of light and of loving helpfulness, which we call "Women's Christian Temperance Unions." We have already twenty-three states organized, with thousands of local auxiliaries. Every day brings fresh accessions of women, translated out of the passive and into the active voice on this great question of the protection of their homes. Of the fifty-four thousand papers published in this country eight thousand have temperance facts and figures regularly provided by members of our societies. Temperance literature is being circulated; *Our Union*, the official organ of the Women's National Temperance Society, has a large subscription list; Sabbath-schools are adopting our plans of temperance instruction; and hundreds of juvenile societies are inscribing on their banners: "Tremble, King Alcohol! We shall grow up." Friendly inns and temperance reading rooms are multiplying; Gospel meetings conducted by women are reaching the drinking class in hundreds of communities; the Red and Blue Ribbon Movements have attained magnificent proportions; and all this many-sided work is fast concentrating its influence to place the ballot in the hand of woman, and thus capture for the greatest of reforms old King Majority. Magnificent is the spectacle of these new forces now rallying to the fray. Side by side with the 500,000 men whose united energies are expended in making and selling strong drink, we are working day by

---

[1] Acts 9:6.
[2] Ecclesiastes 7:23.

day. While they brew beer we are brewing public sentiment; while they distill whisky we are distilling facts; while they rectify brandy we are rectifying political constituencies; and ere long their fuming tide of intoxicating liquor shall be met and driven back by the overwhelming flood of enlightened sentiment and divinely aroused energy.

"To be sure, King Majority gave prohibition to Maine, but prohibition doesn't prohibit," interrupts Sir Sapient, whose remark furnishes a striking illustration of the power of the human mind to resist knowledge. Just take the spyglass of observation, and behold from Kittery to Calais the gleaming refutation of your error.

Less than thirty years ago they had four hundred open hotel bars and ten miles of saloons. To-day Dr. Hamlin, of Constantinople, tells us that, coming home, after forty years' absence, he finds his native state thoroughly renovated from the liquor traffic. Gen. Neal Dow[3] testifies that the law has absolutely driven the sale of strong drink out of all rural districts; and in the larger towns, instead of the free, open sale of former years, it is crowded into secret places, kept by the lowest class of foreigners. Ex-Govs. Dingley and Perham and Senator Blaine and Representative Frye declare that it is as well enforced as the law against stealing; and even sensational journalists have not told us that thieves flourish in the Pine Tree State. Mr. Reuter, of Boston, president of the National Brewers' Convention, held in St. Louis four weeks ago, says: "Formerly Maine produced nearly ten thousand barrels of beer annually, but this has fallen to *seven barrels*, in consequence of the local enforcement of prohibitory law." Surely, this gentleman should be considered as good authority on this subject as a convict is of the strength of his prison bars!

But you say "Maine is different from any other state." Why so? Are not its citizens of like passions with other men? Turn your glass upon a panorama of Maine as it was in former days. See yonder stalwart workers in the harvest-field paying vigorous addresses to the little brown jug; observe its ubiquitous presence at the logging bee, the "raising," the wedding, and the funeral; see it pass from lip to lip around the fireside circle; observe the Gospel minister refreshing himself from the demijohn of his parishioner and host; and be assured that within the memory of men now living these were every-day events. I have this testimony from the most honored residents of Maine, whose recitals involved the words, "all of which I saw and part of which I was." But, as gallant Neal Dow hath it, "Maine was sown knee-deep with temperance literature before we reaped the harvest of prohibition." Let us note the evolution of this seed-planting. Land owners found that two-thirds of their taxes resulted from the liquor

---

[3] Neal Dow; the chief proponent of the 1840 Maine prohibitory law, commonly referred to as the "Neal Dow Law."

traffic (largely in cost of prosecuting criminals and taking care of lunatics and paupers); so they concluded that legalizing saloons for the sake of the revenue was penny wisdom and pound foolishness. Business men discovered that the liquor traffic is a pirate on the high seas of trade, that the more the grog-shop is patronized the fewer customers there are for flour and fuel, boots, shoes, and clothes; and so, in self-defense, they declared for prohibition. Church people found that fifteen times as much money went to the dram-shop as to the church, and that the teachings of the one more than offset those of the other with the young men of the state; so they perceived they could not conscientiously ally themselves with the liquor traffic by their votes. Those interested in education learned that enough money was swallowed in drinks that deteriorate the brain to furnish a schoolhouse for every fifty boys and girls, and to set over them teachers of the highest culture; and they saw it was unreasonable to defend the liquor traffic. In short, the majority came to believe that, between the upper and nether mill-stones of starving out saloons, on the one hand, and voting them out, on the other, they could be pounded to death; and they have so pounded them. The question of selling as a beverage the drinks which we know by centuries of demonstration will so craze men that they will commit every crime and show the subtlest cruelty to those they love the best, is not to-day in Maine an open question with either party, any more than trial by jury or imprisonment for theft. True, the people had a thirty years' war before the declaration of this blessed peace; but what are thirty years when crowned at last by the surrender of King Alcohol to King Majority?

"Ah! but," pursues our doubting friend, "Maine is a peculiar state, in this: it has few foreigners, with their traditions of whisky and of beer."

I grant you, there we are at disadvantage. But go with me to the Cunard wharves of Boston and to Castle Garden of New York, and, as the long procession of emigrants steps across the gangway, you will find *three times as many men as women.* How can we offset their vote for free liquor, on Sundays and all days? Surely, the answer to this question is not far to seek. Strengthen the sinews of old King Majority, by counting in the home vote to offset that of Hamburg and of Cork, and let American customs survive by utilizing (at the point where by the correlation of governmental forces "opinion" passes into "law") the opinion of those gentle "natives" who are the necessary and tender guardians of the home, of tempted manhood and untaught little children.

Hands which have just put aside the beer mug, the decanter, and the greasy pack of cards are casting ballots which undermine our Sabbaths, license social crimes that shall be nameless, and open 250,000 dram-shops in the shadow of the church and public school. I solemnly call upon my countrymen to release those other hands, familiar with the pages of the Book of God, busied with sacred duties of the home and gracious deeds of charity, that they may drop in those whiter ballots, which, as God lives, alone can save the state!

Kind friends, I am not theorizing. I speak that I do know and testify what I have seen. Out on the Illinois prairies we have resolved to expend on voters the work at first bestowed upon saloon-keepers. We have transferred the scene of our crusade from the dram-shop to the council-room of the municipal authorities, whence the dram-shop derives its guaranties and safeguards. Nay, more. The bitter argument of defeat led us to trace the tawny, seething, foaming tide of beer and whisky to its source; and there we found it surging forth from the stately capitol of Illinois, with its proud dome and flag of stripes and stars. So we have made that capitol the center of our operation; and last winter, as one among the many branches of our work, we gathered up 175,000 names of Illinois's best men and women (80,000 being the names of voters), who asked the legislature for a law giving women the ballot on the temperance question. In prosecuting our canvass for these names, we sent copies of our "Home Protection Petition" to every minister, editor, and postmaster in the state; also to all leading temperance men and women, and to every society and corporation from which we had anything to hope.

In this way our great state was permeated, and in most of its towns the petition was brought before the people. The religious press was a unit in our favor. The reform clubs of the state, with ribbons blue and red, helped us with their usual heartiness and efficiency. And what shall be thought of the advance in public sentiment, when (as was often done) all the churches join on Sabbath night in a "Union Home Protection Meeting," and ministers of all denominations (Presbyterians included) conduct the opening exercises, after which a woman presents the religious duty of women to seek and men to supply the temperance ballot; and, to crown all, conservative young ladies go up and down the aisles earnestly asking for signatures, and the audience unite in singing

"Stand up, stand up for Jesus
Ye soldiers of the Cross;
Lift high His royal banner,
It must not suffer loss."

Friends, it means something for women of the churches to take this radical position. America has developed no movement more significant for good since the first dawning of the day we celebrate.

The State of Indiana stands with us; only there the temperance women have worked out the problem of deliverance further than we, and asked for the ballot on all questions whatsoever. They do the same in Minnesota and in Iowa; while at the East the W.C.T.U. of grand old Maine endorses the temperance vote, and Rhode Island sends to Illinois resolutions of approval, while Massachusetts, under Mary A. Livermore, has declared for Home Protection and is preparing for the fall campaign; and within a few days Ohio, the Crusade State, which is the mother of us all, has fallen into line. The most conservative states are Connecticut, New Jersey, Pennsylvania, and New York; but in each of these there are many brave women, who but bide their time for this same declaration, and the whole twenty-three states already joined in the Woman's National Christian Temperance Union will ere long clasp hands in the only work which can ever fulfill the glorious prophecy of the Crusade. History tells us that on the morning of December 23d, 1873, when in Hillsboro, Ohio, the pentecostal power fell on the "praying band" which first went forth, the leading men of that rum-cursed town went out from the church where their wives and mothers had assembled, saying: "We can only leave this business with the women and the Lord." History has repeated itself this winter in our Illinois crusade. Men have placed money in our hands to carry on the Home Protection work, saying: "The women of America must solve this problem. Our business relations, our financial interests, our political affiliations and ambitions have tied our hands; but we will set yours free, that you may rid us of this awful curse."

Yet a few men and women, densely ignorant about this movement, have been heard to say: "Who knows that women would vote right?" I confess that nothing has more deeply grieved me than this question from the lips of Christian people. Have distillers, brewers, and saloon-keepers, then, more confidence in woman's sense of goodness than she has herself? They have a very practical method of exhibiting their faith. They declare war to the knife and the knife to the hilt against the Home Protection Movement. By secret circulars, by lobbyists and attorneys, by the ridicule of their newspaper organs, and threats of personal violence to such women of their families as sign our petition, they display their confidence in womankind.

The only town in Illinois which sent up a delegation of citizens openly to oppose our petition was Belleville, with its heavy liquor interest and ten thousand German to three thousand American inhabitants; and among our 204 legislators there were no other dozen men whose annoyance of the Home Protection Committee was so persistent and so petty as that of the senator who openly declared that he was there to defend the vested interests of his Peoria constituents, who in 1878 produced eight million dollars' worth (?) of ardent spirits. Nay, verily, woman's vote is the way out of our misery and shame, "our enemies themselves being judges";[4] and none see this so clearly as the liquor dealers, whose alligator eye is their pocket-book, and the politicians, whose Achilles heel is their ambition. The women of the Crusade must come once more to judgment—not, as aforetime, with trembling lip and tearful eye; but reaching devout hands to grasp the

---

[4] Deuteronomy 32:31.

weapon of power and crying with reverent voice: *"The sword of the Lord and of Gideon!"*[5]

But, after all, "seeing" is a large part of "believing" with this square-headed Yankee nation; so let us seek the testimony of experience.

In Kansas the law provides that the signatures of women shall be requisite to a petition asking for a dram-shop before that boon shall be conferred upon any given community. This arrangement wrought such mischief with the liquor dealers that they secured an amendment exempting large towns from such bondage. But in small towns and villages it has greatly interfered with the traffic, and has so educated public sentiment that prohibition can—with impunity!—form the theme of a governor's inaugural, and Kansas is on the war-path for a law hardly less stringent than that of Maine.

In Des Moines, Iowa, a few weeks since, as a test of popular opinion, the women voted on the license question; twelve declaring in favor of saloons and eight hundred against them. In Newton, Iowa, at an election ordered by the council, 172 men voted for license to 319 against—not two to one against it; while the women's vote stood one in favor to 394 against licensing saloons. In Kirkville, Mo., ten women favored the liquor traffic, twenty declined to declare themselves, and five hundred wanted "no license." In our Illinois campaign, which resulted in 95,000 names of women who expressed their wish to vote against saloons, not one woman in ten declined to affix her name to our petition.

The attitude of the Catholic Church was friendly to our petition, many priests urging their people to sign. Irish women, as a rule, gave us their names, and saloon-keepers' wives often secretly did so. Scandinavians were generally enthusiastic for the petition. Germans opposed us; but the reply of one of them indicates the chivalric nature which will come to our aid when our invincible argument against beer shall be brought in contact with German brain and German conscience. He said: "If it is not the pledge, I will sign it. I cannot give up my beer, *but I want to help the ladies*." To be sure, German saloon-keepers were universally and bitterly antagonistic, and had so much to say about "women keeping inside their proper sphere."

But the convictions which supply me with unalterable courage and unflagging enthusiasm in the Home Protection work are not based upon any proof I have yet given. No argument is impregnable unless founded on the nature of things.

The deepest instincts and the dearest interests of those who have the power to enact a law must be enlisted for its enforcement before it will achieve success. For instance, the 15th Amendment to the

---

[5] Judges 7:20.

Constitution of the United States is going to be enforced by the ballots of colored men who once were slaves, just so long as those men retain their reason and their color. By parity of reasoning, if you can enlist in favor of a local option or prohibition law the dearest interests of a class in the community which in all the ages of wine and beer and brandy drinking has not developed (as a class) the appetite for them nor formed the habit of their use, you will have something trustworthy on which to base your laws. We temperance people have looked over at the rum power very much as the soldiers of Israel did at Goliath of Gath. We have said: "He has upon his side two of the most deeply-rooted instincts of human nature—in the dealer the appetite for gain, and in the drinker the appetite for stimulants—and we have nothing adequate to match against this frightful pair."

But, looking deeper, we perceive that, as God has provided in Nature an antidote for every poison, and in the kingdom of his grace a compensation for every loss, so in human society he has ordained against King Alcohol, that worst foe of the social state, an enemy beneath whose blows he is to bite the dust. Take the instinct of self-protection (and there is none more deeply seated): What will be its action in woman when the question comes up of licensing the sale of a stimulant which nerves with dangerous strength the arm already so much stronger than her own, and which at the same time so crazes the brain God meant to guide that manly arm that it strikes down the wife a man loves and the little children for whom when sober he would die? Dependent for the support of herself and little ones and for the maintenance of her home, upon the strength which alcohol masters and the skill it renders futile, will the wife and mother cast her vote to open or to close the rum-shop door over against that home?

Then there is a second instinct, so much higher and more sacred that I would not speak of it too near the first. It is as deep, but how high it reaches up toward Heaven—the instinct of a mother's love, a wife's devotion, a sister's faithfulness, a daughter's loyalty! Friends, this love of women's hearts was given for purposes of wider blessing to poor humanity than some of us have dreamed. Before this century shall end the rays of love which shine out from woman's heart shall no longer be, as now, divergent so far as the liquor traffic is concerned; but through that magic lens, that powerful sunglass which we term the ballot, they shall converge their power, and burn and blaze on the saloon, till it shrivels up and in lurid vapors curls away like mist under the hot gaze of sunshine. Ere long our brothers, hedged about by temptations, even as we are by safeguards, shall thus match force with force; shall set over against the dealer's avarice our timid instinct of self-protection, and match the drinker's love of liquor by our love of him. When this is done you will have doomed the rum power in America, even as you doomed the slave power when you gave the ballot to the slave.

"But women should content themselves with educating public sentiment," say one. Nay, we can shorten the process; for we have the sentiment all educated and stored away, ready for use in brain and heart. Only give us the opportunity to turn it to account where in the least time it can achieve the most! Let the great guns of influence, not pointing into vacancy, be swung to the level of benignant use and pointed on election day straight into the faces of the foe! "No; but she should train her son to vote aright," suggests another. But if she could go along with him, and thus make one vote two, should we then have a superfluous majority in a struggle intense as this one is to be? And then how unequal is her combat for the right to train her boy! Enter yonder saloon. See them gathered around their fiery or their foamy cups, according to the predominance in their veins of Celtic or of Teuton blood. What are they talking of, those sovereign citizens? The times have changed. It is no longer tariff or no tariff, resumption of specie payments, or even the behavior of our Southern brethren that occupies their thought. No. Home questions have come elbowing their way to the front. The child in the midst is also in the market-place, and they are bidding for him there, the politicians of the saloon. So skillfully will they make out the slate, so vigorously turn the crank of the machine, that, in spite of churches and temperance societies combined, the measures dear to them will triumph and measures dear to the fond mother heart will fail. Give her, at least, a fair chance to offset by her ballot the machinations which imperil her son.

"But women cannot fight," you say, "and for every ballot cast we must tally with a bayonet." Pray tell us when the law was promulgated that we must analyze the vote at an election, and throw out the ballots of all men aged and decrepit, halt and blind? Do not let the colossal example of Judge David Davis[6] so fill our field of vision that we cannot perceive brain, and not bulk, to be the rational basis of citizenship. Avoirdupois[7] counts greatly among the Zulus; but is a consideration far less weighty with the Americans than it was before the Geneva Arbitration. I venture the prediction that this Republic will prove herself the greatest fighter of the nineteenth and twentieth centuries; but her bullets will be molded into printers' type, her Gatling guns will be the pulpit and the platform, her war will be a war of words, and underneath the white storm of men's and women's ballots

---

[6] Judge David Davis (1815-1886) was a Democratic Congressman who, in exchange for a judgeship, helped elect the Republican Rutherford B. Hayes as president in 1876, even though Democrat Samuel Tilden had garnered a greater number of popular votes.

[7] Avoirdupois: weight, typically in reference to the heaviness of a person.

her enemies—state rights, the saloon, and the commune—shall find their only shroud.

Of the right of woman to the ballot I shall say nothing. All persons of intelligence, whose prejudices have not become indurated beyond the power of logic's sledge hammer to break them, have been convinced already. For the rest there is no cure save one—the death cure—which comes soon or late and will open more eyes than it closes. Of the Republic's right to woman's ballot I might say much. Well did two leaders of public thought set forth that right when Joseph Cook[8] declared that "woman's vote would be to the vices in our great cities what lightning is to the oak"; and when Richard S. Storrs[9] said: "If women want the suffrage they will be sure to have it, and I don't know but when it comes it will turn out to be the precious amethyst that drives drunkenness out of politics."

"But women do not care to vote." This is the "last ditch" of the conservatives. The evolution of temperance sentiment among women hitherto conservative refutes this argument; yet I confess there are many who do not yet perceive their duty. But Jack's beanstalk furnishes only a tame illustration of the growth of women in this direction in the years since the Crusade. Of this swift growth I have already given abundant proof. It is, in my judgment, the most solid basis of gratitude on this national anniversary.

During the past years the women who pioneered the equal suffrage movement, and whose perceptions of justice were keen as a Damascus blade, took for their rallying cry: "Taxation without representation is tyranny." But the average woman, who has nothing to be taxed, declines to go forth to battle on that issue. Since the Crusade, plain, practical temperance people have begun appealing to this same average woman, saying "With your vote we can close the saloons that tempt your boys to ruin"; and behold! they have transfixed with the arrow of conviction that mother's heart, and she is ready for the fray. Not rights, but duties; not her need alone, but that of her children and her country; not the "woman," but the "human" question is stirring women's hearts and breaking down their prejudice to-day. For they begin to perceive the divine fact that civilization, in proportion as it becomes Christianized, will make increasing demands upon creation's

---

[8] Flavius Joseph Cook (1838-1910) was a Boston clergyman and well- known lecturer. His series of "Monday Lectures," in which he reconciled and synthesized modern philosophy, science, and religion, were popularly attended and widely reprinted. Cook was also a close personal friend of Frances Willard.

[9] Richard S. Storrs (1821-1900), a Congregational clergyman and well-known lecturer, was an active civic worker in religious, educational, and philanthropic affairs in New York City.

gentler half; that the Ten Commandments and the Sermon on the Mount are voted up or voted down upon election day; and that a military exigency requires the army of the Prince of Peace to call out its reserves.

The experience which opened the eyes of one cultured conservative in Illinois is here in point.

Mrs. Pellucid[10] was my companion at the Capitol, where, with other ladies, we spent several weeks in the endeavor to secure legislative support for our Home Protection measures. One of the members, when earnestly appealed to, replied, with a rueful grimace: "Ladies, when I tell you the leading towns in the district I represent, you will see that I cannot do as you wish," and he rattled off such names as "Frankfort, Hamburg, and Bremen," wished us "the success that our earnestness merited," and bowed himself out.

"Why—what—does—he—mean?" inquired my lovely Conservative, in astonishment.

A committee clerk stood by, who answered, briskly, "Why, ladies, Mr. Teutonius represents a district in which German voters are in the majority; therefore, he cannot support your bill."

"Why, I thought a lawmaker was to represent his own judgment and conscience," murmured the sweet-voiced lady.

"His judgement, yes; for that tells him on which side the majority of votes in his district is located. His conscience, no; for that would often cost him his chances for a political future," answers the well-instructed youth.

"O-o-oh!" softly ejaculated Mrs. Pellucid, in the key of E flat, minor scale.

By this time Mr. Politicus entered; in response to our invitation, of course—he never would have come on his own motion. After a brief conversation, he pledged himself to vote for our bill and to make a speech in our favor. Nevertheless, if you should glance over the list we are carefully preserving and industriously circulating in Illinois, of men who voted against us, you would find his name. But he is an honest fellow in his way, and we owe it to a motion made by him that women were, for the first time in history, allowed to speak before the legislature of Illinois. He explained his desertion of the temperance cause on this wise: "I tell you ladies, I've got to go back on you. I'm leader of my party in the House, and they've cracked the party whip

---

[10] Pellucid: transparent, clear in meaning, expression. Willard identifies "Mrs. Pellucid" in *Woman and Temperance* as Mrs. E. G. Hibben, who was Willard's successor as President of the WCTU of Illinois. Willard does not reveal the real-life names of the other characters in the story. (New York: Arno, 1972) 370.

mighty lively around my ears. The long and short of it is, I've got to represent the men that voted me in."

Poor Mrs. Pellucid! How appealing was her voice, as she replied: "But I am sure your better nature tells you to represent us." Mr. Politicus brought his great fist down on the table with a stalwart thump and said: "Course it does, Madam; but, Lord bless you women, you can't stand by a fellow that stands by you, *for you hain't got any votes.*" Just here a young lady of the group piped up: "Oh! but we would persuade our friends to vote for you." "Beg pardon, Miss; but you couldn't do nothin' of the kind," said he. "Don't you s'pose I know the lay o' the land in my deestrict?" The young lady now grasped the other horn of the dilemma, saying desperately: "But we will get the temperance men in your district to vote against you if you desert us in this manner." His rejoinder was a deplorable revelation to our simple-minded company: "Never a bit on't, Miss. The temperance men are an easy-going lot, and will vote the party ticket anyhow. Old dog Tray's ever faithful! We've ignored them for years; but they come up smilin' and vote the Republican ticket all the same. You'll see!" "But won't you stand by us for God and home and native land!" pleaded Mrs. Pellucid, with a sweetness that would have captured any man not already caught in the snares of a gainsaying constituency. The worthy politician thumped the table again, and closed the interview by saying: "You women are altogether too good to live in this world. If you could only vote, you'd have this legislature solid. But, since you can't, I'm bound to stand by such a conscience as I've got, and it tells me to stick to the fellows that voted me in. Good-morning!" And he got speedily out of the range of those clear, sad eyes. Mr. Readyright (an ex-senator) came in. With all the vehemence of his Irish nature he anathematized the "weak-kneed temperance men." "Sure as you're living, Politicus told you the truth," said he. "The temperance men are the foot-ball of the parties. There's none so poor to do 'em reverence. Where are the plucky young fellows that were here when we gave Illinois her present local option law?" (By the way, that law bears the name of this valiant senator, who is, by the same token a Democrat.) "Where are they? Out in the cold, to be sure. Did the temperance folks remember their services and send 'em back? Not a bit of it. But the whisky men didn't forget the grudge they owed 'em, and they're on the shelf to-day—every last man of 'em." "I tell you," and the wise old gentleman gesticulated wildly in his wrath, "until you women have the power to say who shall make the laws and who shall enforce 'em, and to reward by re-election them that are faithful to your cause and punish by defeat them that go back upon it, you may hang your bonnets on a very high nail, for you'll not need 'em to attend the funeral of the liquor traffic!" "Why," exclaimed one of the ladies confusedly, "you don't mean to say that the temperance ballot is not enough and that we must follow in the footsteps of Susan B. ———?"[11] The sturdy old gentleman walked out the door, and fired this Parthian arrow back at us: "Susan could teach any one of ye your a-b-abs. This winter's defeat'll be a paying investment to ye all, if ye learn that a politician is now and ever will be the drawn image, pocket edition, safety-valve, and speakin' trumpet of *the folks that voted him in.*"

The ladies drew a long breath. "I begin to see men as trees walking," slowly murmured sweet Sister Pellucid.

"But we must bide the Lord's time," warningly uttered an old lady, who had just arrived. To her the brisk committee clerk ventured this answer: "But Senator Readyright says you'll find the Lord's time will come just about twenty-four hours after the women get their eyes open!"

A temperance member of the House is the last caller whom I will report. He spake in this wise: "Ladies, I pretend to no superior saintship. I am like other men, only I come from a district that would behead me if I did not stand by you. I have a pocket full of letters, received to-day from party leaders at home, assuring me I run no risk." At the close of three weeks of such a school as this, one of our radicals asked Mrs. Pellucid, chief of conservatives, this pointed question: "Are you still for the Home Protection vote alone, or for the ballot on all questions?" She replied, in thrilling tones and most explicit words: "Any woman who could have shared our bitter experience here without desiring to vote on every officer, from constable to President, would be either a knave or a fool."

This lady reasoned that, since we are solemnly bound to be wise as serpents, we must harness self-interest to our on-moving chariot. The great majority of men who are in office desire to be re-elected. By fair means, if they can; but to be re-elected anyhow. Only in one way can they bring this to pass, by securing on their side old King Majority. If we furnish them with a constituency committed to the proposition "The saloon must go," then go it will, and on the double quick. Let the city council know that women have the ballot, and will not vote for them if they license saloons, and they will soon come out for prohibition. Let the sheriff, marshal, and constable know they that their tenure in office depends on their success in executing the law thus secured, and their faithfulness will leave nothing to be desired. Let the shuffling justice and the truckling judge know that a severe interpretation of the law will brighten their chances of promotion, and you will behold rigors of penalty which Neal Dow himself would wince to see.

---

[11] An obvious reference to Susan B. Anthony. In the version published in Willard, *Woman and Temperance*, 373, Anthony's full name is used.

There is also great force in the consideration that, if women, *not themselves eligible to office,* had the power to elect or to defeat *men* (who will alone be eligible for a long while yet), the precise check might by this arrangement be supplied which would keep politics from forming with the worst elements of society that unholy alliance which is to-day the grief of Christians and the despair of patriots. Belonging to no party ourselves, we might be able to lift the Sabbath, the temperance movement, and kindred moral questions out of the mire of merely partisan politics into which they have fallen. It is, at least, worth trying. Into the seething caldron, where the witch's broth is bubbling, let us cast this one ingredient more. In speaking thus I am aware that I transcend the present purpose of my constituency, and represent myself rather than "the folks that voted me in!"

Our temperance women in the West are learning that, while the primary meetings are the most easily influenced, they are the most influential political bodies in America. Ere long the W.C.T.U.s will attend these, beginning in the smaller and more reputable communities. We are confident that nothing would be so effective in securing the attendance of the respectable voter as the presence at the primaries of "his sisters and his cousins and his aunts." To be "in at the birth" of measures vital to the well-being of society seems to us, in the light of last winter's experience, a more useful investment of our influence than to be "in at the death." At Springfield we found the enemy entrenched, while in the primaries his soldiers are not yet even recruited. We intend also to open in each locality books of record; and, by thorough canvass, to secure an informal registration of all men and women—the former as to how they will and the latter as to how they would (mournful potential mood!) vote on the question of permitting saloons. Every such effort helps to obliterate party lines; or, more correctly, to mass the moral elements by which alone society coheres, against the disintegrating forces, which of themselves would drive us into chaos and old night.

New England must lead. Let not the West outstrip you in this glorious race. I appeal to the women of the East. Already New Hampshire and Massachusetts have placed in your hands the educational vote, which has a direct bearing on the temperance question, since by its use the mothers of this land can place on the school committees those who will make the scientific reasons for total abstinence a regular study of the children. I beg you, by its use, to testify your fitness and desire for the more powerful weapon it foretells. It comes to you as the gift of a few earnest, persistent women, who steadily asked your legislators to bestow it, even as they will the larger gift, if you as diligently seek it. Your undertaking will not be so gigantic as ours in Illinois, for with us 34 in the senate and 102 in the house must first agree to a constitutional amendment, and then the concurrence of two-thirds of our voters must be secured. Another contrast further illustrates the favorable conditions here. Negro suffrage at the South was forced upon wide areas occupied by a voting population bitterly hostile to the innovation. Here woman's vote must first be granted by free consent of a majority of the representatives chosen directly by those who are already citizens; and by operating over the small area of a single state at a time it would arouse no violent upheaval of the opposition. Besides, the large excess of women here makes this the fitting battleground of a foregone victory. Women of New England! among all the divisions of our great White Ribbon Army you occupy the strategic position. Truly, your valiant daughter, Illinois, earlier flung down the gauge of the new battle; but your blood is in our veins, your courage nerves our hearts, your practical foresight determines our methods of work. I come from the prairies, where we are marshaling forces for a fresh attack, and solemnly adjure you to lead us in this fight for God and home and native land. Still let dear old New England take her natural place in the forefront of the battle; and from an enemy more hateful than King George let the descendants of our foremothers deliver Concord and Lexington, and wield once more in Boston, with its eight miles of grog-shops, the sword of Bunker Hill! To chronicle the deeds by which your devotion shall add fresh luster to names renowned and hallowed, the Muse of History prepares her tablet and poises her impartial pen.

Friends, there is always a way out for humanity. Evermore in earth's affairs God works by means. To-day he hurls back upon us our complaining cry: "How long? O Lord! how long?"[12] Even as he answered faint-hearted Israel, so he replies to us: *What can I do for this people that I have not done?*[13] *"Speak unto the children of Israel that they go forward.*"[14]

"There's a light about to beam,
There's a fount about to stream,
There's a warmth about to glow,
There's a flower about to blow.
There's a midnight blackness
    Changing into gray;
Men of thoughts, of votes, of action,
    Clear the way!

Aid that dawning tongue and pen;
Aid it, hopes of honest men;

---

[12] This common biblical phrase was also used in "Everybody's War." See fn. 1.

[13] Isaiah 5:4.

[14] Exodus 14:15.

Aid it, for the hour is ripe,
And our earnest must not slacken into play.
Men of thoughts of votes of action,
    Clear the way!

Annual Address, 1881

THE HOME PROTECTION PARTY[1]

When the National Prohibition Party held its Convention in Cleveland, a year ago last Spring, women were invited to attend as delegates. But, while I admired the progressive spirit thus indicated, it seemed to me clearly my duty not to go. Always profoundly interested in politics as the mightiest force on earth except Christianity, and trained to be a staunch Republican, both my education and sympathies were arrayed on Garfield's side. Besides, I labored under the hallucination that the South secretly waited its opportunity to re-open the issues of the war. During all that stormy Summer of the Presidential campaign, I did not hear Neal Dow's candidacy spoken of with interest by the workers of the W.C.T.U., and yet we all honored and gloried in that brave father of the Maine Law. In contrast to the apathy with which we regarded the "Third Party" movement, you will remember the profound enthusiasm that greeted General Garfield's name at our annual meeting in Boston, and that, later on, we hailed his election as an answered prayer.

Dear Sisters, since then, by your commission I have visited the Southern States and met in every one of them representatives and leaders of opinion. I have seen their acceptance in good faith of the issues of the war—a good faith sufficiently manifested toward President Garfield, in spite of his army record, his radical utterances in Congress, and the uncompromising tone of his clear-cut Inaugural. I have

---

[1] "The Home Protection Party" is the fifth section in Willard's Annual Address of 1881.

seen Northern capital pouring into those once-disaffected States in uncounted millions, and I know there is no stronger bridge across the "bloody chasm" than this one woven out of national coin and supported by the iron-jointed cables of self-interest. I have seen their Legislatures making State appropriations for the education of the freedmen and helping to sustain those "colored schools" whose New England teachers they once despised. I have learned how ex-masters cheered to echo the utterances of their ex-slaves in the great Prohibition Convention of North Carolina, and my heart has glowed with the hope of a real "home government" for the South and a "color line broken" not by bayonets nor repudiationists, but by ballots from white hands and black for prohibitory law. Seeing is believing, and on that sure basis I believe the South is ready for a party along the lines of longitude; a party that shall wipe Mason and Dixon's line out of the heart as well as off the map, weld Anglo-Saxons of the New World into one royal family, and give us a really re-United States. With what deep significance is this belief confirmed by the South's tender sympathy in the last pathetic summer, and the unbroken group of States that so lately knelt around our fallen hero's grave!

But this new party cannot bear the name of Republican or Democrat. Neither victor nor vanquished would accept the old war-cry of a section. Besides, "the party of moral ideas" has ceased to have a distinctive policy. Was its early motto "Free Territory?" We have realized it. Later did it declare that the Union must be preserved and slavery abolished? Both have been done. Did it demand negro [sic] enfranchisement and the passage of a bill of Civil Rights? Both are accomplished facts, so far as they can be until education completes the desired work. Was the redemption of our financial pledges essential to good faith? That noble record of the Republican Party cannot be erased. If we contemplate questions still unsettled, as Civil Service Reform—both parties claim to desire it; or a National Fund for Southern Education—each deems it necessary. But when we name the greatest issue now pending on this or any continent—the prohibition of the manufacture and sale of intoxicating liquors as a drink—behold the Republicans of Maine, New Hampshire and Vermont vote for and the Republicans of North Carolina, Ohio and Illinois against it, while the Democrats of Kansas oppose and of South Carolina favor it! Now, I blame neither party for this inconsistency; it is simply the handwriting on the wall, which tells that both are weighed in the balances and found wanting. For they are formed of men who, while they thought alike and fought alike on many great questions, on this greatest of all questions are hopelessly divided, and "a house divided against itself cannot stand." This is saying nothing whatever against the house; it is recognizing the law of gravitation, that is all. In 1868 slavery was the determining factor in American politics. In 1881 that final factor is the liquor traffic. Then, while the prohibitionists of Maine marched to the front with Gen. Neal Dow, the Germans were proud "to fight mit Sigel":[2] but to-day the bayonets of those two champions and their followers no longer point the way. Gen. Sigel approved the Brewers' Sabbath-breaking demonstration at Newark, and Gen. Dow is the chief defender of a law which shuts such men up in jail. John B. Gough and Philip Best, the brewer, voted the self-same ticket; so did Gov. St. John of Kansas, and "Boss Hesing," editor of the *Staats Zeitung*, of Chicago. But it is morally impossible that they should do so now. The Republican Party in Ohio and Illinois can only win through German votes. Hence we behold Legislatures as they bow the knee, and municipal authorities as they grovel in the dust, crying with one accord, "Great is Gambrinus[3] of the Teutonians!" Nay more; to-day Gov. Jarvis, of North Carolina, fights for Prohibition in the same ranks with Gov. Plaisted, of Maine, and all through the North and South the men once at sword's points are now, upon the temperance question, sworn allies.

"But don't take Temperance into politics," is the cry of sundry surface thinkers. I wish every one of these delegates would read Miss Victor's[4] pamphlet on that question, and for this purpose have arranged for its free distribution here. I am proud that a woman—and a Southern woman, too—should have furnished us this earliest and ablest of campaign documents. It will be a discovery to some that, since Beer is already in the political arena shaking its fists, Temperance must go forth to the encounter or fail to exhibit David's faith in the presence of Goliath! "How will you vote on the question of beer?" is the shibboleth of the majority in the Republican Party to-day. By the explicit and unanimous resolutions of every Liquor Dealers' Association from Boston to San Francisco, they put the candidates on trial of their lives. And, as you read Miss Victor's pamphlet, you will see that from the year of their organization in 1862 until to-day, the brewers' wing of the Liquor League "has issued *in the caucus and at the polls* commands which the Republican Party in Congress has scrupulously obeyed." And yet, in this great organization are enough Temperance

---

[2] Brigadier General Franz Sigel (1824-1902) was born in Baden, Germany, and was there trained in life as a military commander. After emigrating to the United States, his prompt and enthusiastic support of the Union rallied many German-Americans to the cause. With his 2nd Missouri brigade, he was largely responsible for keeping Missouri in federal hands.

[3] Gambrinus: a mythical Flemish king, who, according to legend, was the inventor of beer.

[4] "Miss Victor" probably refers to Frances Fuller Victor (1826-1902) who was a widely published author and historian. The name of the pamphlet referred to, however, is not known.

men to hold the balance of power, but they are only members of the great body, and accept the candidates chosen by leaders whom they have so long followed that party allegiance seemed to be second nature to them. For, a party is like some huge, masterful, aggressive man; the head thinks out its orders and the limbs execute them. But when beer has muddled the head, and one of the hands caresses the enemy which the other hand attempts to crush, there is no more absurd figure above ground. In this imbecile attitude stands the Republican party of to-day, while at the North the Democratic openly espouses the cause of the saloons, against which in the South it is beginning to contend. And yet, in the magnificent arena of public opinion, opposing parties are the only gladiators worthy of the scene, and upon their victory or defeat depends the weal or woe of nations.

We point to the non-partisan homage of which our murdered President is the subject, but we must not forget that when fifty millions gathered around his dying couch, it was to lament over a man who was one of the most loyal partisan leaders of his day, a man, too, whose name they would never have heard except as he became the standard bearer of the party which for a generation had never known defeat.

No, parties are the moulds into which God pours the principles that are to bless humanity. But when these have crystallized into the law and the life of a people God breaks the mould for which he has no further use. Parties, like men, travel the long road from cradle to coffin, but, unfortunately, when dead they are not so sure of burial as men. In Illinois we have two that sadly need interment. Parties are organic—they grow by gradual accretions, and require nourishment and care. As a whirlwind begins with a few leaves or particles of dust, so a party begins with a few individuals, often obscure, but if God's breath sets them in motion, the widening and ascending spiral of their progress draws in the multitudes. But parties have their best analogy in well-disciplined armies, under intelligent and faithful leadership. First the soldiers must be recruited, one by one, for a well understood contest against a foe detested by them all. Our Temperance women have long been petitioning Legislatures which were, as a rule, companies of soldiers enlisted for no other purpose than to defeat their measures. Is it any wonder we have grown tired of it and decided to invest our valuable time where it promises better results—namely, in recruiting, one by one, from the people of the country, soldiers committed to the proposition, *"The saloon must go?"*[punctuation *sic*]

But in a military exigency recruiting is not enough. The commander is obliged to order a draft including those ordinarily exempt from service. Precisely this crisis is upon us, and our most experienced leaders, both men and women, have called out the *Home Guards*, the gentle, soft-voiced creatures who are afraid of guns and gunpowder, but who, upon a moral battle-ground, can march side by side with the gallant and the strong. Behold the two armies deploying now for the most glorious conflict this world has ever seen—one side marches from distilleries, breweries, saloons, the other from churches, schools and homes!

Believing that the hour had come for us, the Woman's Christian Temperance Union of Illinois, at its annual meeting nearly two months ago, endorsed the following action of the Lake Bluff Convocation, held a few days earlier, and composed of representative Temperance men and women from twelve different states:

The union of the best elements of the North and South, upon the principles of the Temperance reform is a happy omen of the destruction of that sectionalism which is so dangerous to the welfare of our country, and which is the cause of bitterness, wrangling and corruption.

A political party, whose platform is based on constitutional and statutory prohibition of the manufacture and sale of alcoholic beverages in the State and the Nation, is a necessity, and to give those who suffer the most from the drink curse a power to protect themselves, their homes and their loved ones, the complete enfranchisement of women should be *worked for* and welcomed.

The Temperance people of the several States should call conventions for the purpose of organizing in every State a Home Protection Party upon the basis of the foregoing article.

We hereby authorize the officers of this Convocation to carry out the provisions of the foregoing article by correspondence with prohibition leaders and the calling of National, State and Legislative Home Protection Conventions.

In many a meeting of our Temperance women I have seen the power of the Highest manifest, but in none has the glow of crusade fire been so blessed as when these daughters of heroic sires who in the early days of the great party whose defection we deplore, endured reproach without the camp, solemnly declared their loyalty to the Home Protection Party, wherein dwelleth righteousness. Let me read you the statement of doctrine to which we women of Illinois subscribed:

"We recommend that, looking to the composition of the next Legislature, we request and aid the Home Protection Party to put in nomination in each district a Home Protection candidate, committed not more by his specific promise than by his well-known character to vote for the submission of a constitutional amendment giving the full ballot to the women of Illinois as a means of protection to their homes.

"Finally to these advance positions we have been slowly and surely brought by the logic of events and the argument of defeat in our seven years' march since the Crusade. We have patiently appealed to existing parties, only to find our appeals disregarded. We now appeal to the manhood of our State to go forward in the name of God, and Home and Native Land."

Ten days later the Liquor League of Illinois held its convention, the day being universally observed by our Unions in that State in fervent prayer that God would send confusion and defeat as the sequel to their machinations. Let me read you their declaration:

Resolved: That the District Executive Committees be instructed to make a vigorous fight against all such candidates for the General Assembly, no matter what political party they may belong to, who cannot be fully relied upon to vote in favor of personal liberty and an equal *protection* of ours with all other legitimate business interests.

They want protection, too! and they know the Legislature alone can give it. But we know, as the result of our Local Home Protection ordinance, under which women have voted in nearly a dozen widely separated localities of Illinois, and have voted overwhelmingly against license, that our enfranchisement means confusion and defeat to the liquor sellers. Therefore, since for this we have prayed, we must take our places at the front and say, with the greatest reformer of the sixteenth century:
"Here I stand. I can do no other. God help me. Amen!"[5]
The "Home Protectionists" have flung their banner to the breeze in Illinois, inscribed with the motto, "Falter who must, follow who dare!" The W.C.T. Unions of Maine, New Hampshire and Delaware have wheeled into line beside us, which we regard as the best possible endorsement of our action; while the Vermont, Pennsylvania and Michigan Unions have sent us hearty greetings. This, then, is our response to you, brave men of Ohio, who have dared to break away from party leadership, and who in your June convention asked the help of the Woman's Christian Temperance Union. We are here and hope that since we have come over to your principles you will graciously condescend to take our name "Home Protection" being a dearer word to us than Prohibition even, since it also includes the idea of placing in our weaponless hands those munitions of war, so mighty for pulling down the enemy's stronghold.
In conclusion let me ask your careful thought to these considerations.

First. The formation of this party, or, if its leaders so determine, the rechristening of the Prohibition Party under a name sure to enlist more of our women workers, because it emphasizes their enfranchisement, will place the work done by us for that end under the auspices of a political party. This has long been claimed by our conservative sisters as a consummation devoutly to be wished. They have declared

---

[5] Quoted from Martin Luther's speech at the Diet of Worms, April 18, 1521.

their willingness to use the ballot whenever it should be placed in their hands, and notably in New York, Massachusetts and Vermont have nobly bestirred themselves to exercise their new right to vote on questions connected with the public schools. But they have not been willing to join those of us who made the Home Protection Ballot an article of our faith as members of the W.C.T.U. Now, however, for a party whose candidate must, of course, be men, but which welcomes us to its primaries and conventions, those of us whose convictions compel us so to do, can work to our hearts' content, investing for its success the time we once spent in the vain attempt to persuade unfriendly Legislatures, and going directly *to the individual voter* with a pledge of his allegiance to the Home Protection candidate.

Second. In States where a constitutional Amendment is pending, as in Iowa and Indiana, we can hold this party in abeyance until they reach a final decision, which will be within two years. But, meanwhile, the pressure of this new movement, as carried forward in adjoining States, will react favorably upon our Temperance friends who can not as yet affiliate with us for political action.

Third. In some States it may be deemed best to make Constitutional and Statutory Prohibition the main issues, and woman's vote subsidiary. This will be for the leaders in each State to determine. While at first our Southern friends may hold aloof from the latter movement, and should not be prematurely urged to join it, a few more defeats like that in North Carolina (resulting from the vote of ignorant colored Republicans under party leadership), may perhaps lead them to apply to the ballot an educational pre-requisite, and summon to their aid in this non-sectional and prohibitory party of which I speak, their mothers, wives and daughters.

Fourth. The men who will naturally unite in this party will also strongly support Civil Service Reform, anti-monopoly and anti-Mormon legislation; and commit the organization heartily to the cause of Compulsory Education. The best elements of the disintegrating parties of the past will gravitate toward this; from their out-worn hulls the sound timbers will help make up our life rafts.

Very soon this new "party of great moral ideas" will hold the balance of power. When we see a David Davis[6] or a Mahone[7] determining which of two existing parties shall aspire to national

---

[6] Judge David Davis (1815-1886) was a Democratic congressman who, in exchange for a judgeship, helped elect the Republican Rutherford B. Hayes as president even though Democrat Samuel Tilden had garnered a plurality of the popular vote.

[7] William Mahone (1826-1895), also known as the "King of the Lobby," was a railroad president, Virginia senator, and the political boss of the Republican party in Virginia.

ascendancy, when we review the record of the Greenbackers[8] in and out of Congress, the prediction should not seem to us absurd that ere long our new party will hold the balance of power. At first, perhaps, this will occur in some obscure but carefully canvassed locality, later in a State, and finally by the inevitable sequence of party evolution, in the nation itself.

Here, then, at the nation's capital, let us declare allegiance; here let us turn our faces toward the beckoning future; here, where the liquor traffic pours in each year its revenue of gold, stained with the blood of our dearest and best, let us set up our Home Protection standard in the name of the Lord!

---

[8] The Greenback party was also variously called the Independent National, National, and Greenback Labor party. Formed in 1876, the party urged that paper money (greenbacks) be freed from the gold standard and be given status as legal tender, in order that the money supply be increased and debts more easily repaid. Later they added woman suffrage and a graduated income tax to their list of reforms. Their largest success was in 1880, when James B. Weaver received 300,000 popular votes for president.

Tenth Annual Address, 1889

Beloved Comrades:
"Immortal things have God for architect.
And men are but the granite He lays down."

Ruskin[1] says, "What woman wills will be accomplished." The 4,000 dram-shops of Chicago have here in Battery D an object-lesson of what woman wills. But the great English seer and greatest prose poet of any age meant only that woman's simplicity and sufferings have made her, more than man, receptive of the will of God, for nothing upon earth is worth doing except that will.

Some of us have desired in other days the lion's will bound up in heart of dove, but the disintegration of our wills, that God's may take their place, is slowly dawning on us as life's one beatitude.

Every person is a trinity in which a physical man wars against an intellectual, and an intellectual against a spiritual. This is the evolution, and happy are we if the spiritual comes fully to its kingdom. Nothing less should be the definite, solemn and joyful purpose of white-ribboners born of the crusade.

One of the greatest spirits of our age gave a prophetic voice to the purpose of this convocation when he cried out in words not unlike these that follow:

---

[1] John Ruskin (1819-1900) was an English writer, sociologist, and philanthropist. In *Unto this Land*, a series of essays published in *Cornhill* magazine in the 1860s, Ruskin attacked the dehumanized ethics of modern capitalism.

"Sacrifice to 'the mob,' O poet and reformer! Sacrifice to that unfortunate, disinherited, vanquished, vagabond, shoeless, famished, repudiated, despairing mob; sacrifice to it, if it must be, and when it must be, thy repose, thy fortune, thy joy, thy country, thy liberty, thy life. *The mob is the human race in misery. The mob is the mournful beginning of the people. The mob is the great victory of darkness. Sacrifice to it! Sacrifice thyself!* Let thyself be hunted, let thyself be exiled like Juvenal to Syene, life D'Aubigne to Geneva, like Dante to Verona, like Elijah to Horeb, like Isaiah to Ezion-geber, like Christ to Calvary! Sacrifice to the mob; sacrifice to it thy gold, and thy blood, which is more than thy gold, and thy thought which is more than thy blood, and thy love which is more than thy thought. Receive its complaint, hear its accusation. Give it thy ear, thy hand, thy arm, thy heart. Do everything for it excepting evil. *Alas! it suffers so much, and it knows nothing.* Correct it, warn it, instruct it, guide it, *train it.* Make it spell truth, show it the alphabet of reason, teach it to read virtue, probity, generosity, mercy. Hold thy book wide open. Be there, attentive, vigilant, kind, faithful, humble. *Light up the brain, inflame the mind, extinguish selfishness; and thyself give the example.* "[2]

But, as Christian women, we should set before our minds the ideal toward which we move in individual life, social custom and national law, nothing less than an agreement as complete between the Bible and them all, as is the agreement between a healthy eye and the light of a June day.

Egyptian astronomers caused a slanting shaft of stone to be cut through one of their great pyramids. It pointed to a star near the pole. But that was so long ago that the wild men of Great Britain could see in their now cold skies the Southern Cross. If we could look through that stone spyglass of the pyramid to-night, the star that shone there once would be no longer visible, so greatly has the earth's axis changed its place. It is so with the human soul; its axis changes, and stars once bright before the telescope of aspiration pass everlastingly from view.

"When, marshaled on the nightly plain,
    The glittering host bestud the sky,
One star alone of all the train,
    Can fix the sinner's wandering eye.
Hark! hark! to God the chorus breaks,
    From every host, from every gem;
But one alone the Savior speaks,—
    It is the Star of Bethlehem."[3]

---

[2] Source unknown.
[3] Source unknown.

Beloved comrades, we are here to guide the old white-ribbon ship by that one star!

THE SITUATION

Patriotism has always been part and parcel of my religion. From the first flag I ever saw, made for me by my mother when I was a little prairie girl, out of an old pillow-case with red calico stripes sewed on, and gilt paper stars pinned in the corner, I have always looked upon America as the Majestic Mother whom her grateful daughters should gladly live to serve or die to save. This fact I mention because I know the annals of your lives, beloved comrades, would reveal the same sacred passion of the patriot. God always has one more arrow in His quiver, one more force as yet untried, one more division of His army to deploy upon the field, and this convention of representative delegations, is one of God's condensations of celestial power. Surely the time is ripe for it, and the occasion fit. You are in Chicago, the Cronin murder trial[4] is in full blast, the National flag was hissed and the red flag of the Commune applauded not far from here but a few weeks ago.

For the experiment of free government in our large towns and cities is a failure loudly confessed by men themselves. Nor are the reasons for this monumental catastrophe mysterious.

America has become the dumping ground of European cities. The emigration has steadily deteriorated in proportion as its quantity has grown. This is a fact so notorious that our reputable foreign population now protests against the present wholesale exodus from European slums more bitterly than we do.

To-day we have a hundred thousand anarchists among us in this country who claim to have twenty-five thousand drilled soldiers at their call, as many as the entire regular army of the United States. It has been said that the explosion of a little nitro-glycerine under a few water mains would make our great city uninhabitable; the blowing up of a few railway bridges would bring famine; the pumping of atmospheric air into the gas mains and the application of a match would tear up every street and level every house.

The multiplication of inventions, the enormous accumulations of capital, the corporate combinations and octopus grip of the "Trusts" render our wage-workers uneasy. A new machine may any day make the work of scores of men superfluous. "Bread or blood" is the

---

[4] On May 4, 1889, three men, apparently drunk, robbed and murdered Dr. Cronin and put his body down a sewer. The murder and subsequent trial gained national attention and notoriety.

inscription on many a concealed red flag and the motive of many a hidden bomb. Note the sullen look on grimy faces in mine and manufactory and on the streets;—read the labor organs of the day, and see if well-to-do Americans are not asleep on the edge of a volcano.

Over 800 papers printed in foreign languages circulate constantly throughout the nation, a majority of which contain ideas concerning home and women, temperance and the Sabbath, that are European and revolutionary, not American and Christian.

At Castle Garden eighty-four large steamships land their passengers each month, thirty-two of these steamers being from Great Britain and Ireland. In the First Ward of New York, where Castle Garden stands, are five churches and chapels and four hundred saloons, "and this is their welcome home."

In May of last year, one hundred and forty-three thousand emigrants landed at Castle Garden. A million feet yearly sound the signal of an ominous invasion on our wharves as these strange people come. Whether this swift tattoo shall prove to be the reveille of hope or the requiem of despair for America, doth not yet appear, and depends decisively upon the amount of Christian endeavor that is put forth in the next quarter of a century.

Twenty-six per cent of our entire population is either foreign-born or of foreign parentage.

Of one hundred persons in New York City, only twelve are born of American parentage, and in Chicago only nine out of one hundred. You see we women have entered on foreign missionary work without crossing the sea to do so.

In San Francisco, with three hundred and fifty thousand inhabitants, only forty thousand go to church. In "Pilsen," the Bohemian quarter of Chicago, the entire church facilities would accommodate, sitting and standing, about twenty-five hundred persons, but there are not less than forty thousand inhabitants. The largest missionary work done in this foreign city, that forms a section of Chicago, is by disciples of Robert Ingersoll. His writings the people have in their own language. Indeed, his books have been translated into every European tongue, several languages of India, Chinese, Japanese, and others. The man in this country who relishes these books is apt to read them in saloons on Sunday with a pipe in his mouth and in his hand a mug of beer. Nearly half a million Chicagoans would be kept out of church for lack of sittings, had they no other reason for remaining absent, but even under the magic method of High License all who wish sittings in the *saloon* can be accommodated.

There are seven million young men in America to-day, of whom over five million never darken a church door. Seventy-five out of every one hundred of these young men do not attend church; ninety-five out of every hundred do not belong to the church and ninety-seven out of every hundred do nothing to spread Christianity. But on the other hand, sixty-seven out of every one hundred criminals are young men, and young men are the chief patrons of the saloon, the gambling house, the haunt of infamy. It was noticed recently that into a single saloon of Cincinnati and within a single hour went 252 men, 236 of whom—or all but sixteen—were young men. As a result the death rate steadily increases from 14 to 25 years of age, their evil habits reporting themselves in deteriorated bodies and distempered souls at the age when they should have attained their manly prime.

We spend fifteen hundred millions a year for liquor and tobacco—ten times as much as for education and religion. We have two hundred and fifty thousand saloons, enough to form a line from Chicago to New York, and in making alcoholic beverages we waste enough grain annually to pave a street a thousand miles long with loaves of bread. East of the Mississippi we have one saloon for every 107 voters, west of it, in the eleven mountain States and Territories, one for every forty-three.

A valiant old white-ribboner from the country was a guest in one of our large cities, and among other wonders of the place, saw a distillery, a brewery and a tobacco factory in congenial juxtaposition, whereupon she remarked in soliloquizing fashion, "They say we women have a hard time of it, and that we have n't got our rights, but anyhow we hain't got all the stuff in them three buildings to chew and smoke and swaller down."

We have seventy-thousand criminals, while our population doubles every twenty-five years, the number of criminals doubles every ten. It is but just to say that this increase is almost wholly among the native-born, the proportion of foreign-born being about what it was ten years ago.

We have 492 towns and cities containing over five thousand persons each. They make up one-fourth of the population and contain a standing army of fifteen thousand policemen. These men cost us fifteen millions per year and make on an average fifty arrests each. Figure out the cost of each arrest and see if prohibition would not be a great economy.

The ratio of women prisoners to men prisoners is as one to ten, of foreign to native born nearly double; the average age a little more than twenty-nine and one-half years. About five per cent of our entire population is placed under arrest each year, and in that period about one hundred thousand persons are put in the common jail for the first time. We have at present with us four thousand murderers, five thousand convicted of assault, nine thousand burglars, seventeen thousand common thieves—these are some of the figures of our degradation.

Light is thrown upon the temptation to crime in great cities by the fact that in Chicago we have women who make twelve shirts for 75 cents and furnish their own thread; women who "finish off" a costly cloak for 4 cents; children that work twelve hours a day for a dollar a week. "Alas that gold should be so dear and flesh and blood so cheap!"

The conditions across the water, in the most favored land whence our foreign people come, is thus hinted at by one of the experts belonging to the famous "American Workingmen's Expedition" to the World's Fair in Paris. He says of English factory hands:

"The greatest portion of the help employed in the mills I have visited are females, and they range from the child of 10 or 12 years of age to the gray-haired matron. The children are rather puny, and the mothers are gaunt, hungry-looking creatures, and have a pallid look that is far from interesting. Their working clothes would not bring a shilling to the individual; they work in their bare feet on stone floors, and their heads look as though the use of a comb would be a torture. Bread and beer seem the staple articles of diet, and it is the common practice to send a girl child of about the size of the can she carries for the beer that is to wash down the bread. How the bread comes to the house is beyond my ken. The child and the beer are as common a sight as beer and children, and there is no lack of either in old England. The streets are paved with the latter, or, in lieu of that, they are numerous enough to cover the pavements. The lives of this class of workers are but one remove from poverty, and their escape in that direction must be a very narrow one.

"To the average working man and woman of America it would be a life not worth living, and whatever betides the future of the American toiler, God preserve him from the fate of his English brother and sister worker."[5]

For the ills of such an emigration and the degeneracy of our people as proved by the defeat this year of prohibition in six States, there is one remedy—one only—and that is Christianity in action; not fashionable church-membership, but actual Christian living and Christlike reaction on the work around us. But so long as religion is kept like canned fruit bottled up at a fixed price of pew rent or other contribution, so long will the crime list continue to increase. God be thanked that the womanhood of Christendom begins to go out into the highway and hedge, shaking into the laps of the people the rich ripe fruit of the gospel trees without money and without price.

The Chicago Training School, for women workers, founded by Methodists and presided over by Lucy Rider Meyer, is one of the brightest beacons that gleams through the smoke of our city of sin. For I have seen this Bible pressed against a forehead cold as the Alps by moonlight, and ever afterward it has been roseate as sunset heavens with the sweet light of faith. I have seen it pressed against a heart hard

---

[5] Source unknown.

as an iceberg and it was melted and made mellow as the rhythmic flow of summer brooks. I have seen it pressed against lips that were querulous and complaining, and they complained no more.

Mr. Moody's Chicago Bible Institute, to which women are admitted on equal terms with men, has been quite recently established and promises to set a key-note for this land like that of the "McAll Mission" for the old world. There is nothing in Chicago better worth a visit than these two institutes situated near each other on the North Side, and the great "Armour Mission" on the South Side.

Some are born mothers, some achieve motherhood, some have it thrust upon them. Blessed beyond all the rest is she who has carried a motherly heart in her breast since ever that heart began to beat, and in these gospel days her holiest work will be to play the part of mother to the thousands worse than motherless to whom she goes with Bible in her hand and Christ enshrined in body and soul.

SUNDAY CLOSING

In the spring of 1874 Chicago was the scene of one of the most thrilling dramas of the crusade. Fourteen thousand names of our best citizens were gathered in ten days by such women as Mrs. Matilda B. Carse, Mrs. J. B. Hobbs and Mrs. C. H. Case, to a petition for the enforcement of our law prohibiting open saloons on Sunday. Led by Mrs. Rev. Moses Smith, a procession of ladies marched from Clark Street M. E. Church, where they left their sisters at prayer, to the City Hall and presented their petition to the Mayor and Common Council, whereupon, in their presence, the petition was tabled and the opposite of what it called for was indorsed. Meanwhile a mob made up of the city's most dangerous elements swarmed into the square and up the steps of our City Hall almost into the Council Room itself; and only by the prompt action of such men as Dr. Arthur Edwards and other leading ministers, did our ladies, by slipping out a side door, escape the angry insults of the mob.

Let any who are alarmed lest the temperance cause is waning, read the Chicago papers of to-day, note the uprising tide against Sunday saloons and gambling dens, in this and nearly all our cities, if he needs proof that God is not yet dead, neither is the devil crowned.

To the everlasting credit of the wage-workers let it be said, *they do not obstruct the enforcement of the Sunday prohibition law,* though on that day they are out in force, seeking pleasure, and are the chief patrons of the average saloon. The saloon-keepers and ward sneak-thieves of the ballot box, the bosses of politics whose booty is boodle and whose worst villainy is beer-bribed votes, form the pitiful minority that has alone hindered, throughout all the fifteen years since our good women failed in their crusades, the enforcement of Sunday prohibition.

But alas, my sisters, you have come to the city that gave to evangelization a Dwight L. Moody, to sacred song a Philip Bliss, to temperance work a Matilda B. Carse, and to the world a Woman's Temperance Publication House, only to find that this riff-raff handful of saloon-keepers and pot-house politicians still holds our people by the throat, while red flag riots, dynamite plots and Cronin murders are begotten by alcoholized brains and hatched in the high-license grog shops of Chicago.

Why is the vote of reputable men thus "solid" for municipal officers who trample on their solemn oath to enforce all the laws, and among them those against saloons and gambling dens? Because, for instance: In a certain city (which is a sample of all the rest) *one* firm of brewers holds mortgages on the fixtures of *six hundred saloons;* another holds mortgages on over *two hundred*, and altogether, nearly *five thousand* chattel mortgages were given last year by brewers to the nominal proprietors of saloons. As a consequence, the saloon-keeper is the political chattel of the brewer who in secret counsel with the political boss decides who shall have the political sugar plums of office, and the "dear people" simply "vote the regular ticket" of their respective parties, and thus ratify the bargain.

In a New England town there were five saloons. High license reduced them to one and the proprietor of that one employed the former owners of the other four! If I were allowed to blot out one-half of Chicago's saloons, it should be the most reputable half, not the most disreputable, for an attractive temptation is the most dangerous of all.

A veteran Crusader of Ohio, now a white-ribboner of fifteen years' standing, condensed into a sentence the whole argument for our position when she said, "On our knees in the saloons we prayed God to raise up men who would put away from our homes this awful curse, and now can we do less than to thank and pray for those men who consecrate their votes to prohibition?"

Where can experts and specialists of any reform movement be, if true to their light, except right at the front of the army? They were the ordained scouts from the beginning. Conservatives come along slowly enough at best; "bringing the regiment up to the colors" implies both colors and standard-bearers who have gone on ahead. Many a good man in the old parties has said to me (if at the North a Republican, if in the south a Democrat), "We don't like all this prodding that we get from the Prohibition party, but all the same it wakes us up, and crowds us to advance positions in localities where we can best afford to take a step ahead."

But the managers of the Republican and Democratic *National* liquor parties are solidly against us, and which of the two parties has reason to hate white-ribboners most cordially, will probably be answered ten years later by the famed Hibernicism, *"Both of them."*

In all this steadfast forward movement let us take for our motto: *"The Lord hath not given me the spirit of fear, but of power and of love and of a sound mind,"*[6] and let us remember the wise words of a simple heart that said that *"Goin' to work gently about a thing won't hinder it's [sic] being done."*

*   *   *

PURITY IN LITERATURE AND ART[7]

The aggregate self-respect of women, if it could but be brought to bear upon such public atrocities as smite our eyes from theatrical bill posters, saloon and tobacconist's windows, and too often also in the ballet, the picture gallery, and the pages of current literature, would banish such exhibitions in a twelvemonth. But so little have we understood our power that while every woman of chaste mind as well as body, protests in righteous indignation when these abominations strike her eye, that protest falls to the ground like a spent arrow. No attempt is made to utilize it in a practical reaction on this public defilement and disgrace. Sometimes a brave woman, like our white-ribbon lawyer in Illinois, Mrs. Ada H. Kepley, of Effingham, dares to tear down disgraceful pictures when she sees them and does not lose her courage though arrested for her valorous deed. One week ago, this woman, with her lawyer-husband at her side, stood her trial and was acquitted, the judge declaring that *such pictures are common nuisances and have no right under the law.* Indeed he said she ought not to have been arrested at all. Mrs. Kepley made her own plea and I hope we may have it to scatter as a leaflet, helping inspire other women to *protest on the spot* against exhibitions that are a public insult to all virtuous women. Be it remembered that the W.C.T.U. was with her in this work, and had already petitioned the mayor to forbid the exhibitions ("for men only") of which these nude figures of women were the advertisement. Four women said, "We will take that obscene and indecent picture from the bulletin board." When this decision was made, the company knelt, and one of their number poured out a fervent prayer to God, asking Him to give them courage to perform this righteous, needed action, to fear no consequences that might befall them, and to be given divine direction in their endeavor. The other women said, "We will pray for you as you go." Quietly the four went

---

[6] 2 Timothy 1:7.

[7] Seven major sections intervene between Sunday Closing and Purity in Literature and Art: Politics, The Defeats, National Prohibition, Woman's Ballot, The Labor Question, Moderate Drinking, and White Cross and White Shield.

down to the post-office door, and, with a prayer in each heart, the picture was quickly removed and destroyed. Mrs. Kepley's prominence caused her to be the only one arrested. She is Superintendent for Illinois W.C.T.U. of work against impure literature and art, and through her efforts our helpful new law on this subject was last winter secured. God's word to every atom is "Combine!" and the difference between weakness and strength is always combination, whether on the human or the spiritual plane. Let us then, as white-ribbon women, combine to put away from sight these advertisements that are wholesale demoralizers of the young,—and they were never more boldly flaunted than along Chicago's streets to-day.

In the interest of public decency we ought to go before the municipal authorities everywhere asking for protection from the three chief sources of this leprosy, viz., saloon and theatrical advertisements, and cheap literature. Let it be noted also that high-license saloons pander even more than others to meretricious tastes.

But we can not forget that some women sin against public modesty so woefully that no explanation can be offered for their conduct which is not in itself the most scathing arraignment—I mean the women who parade what ought to be the mysteries of the dressing-room before the public gaze of men; who, bewilderingly attired, emulate in the waltz, the fascinations that in haunts of infamy beguile these same men to dishonor, and whose effrontery in defending their outrageous conduct with the time-worn phrase: *"Evil to him who evil thinks,"* proves them to be as barefaced mentally and bare-footed morally, as they are bare-necked and shouldered in the dance-delirium. From this horrible category let me exempt very young and very giddy women, also those bound in the toils of half-barbarous social usage. All these, while good in themselves, are pitifully bad in the results of their fashion-idolatry upon their tempted brothers.

Our National Superintendent, Mrs. Clements, of Ogontz, Pa., is hard at work to arouse the local Unions to the possibilities of good work along all lines to which reference has here been made, and I ask especial attention to her report.

HOME FOR INCAPABLES

Think of the peace, order and quiet that pertain to a normal idea of home. Then think of making home an asylum or a small-pox hospital. No one would for a moment tolerate the idea, but the kleptomaniac, the libertine, gambler and drunkard, all of them morally insane and totally unfit to be harbored within home's sacred walls, are still retained there because society makes no provision to place them where they ought to be, within the walls of institutions where they can have expert care and treatment, be self-supporting, and best of all, *be delivered from themselves.* There are thousands of these "scourges of God," these embodied penalties of the violation of natural law in some ancestral or pre-natal state, and they are the curse of the homes in which their youth is spent. Those homes deserve protection from society, those victims of an abnormal make-up, as visible to the spirit's eyes as a humped back or goitered neck are to the physical, deserve protection from themselves. The drunkard in Chicago who pounded his sick wife to death with the body of their new-born child, was an illustration, carried to the supreme degree, of the cruelty to which the state is not yet awakened, on behalf of the home. When women statesmen come to their own, let us hopefully believe, the home will not be left so shelterless as it is now.

There is another class not yet provided for and that is the adult imbeciles, in mind or body, who as children are received in institutions but, after a stipulated length of time, are sent home to be and to make others miserable. For these, whose lives are the outcome, largely, of diseased conditions originating from alcohol, nicotine and impurity, provision must be made.

There is still another class, blessedly removed from all that have been named, and they are boys and girls of good endowment, physically and otherwise, who can never be educated unless the state founds for them industrial schools. This is most of all true of girls from homes that are financially impoverished; and last of all, the boys and girls who have begun a life of sin and laid themselves liable to law, should be strictly secluded from the company of old offenders and helped to learn a trade and to be translated from the criminal to the self-supporting class.

The people are sure to be taxed; the disbursers of their money often trick them out of any equivalent; and if woman, now coming on the stage as a power for good can but secure some of that money for the people's deliverance, the home's safety and the bettered condition of the depraved and the delinquent classes, her advent will help to make the desert blossom as the rose.

Let us then *crusade the public treasury* in the interest of our proteges—the ill-conditioned and ill-endowed; white ribbon women in Maine and Michigan, Kansas and Mississippi, New Hampshire and Iowa, have already done this to good effect. I wish we had a sort of universal Dorthea Dix, who would marshal the forces in this Holy War.

PHYSICAL CULTURE

It will be observed that, as usual, large room is given on our program to this truly "vital issue." Miss Julia Thomas, of New York City, one of the most successful specialists, Mrs. Col. F. W. Parker, of Englewood, well known as a Delsartean[8] and Dress Reformer; Prof. Wm. T. Anderson, of Brooklyn, who stands at the head of gymnastic culture in that city of schools, are with us, besides Dr. Bessie Cushman, our veteran Superintendent of Hygiene. For if any subjects in this world relate to the temperance movement, they are health-studies and dress reform for women.

A physician has made this momentous declaration: "In all my experience I have never known but one man who died *a natural death.*"[9] *One-third* of all mortality occurs among children under five years of age. Would this have been true under normal conditions of genesis and birth? One of our best trained women physicians has the following in a recent article on "National Hygiene":

"The little ones come already weak and tired,—bearing on their innocent shoulders the sins of many ancestors,—make a brief struggle against the adverse conditions which surround them only to fall on the threshold of life, victims to heredity and ignorance. *There is no effect without a cause.*

"We see whole cities depopulated by some terrible disease—we see crime running rampant in a land blest with an army of good and intelligent men and women. We see starvation in the midst of plenty—sickness, misery and death in a world where there should be perfect health, happiness and life, and we no longer rest satisfied with the assurance that as an enlightened people we are in no way responsible. Surely these evils are no law of nature. There must be a cause, and we can not shirk the responsibility. Reason tells us we are directly responsible, and the cause must be found.

"If we aspire as we should, to once more having upon the earth a race of healthy men and women, we must begin with the children. Teach them that it is their sacred duty to care for their bodies, that a sound mind in a sound body is the best gift of the gods, and that this is in their power to obtain. Teach them that death from disease is unnatural and the direct result of a broken law; that the young should never die; that only the old die well. Make the rules of hygiene and of right living part of the curriculum of every school and college in our land. Let physiology be taught on a scientific basis. Let the children learn the structure and functions of their own bodies, as openly and as plainly as they learn their problems in mathematics. Ignorance is not innocence, and knowledge is a powerful weapon against temptation. Let them know and realize the interdependence of mental, moral and physical health. Surround them with every hygienic condition and teach them the fear of nature's laws and penalties."[10]

This fearless M.D. deplores the fact that *four thousand* doctors are let loose on the population every year, and says that by the latest census there were 65,000 physicians in the United States, an excess

---

[8] Delsartean: after the French actor and teacher Francois Delsart (1811-1871), the study of human behavior by observing body movement.

[9] Source unknown.

[10] Source unknown.

over any European country of *fifty thousand*. And besides all this there are over *thirty-six thousand patent medicines;* meanwhile the number of habitual opium eaters has increased in twenty years from ninety thousand to half a million; and in the statistics of insanity, we lead the horrible majority.

"It is estimated that there are now in the United States, 168,900 insane. In 1850 the ratio of insane in our population was one in 1,500—in 1860, one in 1,300—in 1870, one in 1,000—and in 1880, one in 550—an enormous increase in ten years. In comparing the statistics of our own country with England, France and Germany, we lead with a horrible majority. England has, within 15,000,000, as large a population as our country, and not half the number of insane. France has a population by 13,000,000 less than the United States and only a trifle over half the number of insane. Germany has only 5,000,000 less in population, and 50,000 less insane. Late statistics from New York State show an increase during the year '87-'88, of 710 over the last year, there being in 1888, 14,722 insane in the state of New York alone. This was the greatest increase in a year in the history of the state. The asylums are full, many of them overcrowded. In our own state the public asylums are taxed to the utmost, to care for all who apply.

"The statistics in regard to some of the principal diseases of modern life are almost beyond belief; in Massachusetts, for instance, the increase of death from Bright's disease.[11] In 1850, the mortality was one and a fraction in 1,000 deaths; in 1860, two and a fraction; in 1870, 10 and a fraction; in 1880, 19 and a fraction, and in 1886, 30 and a fraction."

The enormous quantity of beer consumed nowadays helps to explain the cumulative miseries involved in these last figures.

A State Board of Health, which shall have exclusive power to authorize the practice of medicine would be the surest way to get rid of the surplus, and well-educated women physicians should in every case be on that board, for as sanitarians they are unexcelled if not unrivalled.

But woman's everlastingly befrilled, bedizened and bedraggled style of dress is to-day doing more harm to children unborn, born and dying, than all other causes that compel public attention.   With ligatured lungs and liver as our past inheritance and present slavery, the wonder is that such small heads can carry all we know! Catch Edison and constrict him inside a wasp-waistcoat, and be assured you'll get no more inventions; bind a bustle upon Bismarck, and farewell to German unity; coerce Robert Browning into corsets, and you'll have no more epics; put Parnell in petticoats, and Home Rule is a lost cause; treat Powderly in the same fashion, and the powder mine of failure will blow up the Labor Movement. Niggardly waists and niggardly brains go together. The emancipation of one will always keep pace with the other; a ligature around the vital organs at the smallest diameter of the

---

[11] Bright's disease: a synonym for nephritis, a general term for an acute or chronic inflammation of the kidneys.

womanly figure means an impoverished blood supply in the brain, and may explain why women scream when they see a mouse, and why they are so terribly afraid of a term which should be their glory, as it is that of their brothers—viz., *strong-minded.*

Our degradation in the line of bandaging the waist has reached such a point, that Helen Campbell says it is a requisite in fashionable London stores to have women clerks not larger around than twenty inches, "and eighteen-inch waists are preferred." Look at the monstrous deformity produced by constrictive surgery as applied to the average fashion-plate; and think what belittlement of power and happiness it means to the poor creatures who will wear these waists, and to their children! We shall, I hope, see something less humiliating in *Harper's Bazar* [sic] than its immemorial abominations of "fashionable style," now that so true a Christian woman as Margaret Sangster edits that otherwise excellent paper. Col. Higginson's keen, progressive articles are horribly neutralized.

Bonneted women are not in normal conditions for thought; high-heeled women are not in normal conditions for motion; corseted women are not in normal conditions for motherhood. Each of the constrictions and contortions involved by these crimes in dress is a distinct violation of loving laws given by our Heavenly Father for our highest happiness and growth. I wonder that men, in their broader outlook and magisterial power, do not forbid this thing by statute, in the interest of their sons that are to be.

But ethics and aesthetics must go side by side in the blessed work of dress-reform, for that is Nature's way. The pioneers did not see this, and their "bloomers" speedily dropped into innocuous desuetude. But the moderns—led by Mrs. Annie Jenness Miller, "that Hebe[12] of the new fashionplate"—have sat at Nature's feet, and on my recent eastern trips I learned what I know to be true in progressive Chicago—that the best are also coming to be the bravest women, that among them there is an absolute craze for getting rid of corsets, and that the divided skirt is worn by tens of thousands whom you might not suspect of so much good sense and courage.

Much as I am devoted to the ballot for woman, I would to-day rather head a crusade against bandaged waists, street-sweeping skirts, and camel's hump bustles than—do I live to say it?—yea, verily, *than to vote* at Chicago's next election for a Sunday-closing mayor![13]

---

[12] In Greek mythology, Hebe was the goddess of spring and youth.

[13] The address, totaling seventy-one pages, continues through various topics for another twenty-eight pages. It closes with a memorial to Willard's recently deceased mother.

A White Life for Two, 1890

America may well be called "God's Country," a gracious Mother-land that women well might live to serve or die to save. For in America, home questions have become the living issues of the time, and "Home Protection" is the battle cry of preachers, publicists and politicians. The mighty war of words that culminated in the Presidential election of 1888, was waged on both sides in the interest of the home, but only on a materialistic money basis. The three questions that alone engross our people are the Temperance, the Labor, and the Woman Questions, and these three agree in one. Only by convincing Labor that a high tariff meant material protection for the home, was that election won; only by convincing wage-workers and women that the outlawing of the saloon means protection for those who dwell within the home, will Prohibition ever gain the day; only by convincing wage-workers and temperance voters that through equal suffrage women will help to protect both the external and internal interests of the home, will the Woman Question ever be wrought out in government. But beneath this trinity of issues is the fount from which they flow and that is Home itself, and back of Home is the one relationship that makes it possible. In view of this, I dare affirm that the reciprocal attraction of two natures, out of a thousand millions, for each other, is the strongest,

The author is indebted to Karlyn Kohrs Campbell's well-referenced reprint of this speech in *Man Cannot Speak for Her*, vol. 2 (New York: Praeger, 1989). Readers wanting more detailed reference footnotes should consult that text.

though one of the most unnoted proofs of a beneficent Creator. It is the fairest, sweetest Rose of Time, whose petals and whose perfume expand so far that we are all inclosed and sheltered in their tenderness and beauty. For, folded in its heart, we find the germ of every home; of those beatitudes, fatherhood and motherhood; the brotherly and sisterly affection, the passion of the patriot, the calm and steadfast love of the philanthropist. For the faithfulness of two, each to the other, alone makes possible the true home, the pure church, the righteous Nation, the great, kind brotherhood of man.

The inmost instincts of each human spirit must cry out to God,

> Comfort our souls with Love,
> Love of all human kind,
> Love special, close, in which like sheltered dove
> Each heart its own safe nest may find;
> And Love that turns above adoringly, contented to resign
> All love if need be, for the love divine.

Marriage is not, as some surface-thinkers have endeavored to make out, an episode in man's life and an event in woman's. Sup your fill of horrors on the daily record of suicides by young men who are lovers, or sweethearts shot, and murdered wives, if you have ever fancied marriage to be the unequal thing that such phrasing indicates. Nay, it is the sum of earthly weal or woe to both. Doubtless there are in this modern land and age, almost as many noble men unmated because of a memory cherished, an estrangement bravely met, many of the best men living go their way through life alone. Sometimes I think that of the two it is a man who loves home best; for while woman is hedged into it by a thousand considerations of expediency and prejudice, he,

. . . . . . "With all the world before him which to choose,"

still chooses home freely and royally for her sake who is to him the world's supreme attraction.

The Past has bequeathed us no records more sublime than the heart-histories of Dante, of Petrarch, of Michael Angelo, and, in our own time, of Washington Irving, Henry Martyn[1] and others whom we dare not name. It was a chief among our own poets who said:—

> I look upon the stormy wild,
> I have no wife, I have no child;

---

[1] Henry Martyn (1781-1812), influential English missionary in India and Persia.

For me there gleams no household hearth
I've none to love me on the earth.[2]

We know that "he who wrote home's sweetest song ne'er had one of his own," and our gracious Will Carleton[3] [*sic*] oncerning John Howard Payne[4]—

Sure, when thy gentle spirit fled
  To lands beyond the azure dome,
With arms out-stretched God's angels said,
  "Welcome to Heaven's home, sweet home.

There are men and women—some of these famous, some unknown—the explanation of whose uncompanioned lives may be found in the principle that underlies those memorable words applied to Washington: "Heaven left him childless that a Nation might call him Father."

In such considerations as I have here urged, and in this noblest side of human nature, a constant factor always to be counted on, I found my faith in the response of the people to the work of promoting social purity. "Sweet bells jangled, out of tune," now fill the air with minor cadences, often, alas, with discords that are heart-breaks, but all the same they are "sweet bells," and shall chime the gladdest music heaven has heard, "Some sweet day, by and by." This gentle age into which we have happily been born, is attuning the twain whom God hath made for such great destiny, to higher harmonies than any other age has known, by a reform in the denaturalizing methods of a civilization largely based on force, by which the boy and girl have been sedulously trained apart. They are now being set side by side in school, in church, in government, even as God sets male and female everywhere side by side throughout His realm of law, and has declared them one throughout His realm of grace. Meanwhile, the conquest, through invention, of matter by mind, lifts woman from the unnatural subjugation of the age of force. In the presence of a Corliss engine, which she could guide as well as he, men and women learn that they are fast equalizing on the plane of matter, as a prediction of their confessed equalization upon the planes of mind and morality.

---

[2] Verse written by Bayard Taylor (1825-1878), according to Frances Willard, *Glimpses of Fifty Years*, (Chicago, IL: Woman's Temperance Publication Association, 1889) 605.

[3] Will Carlton (1845-1912), American poet.

[4] John Howard Payne (1791-1852), wrote the lyrics of the song "Home, Sweet Home."

We are beginning to train those with each other who were formed for each other, and the American Home, with its Christian method of a two-fold headship, based on laws natural and divine, is steadily rooting out all that remains of the mediaeval continental and harem philosophies concerning this greatest problem of all time. The true relations of that complex being whom God created by uttering the mystic thought that had in it the potency of Paradise: "In our *own* image let *us* make man, and let *them* have dominion over all the earth,"[5] will ere long be ascertained by means of the new correlation and attuning, each to other, of a more complete humanity upon the Christ-like basis that *"there shall be no more curse."*[6] The Temperance Reform is this correlation's necessary and true fore-runner, for while the race-brain is bewildered it can not be thought out. The Labor Reform is another part, for only under co-operation can material conditions be adjusted to a non-combatant state of society, and every yoke lifted from the society, and every yoke lifted from the laboring man lifts one still heavier from the woman at his side. The Equal Suffrage Movement is another part, for a government organized and conducted by one half the human unit, a government of the minority, by the minority, for the minority, must always bear unequally upon the whole. The Social Purity Movement could only come after its heralds, the three other reforms I have mentioned, were well under way, because alcoholized brains would not tolerate its expression; women who had not learned to work would lack the individuality and intrepidity required to organize it, and women perpetually to be disfranchised, could not hope to see its final purposes wrought out in law. But back of all were the father and mother of all reforms—Christianity and Education—to blaze the way for all these later comers.

The Woman's Christian Temperance Union is doing no work more important than that of reconstructing the ideal of womanhood. The sculptor Hart[7] told me, when I visited his studio in Florence many years ago, that he was investing his life to work into marble a new feminine type which should "express, unblamed," the Twentieth Century's womanhood. The Venus de Medici, with its small head and button-hole eyelids matched the Greek conception of woman well, he thought, but America was slowly evolving another and loftier type. His statue, named by him "Woman Triumphant," and purchased by patriotic ladies of his native state, Kentucky, adorns the city hall at Lexington, and shows

A perfect woman, nobly planned

---

[5] Genesis 1:26.
[6] Revelations 22:3; Galatians 3:13.
[7] Joel T. Hart (1810-1877).

To warn, to comfort, and command;
A creature not too bright or good,
For human nature's daily food,
And yet a spirit pure and bright,
With something of an angel's light.[8]

She is the embodiment of what shall be. In an age of force, woman's greatest grace was to cling; in this age of peace she doesn't cling much, but is every bit as tender and as sweet as if she did. She has strength and individuality, a gentle seriousness; there is more of the sisterly, less of the syren—more of the duchess and less of the doll. Woman is becoming what God meant her to be, and Christ's Gospel necessitates her being, the companion and counsellor not the incumbrance and toy of man.

To meet this new creation, how grandly men themselves are growing; how considerate and brotherly, how pure in word and deed! The world has never yet known half the aptitude of character and life to which men will attain when they and women live in the *same* world. It doth not yet appear what they shall be, or we either, for that matter, but in many a home presided over by a Temperance voter and a White Ribbon worker, I have thought the Heavenly Vision was really coming down to terra firma.

With all my heart I believe, as do the best men of the nation, that woman will bless and brighten every place she enters, and that she will enter every place on the round earth. Its welcome of her presence and her power will be the final test of any institution's fitness to survive.

Happily for us, every other genuine reform helps to push forward the white car of Social Purity. The great Peace Movement, seeking as its final outcome a Court of International Arbitration as a substitute for war, promises more momentum to our home cause than to almost any other. For as the chief corner-stone of the peaceful State is the hearthstone, so the chief pulverizer of that corner-stone is war.

An organized and systematic work for the promotion of Social Purity was undertaken in 1885 by the Woman's Christian Temperance Union. Under the three subdivisions of Preventive, Reformatory and Legal Work, this society has gone steadily forward until the White Cross Pledge, appealing to the chivalry of men, has grown familiar in thousands of homes, and the White Shield Pledge, appealing to the chivalry of women, is following after the first.

---

[8] From William Wordsworth's "She was a Phantom of Delight." According to Campbell, it was "often quoted by feminist abolitionists to describe their ideal woman." *Man Cannot Speak for Her*, vol. 2, 325.

Its pledges are based on the belief that you can not in mature years get out of a character what was not built into it when the youthful nature was like "wax to receive the marble to retain"; that the *arrest of thought* must be secured by mother, minister and teacher, before the common talk of street and play-ground has wrenched that thought away from the white line of purity and truth. Innocence may be founded on ignorance, but virtue is ever more based upon knowledge. In the presence of temptation one is a rope of sand, the other, a keen Damascus blade. To be forewarned is the only way to be fore-armed. A precipice lies before every boy and girl when they emerge beyond the sheltering fortress of their home, but a safe, sure path leads around it; we must gently warn them of the one; we must tenderly lead them to the other.

The personal habits of men and women must reach the same high level. On a low plane and for selfish ends primeval and mediaeval man wrought out, with fiercest cruelty, virtue as the only tolerated estate of one-half the human race. On a high plane of Christianity working through modern womanhood, shall yet make virtue the only tolerated estate of the other half of the human race, and may Heaven speed that day! A woman knows that she must walk the straight line of a true life or men will look upon her with disdain. A man needs, for his own best good, to find that in the eyes of women, just the same is true of him.

Evermore be it remembered, this earnest effort to bring in the day of "sweeter manners, purer laws" is as much in man's interest as our own.

Why are the laws so shamelessly unequal now? Why do they bear so heavily upon the weaker, making the punishment for stealing away a woman's honor no greater than that for stealing a silk gown; purloining her character at a smaller penalty than the picking of a pocket would incur? Why is the age of protection or consent but ten years in twenty states, and in one, only seven years? Who would have supposed, when man's great physical strength is considered, he would have fixed upon an age so tender, and declared that after a child had reached it, she should be held equally accountable with her doughty assailant for a crime in which he was the aggressor? And who would not suppose that the man who had been false to one woman would be socially ostracized by all the rest of womankind? What will explain the cruelty of men and the heartlessness of women in this overmastering issue of womanhood's protection and manhood's loyalty?

The answer is not far to seek. Women became, in barbarous ages, the subjects of the stronger. Besides, what suits one age becomes a hindrance to the next, and as Christianity went on individualizing woman, uplifting her to higher levels of education and hence of power, the very laws which good men in the past had meant for her protection, became to her a snare and danger.

But, while all this heritage of a less developed past has wrought such anguish and injustice upon woman as she is to-day, it has been even more harmful to man, for it is always worse for character to be sinning than to be sinned against. Our laws and social customs make it too easy for men to do wrong. They are not sufficiently protected by the strong hand of penalty, from themselves, from the sins that do most easily beset them, and from the mad temptations that clutch at them on every side. Suppose the outragers of women, whose unutterable abomination crowd the criminal columns of our newspapers each day, knew that life-long imprisonment might be the penalty, would not the list of their victims rapidly diminish? The Woman's Christian Temperance Union has taken up this sacred cause of protection for the home, and we shall never cease our efforts until women have all the help that law can furnish them throughout America. We ask for heavier penalties, and that the age of consent be raised to eighteen years; we ask for the total prohibition of the liquor traffic, which is leagued with every crime that is perpetrated against the physically weaker sex, and we ask for the ballot, that law and law-maker may be directly influenced by our instincts of self-protection and home protection.

We hear much of physical culture for boys, but it is girls that need this most. We hear much of manual training schools to furnish every boy at school with a bread-winning weapon; but in the interest of boys and girls alike, girls need this most. Hence it is in our plans to work for these. Mothers' Meetings are becoming one of the most familiar features of the W.C.T.U. For these we prepare programs, leaflets, and courses of reading at the Woman's Temperance Publishing House, Chicago, from which hundreds of thousands of pledges and pages of literature have gone, as pure and elevated in style and spirit as consecrated pens could render them.

REFORMATORY WORK is the most difficult of all and yet has been of all others most earnestly carried forward thus far by women. Matrons have been placed in the police stations to look after arrested women, Reading Rooms, Lodging Houses and Industrial Homes for Women are multiplying now on every hand. State care for moral as well as mental incapables is being urged and with some small beginnings of success. Statistics of such work are difficult to gain. A single fact vouched for by the women who have in charge one of these homes in Massachusetts, is fitted to encourage every worker in this trying field. They tell us that one woman who had been arrested forty-five times was taken to the home, lifted by kindness from the depths, put into self-supporting lines and for seven years has been an honorable, hard-working woman, happy in her rescued life.

The awful deeds done by white men in the great woods of Alaska, the brutal relations of our soldiery to the Indian women of the plains; the unspeakable atrocities of the lumber camps in Wisconsin and in

Michigan; the daily calendar of crimes against women set forth by the
press, and the blood-curdling horrors of Whitechapel, London,[9] have
aroused the civilized world. Womanhood's loyalty to woman has
overleaped the silence and reserve of centuries and Christendom rings
with her protest to-day. It is now the deliberate purpose of as capable
and trusty women as live, that the *laissez-faire* method of dealing with
these crimes against nature, shall cease; that the method of license,
high or low, shall never be for one moment tolerated, and that the
prohibitory method shall come and come to stay.

Within three years immense advances have been made in legislation. England has cleared the Blue Books of the "Contagious Diseases
Acts";[10] has repealed the atrocious army regulations of India, and
raised the age of protection to sixteen years. America is moving
forward rapidly, improved legislation having been obtained in almost
every State and Territory. The following petition is being everywhere
circulated and its plea, already partially responded to in several States,
is now before the National congress:

"The increasing and alarming frequency of assaults upon women, and
the frightful indignities to which even little girls are subject, have
become the shame of our boasted civilization. A study of the statutes
has revealed their utter failure to meet the demands of that newly
awakened public sentiment which requires better legal protection for
womanhood and girlhood. Therefore we do most earnestly appeal to
you to enact such statutes as shall provide for the adequate punishment
of crimes against women and girls."

But, as I have said, we are not working for ourselves alone in this
great cause of Social Purity. As an impartial friend to the whole
human race in both its fractions, man and woman, I, for one, am not
more in earnest for this great advance because of the good it brings to
the gentler than because of the blessing that it prophesies for the
stronger sex. I have long believed that when that greatest of all
questions, the question of a life companionship, shall be decided on its
merits, pure and simple, and not complicated with the other questions,
"Did she get a good home?" "Is he a generous provider?" "Will she

---

[9] In reference to Jack the Ripper, who, in the fall of 1888, had
stabbed to death five prostitutes in the Whitechapel section of London.

[10] The "Contagious Diseases Acts" required women suspected of
being prostitutes to be inspected regularly for venereal disease. As
Campbell writes, many like Willard condemned such laws because they
"believed all women were debased by these acts because 'in them the
buying and selling of the female body was sanctified by statute law.'"
Man Cannot Speak for Her, vol. 2, 330.

have plenty of money?" then will come the first fair chance ever enjoyed by young manhood for the building up of genuine character and conduct. For it is an immense temptation to the "sowing of wild oats," when the average youth knows that the smiles he covets most will be his all the same, no matter whether he smokes, swears, drinks beer and leads an impure life, or not. The knowledge on his part that the girls of his village or "set" have no way out of dependence, reproach or oddity except to say "yes" when he chooses to "propose"; that they dare not frown on his lower mode of life; that the world is indeed all before him where to choose; that not one girl in one hundred is endowed with the talent and pluck that make her independent of him and his ilk—all this gives him a sense of freedom to do wrong which, added to inherited appetite and outward temptation, is impelling to ruin the youth of our day with a force strong as gravitation, and relentless as fate. Besides all this, the utterly false sense of his own value and importance which "Young America" acquires from seeing the sweetest and most attractive beings on earth thus virtually subject to him, often develops a lordliness of manner which is ridiculous to contemplate in boys who, otherwise would be modest, sensible and brotherly young fellows such as we are most of all likely to find in co-educational schools, where girls take their full share of prizes, and where many young women have in mind a European trip with some girl friend, or mayhap 'a career.'

Multiplied forces in law and gospel are to-day conspiring for the deliverance of our young men from the snares of the present artificial environment and estimate of their own value; but the elevation of their sisters to the plane of perfect financial and legal independence, from which the girls can dictate the equitable terms, "You must be as pure and true as you require me to be, ere I give you my hand," is the brightest hope that gleams in the sky of modern civilization for our brothers; and the greater freedom of women to make of marriage an affair of the heart and not of the purse, is the supreme result of Christianity, up to this hour.

There is no man whom women honor so deeply and sincerely, as the man of chaste life; the man who breasts the buffetings of temptation's swelling waves, like some strong swimmer in his agony, and makes the port of perfect self-control. Women have a thousand guarantees and safeguards for their purity of life. "Abandon hope, all ye who enter here,"[11] is written in letters of flame for them above the haunt of infamy, while men may come and go and are yet smilingly received in the most elegant homes. But in spite of all this accursed latitude, how many men are pure and true!

---

[11] The phrase that is written on the gates of hell in Dante's *Inferno*.

It is said, that when darkness settles on the Adriatic Sea, and fishermen are far from land, their wives and daughters, just before putting out the lights in their humble cottages, go down by the shore and in their clear, sweet voices sing the first lines of the Ave Maria. Then they listen eagerly, and across the sea are borne to them the deep tones of those they love, singing the strains that follow, "Ora pro nobis," and thus each knows that with the other all is well. I often think that from the home-life of the Nation, from its mothers and sisters, daughters and sweethearts, there sounds through the darkness of this transition age the tender notes of a dearer song, whose burden is being taken up and echoed back to us from those far out amid the billows of temptation, and its sacred words are, "Home, Sweet Home!" God grant that deeper and stronger may grow that heavenly chorus from men's and women's lips and lives! For with all its faults, and they are many, I believe the present marriage system to be the greatest triumph of past Christianity, and that it has created and conserves more happy homes than the world has ever before known. Any law that renders less binding the mutual, life-long loyalty of one man and woman to each other, which is the central idea of every home, is an unmitigated curse to that home and to humanity. Around this union, which alone renders possible a pure society, and a permanent state, the law should build its utmost safeguards, and upon this union the gospel should pronounce its most sacred benedictions. But while I hold these truths to be self-evident, I believe that a constant evolution is going forward in the home as in every other place, and that we may have but dimly dreamed the good in store for those whom God for holiest love hath made.

In the nature of the case, the most that even Christianity itself could do at first, though it is the strongest force ever let loose upon the planet, was to separate one man and one woman from the common herd, into each home, telling the woman to remain there in grateful quietness, while the man stood at the door to defend its sacred shrine with fist and later on, to represent it in the State. Thus, under the conditions of a civilization crude and material, grew up that well-worn maxim of the common law, "Husband and wife are one, and that one is the husband." But such supreme power as this brought to the man supreme temptation. By the laws of mind he legislated first for himself and afterward for the physically weaker one within "his" home. The *femme couverte* is not a character appropriate to our peaceful, home-like communities, although she may have been and doubtless was a necessary figure in the days when women were safe only as they were shut up in castles and when they were the booty chiefly sought in war. To-day a woman may circumnavigate the world alone and yet be unmolested. Our marriage laws and customs are changing to meet these new conditions. It will not do to give the husband of the modern woman power to whip his wife, "provided the stick he uses is not larger than his finger"; to give him the right to will away her unborn child; to have control over her property; to make all the laws under which she is to live; adjudicate all her penalties; try her before juries of men; conduct her to prison under the care of men; cast the ballot for her; and in general, hold her in the estate of a perpetual minor. It will not do to let the modern man determine the age of "consent," settle the penalties that men should suffer whose indignities and outrages upon women are worse than death, and by his exclusive power to make all laws and choose all officers, judicial and executive, thus leaving his own case wholly in his own hands. To continue this method is to make it as hard as possible for men to do right, and as easy as possible for them to do wrong; the magnificent possibilities of manly character are best prophesied from the fact that under such a system so many men are good and gracious. My theory of marriage in its relation to society would give this postulate. Husband and wife are one, and that one is—husband and wife. I believe they will never come to the heights of purity, of power and peace, for which they were designed in heaven, until this better law prevails. One undivided half of the world for wife and husband equally; co-education to mate them on the plane of mind; equal property rights to make her God's own free woman, not coerced into marriage for the sake of support, nor a bond-slave after she is married, who asks her master for the price of a paper of pins, and gives him back the change; or, if she be a petted favorite, who owes the freedom of his purse wholly to his will and never to her right; woman left free to go her honored and self-respecting way as a maiden *in perpetuo*, rather than marry a man whose deterioration through the alcohol and nicotine habits is a deadly menace to herself and the descendants that such a marriage has invoked—these are the outlooks of the future that shall make the marriage system, never a failure since it became monogamous, an assured, a permanent, a paradisiacal success.

In that day the wife shall surrender at marriage no right not equally surrendered by the husband, not even her own name. Emile Ollivier,[12] that keen-sighted writer of France, says that it is so much easier, for obvious reasons, to trace ancestry along the mother's line, that historic records have incalculably suffered by the arbitrary relinquishment of her name. Probably the French have hit upon the best expedient—the union of the two. Thus I recall that in Paris my home was with an accomplished lady whose name was Farjon and whose husband's was Perrot; her visiting card always bore the inscription:

MADAME EGLANTINE PERROT-FARJON

---

[12] Emile Ollivier (1825-1913), a liberal, reform minister in the government of Napoleon III.

The growing custom, in this country at least, to give the mother's name to son or daughter indicates the increasing, though perhaps unconscious, recognition of woman as an equal partner in the marriage bond. But the custom, even among men of intelligence, of signing themselves, "John Jones, wife, child and nurse," as we see it in the registers of fashionable hotels, is a frequent reminder of the pit from which wives are slowly being digged. The man who writes Mr. John and Mrs. Jane Jones," may be regarded as well on the road to a successful evolution, though "Mr. and Mrs. John Jones" seems to most of us about the correct thing up to this date!

The time will come when the mother's custody of children will constructively be preferred in law to that of the father, on the ground that it is surer and more consonant with natural laws. Last of all, and chiefest, the *magnum opus* of Christianity and Science, which is its handmaid, the wife will have undoubted custody of herself, and as in all the lower ranges of the animal creation, she will determine the frequency of the investiture of life with form. My library groans under the accumulations of books written by men to teach women the immeasurable iniquity of arrested development in the genesis of a new life, but not one of these volumes contains the remotest suggestion that this responsibility should be equally divided between husband and wife. The untold horrors of this injustice dwarf all others out of sight, and the most hopeless feature of it is the utter unconsciousness with which it is perpetuated. But better days are dawning; the study of heredity and pre-natal influences is flooding with light the Via Dolorosa[13] of the past; the White Cross army with its equal standard of purity for men and women is moving to its rightful place of leadership among the hosts of God's elect.

> "Then reign the world's chaste bridals, chaste and calm
> Then springs the crowning race of humankind.
> *May these things be!*"

I believe in uniform national marriage laws, in divorce for one cause only; in legal separation on account of drunkenness; but I would guard the marriage tie by every guarantee that could make it at the top of society, the most coveted estate of the largest-natured and most endowed, rather than at the bottom, the necessary refuge of the smallest-natured and most dependent women. Besides all this, in the interest of men—i.e., that their incentives to the best life might be raised to the highest power—I would make women so independent of marriage that men who, by bad habits and niggardly estate, whether

---

[13] Originally, Jesus' route from Pilate's hall of judgment to Golgotha. It metaphorically refers to any difficult or sad experience.

physical, mental or moral, were least adapted to help build a race of human angels, should find the facility with which they now enter its hallowed precincts reduced to the lower minimum. Until God's laws are better understood and more reverently obeyed, marriage cannot reach its best. The present abnormal style of dress among women, heavily mortgages the future of their homes and more heavily discounts that of their children. Add to this the utter recklessness of immortal consequences that characterizes the mutual conduct of so many married pairs and only the everlasting tendency toward good that renders certain the existence and supremacy of a Goodness that is infinite, can explain so much health and happiness as our reeling old world persists in holding while it rolls onward toward some far-off perfection, bathed in the sunshine of our Father's Omnipotent Love. Our own Julia Ward Howe[14] has given us our noblest motto for Social Purity:

> "In the beauty of the lilies Christ was born across the sea;
> With a glory in his bosom that transfigures you and me;
> As He died to make men holy, let us die to make men free,
> While God is marching on."

---

[14] Julia Ward Howe (1819-1910), most famous for authoring the "Battle Hymn of the Republic," the final verse of which Willard quotes here. Howe was also a leader in the American Woman Suffrage Association and co-founder of *Woman's Journal*.

President's Address, 1897

LABOR[1]

Nothing proves the growing solidarity of the people more than the fact that since the succession of the Queen the number of letters passed through the mails in Great Britain has grown from 80 to 2,000 millions in a year, and that before her reign shall close it is probable that the earth can be circumnavigated in a little over thirty days when the Siberian and Alaska railroads shall be in operation. Nothing is more certain than that people, when they can thus freely communicate their thoughts and come together for their purposes, will first of all seek to improve their condition.

One of the cardinal doctrines of the labor movement is the Eight Hour Law, and I greatly desire that this convention may declare in favor of it, not only because the present hours are oppressively long, but for the reason that if eight hours were the fixed period a great many more wage-workers would be employed. It is a hopeful symptom for Sabbath reform that the labor people have taken it up with so much enthusiasm; they feel that the Sabbath is their day, and that it is a species of tyranny so to arrange the business of the country that they have no period of recreation. This position is well taken, and I am glad that in the interest of human brotherhood, as well as a reverent observance of what we believe to be a divine command, the White Ribbon women can join hands with the wage workers for the protection of the pearl of days. As we have in the past heartily co-operated with

---

[1] "Labor" is the twenty-third section of Frances Willard's 1897 annual address.

all who sought this end, so let us do in the future, but we must be careful always to let it be understood that those who observe some other day than the seventh are to be respected in their belief by any law that we are working to help obtain.

The divinest right on this earth is the right of the people to take corporate care of their own affairs.

There is a commodity in the market which has the magic power of creating more than it costs to produce it. This is the labor power of the human being, of a free wage-worker. He sells it for a certain amount of money, which competition reduces to the average necessaries of life to produce it; to so much food, clothing and shelter, which are absolutely necessary to recuperate his lost powers on the next morning, and to reproduce a new generation of wage-workers after this one is gone. Almost all above this goes to the employing class, and is called "the surplus value."

The human hand will yet become the adequate emblem of the only aristocracy; it is the wizzard's wand. Our great Emerson[2] said, "A little waving hand reared these huge columns," and the touch of a child's finger has set free the power that made magnificent the harbor of our great metropolis. There is no limit to the forces that man's thoughts will yet start into motion, so that the plains shall be diversified by hills and valleys, and the inaccessible heights lowered to the level where man may build his happy home upon them, and the poles brought within the range of pleasant weather, and the poet's famous line about "the looks that commerce with the skies," made everyday experience, while we are signalling our sister planets, and the navigation of the air becomes as simple and homelike a thing as the swift whirl of a bicycle is now upon the street. But back of all must be that faithful little hand, directed by the "gray matter" which is the condensation of development upon this earth, and warmed at the friendly fires of a heart big with the indwelling sense of God and Brotherhood.

It looks as if electricity would bring back those better times when men did their work in their own homes, instead of flocking to the factory to make machines of themselves as they do now. In the old days one man made a whole shoe, in these he only holds the hammer that drives home a peg, or the instrument that cuts a string, and he and his occupation have become equally fractional; but when the people can take the power that drives the wheels into their own houses, they will live a much more complete and independent life. May the day hasten when their liberty shall be given back again by the new down-pour of Promethean fire.

---

[2] Ralph Waldo Emerson (1803-1882) was an American essayist and poet.

I do not wish to know what the country does for the rich, they can take care of themselves; but what it does for the poor determines the decency, not to say the civilization, of a government. How to develop the downmost man and woman—that is our problem. Nothing proves the incapacity of our rulers like the tenement-house abomination. If we had statesmen this could not continue; if but one more Shaftsbury[3] would arise in the British Parliament, or Richard H. Gilder[4] in the New York Legislature, a peaceful revolution would be set in motion.

Though we have nothing to hope for as temperance people from the present Government, we rejoice that they have championed, and Parliament has adopted the bill giving universal compensation to injured wage-workers, except agriculturalists. It speaks well for human nature that Lord Salisbury and Mr. Chamberlain carried the bill through, and capitalists voted for it, knowing that it would cost them dear.

Germany provides an insurance taken from the wages of the work-people and from their employers, whereby if ill they will have resources to fall back upon, and when old they need not go to the workhouse, but will have enough to support them in comfort.

These laws are intended "to check the socialists," and they show the good that the socialistic movement has already accomplished, and predict the infinitely greater good that is to come. The next move is likely to be the enactment of laws whereby the unemployed, who are good and respectable men and women, may have provision made for their necessities when they are out of work.

There is no class more dependent than what is called "the servant class." They with laundry women must, as a rule, rely upon the good-will of their employers, for they have but little moral or legal protection. Oftentimes they live in rooms that have no fire, and lie down to sleep on beds that are less comfortable than those they have provided for their master's horses. As a rule, small provision is made for their personal cleanliness by means of baths, etc. They have no stated hours, but their work, like that of the farmer's wife, is never done. They have no understanding as to holidays, of recreation and recupera-

---

[3] Anthony Ashley Cooper (1801-1885), the seventh earl of Shaftesbury, was a leading Victorian reformer. He was largely responsible for the creation of the Sanitary Commission in Britain, better treatment of the insane, and regulated working conditions and hours for women and children.

[4] Richard Watson Gilder (1844-1909) was a poet and editor of *Century* magazine. He was particularly active in civic work in New York, as president of the Fellowship Club and the Free Kindergarten Association, and as chairman of the Tenement House Committee. He was actively anti-Tammany Hall in many municipal campaigns.

tion, either during the week or during the year. In short, they are not looked after as they ought to be. We believe that the great majority who employ servants treat them with a measure of consideration and good-will, but the fate of so many persons ought not to be dependent in anywise on the peculiarities of those who employ them. Servants should organize as other working people are organized, and there should be inspection to know whether the sanitary condition and comfort of the rooms that they inhabit is adequate to the degree of civilization that we have reached.

The same should be remembered of all women who do laundry work, a most taxing and difficult employment, and one in which, so far as we can learn, they are expected to begin very early and continue until very late. There should be inspection for them as well, and we believe the time will come when there will be an eight-hour law for laundry women and servants as well as for the more independent classes of workers. Until there is a move made in this direction we are far from having reached a Christian standard in respect to the condition and lives of our fellow men and women who hold the position of servants, or, as our New England people used to say, with far more refinement, "helpers."

In England, especially among the nobility, these are much better looked after than in any other country, and after sixty, or thereabouts, they are pensioned off, if faithful.

In Denmark there is a statute called the "Old Age Relief Law," whereby the aged and infirm receive certain sums from the Government. They are not sent to the poor-houses, but have the happiness of paying out their own money, which enables them to retain their self-respect.

We favor postal savings banks and direct legislation whereby the "representative government" of which we have been so proud and which is becoming the most colossal of all failures, can be replaced by the skilful method invented by the only real Republic in the world, that of Switzerland, where the people originate or confirm their own laws by a popular vote.

The firing of Sheriff Martin and his deputies on unarmed miners at Hazelton, Pennsylvania, is likely to prove one of the "shots heard around the world." The American people are patient, but like all patient natures when aroused they make quick work. Every patriot must rejoice that the revenges of the citizen can be speedily worked out at the ballot box, and in the elections of this autumn we shall doubtless see some curious things, and among them a vigorous attempt of the people to shake themselves loose from the tyranny of the "Boss." No attempt has ever been made on so large a scale since we had a country, as that of the Citizens' Union, which has put forward the name of Seth Low for Mayor of Greater New York with its three million and a half people. Mrs. Charles Shaw Lowell stands at the head of the Woman's

Municipal League that did a large part of the work of securing a hundred and fifty thousand names of the best citizens, urging Mr. Low to stand.

As a matter of course, our sympathies are still more strongly with the Prohibition candidate, William Wardwell, and I confess that I should hear of the election of Henry George with solid satisfaction, while the high character of General Tracy promises good government in case he is elected;[5] so that as Tammany[6] seems to be check-mated this time, it is quite probable that the Mayor who will wield the power never before committed by so large a number of people in one municipal group to any man, will have the public confidence and will predict great things for the redemption of municipal politics.

The resurrection of Christ is the need of our day. He has dwelt behind a curtain of mysticism; He has been buried in the grave of ecclesiastical formulae, wrapped about by the cerements of superstition, until the common people, who would hear Him gladly if He were permitted to speak the language of their common life, have grown weary and sad, saying, "They have taken away my Lord, and I know not where they have laid Him."[7]

Look about you; the products of labor are on every hand; you could not maintain for a moment a well-ordered life without them; every object in your room has on it, for discerning eyes, the mark of ingenious tools and the pressure of laborious hands. Our Mary Allen West[8] always prayed, among other things, when asked to say grace before meat, "God bless the hands that prepared this food for us." She was the only person I ever met who seemed to have given thought to those invisible human forces on which we are dependent for our daily bread. Why is it that the men and women who made the furniture in our rooms would by no means be recognized as our equals or companions? Why is it that those who make our food are usually as much forgotten by those who eat as if they were machines like the stoves on which the food is cooked? Why is it that even the higher class of draftsmen, clerks and helpers whose toil is largely mental, have no more social recognition than if a law had barred them out? Indeed just this has happened. It is that unyielding, unwritten law of caste which says: "Labor is under foot, money is on top; idleness is a token of refinement; pleasure is the mark of birth and breeding;

---

[5] Wardwell, George, and Tracy were all candidates for the New York mayoral elections.

[6] Tammany: an organization within the New York City Democratic party, known for its graft and corruption; from Tammany Hall, the group's meeting place.

[7] John 20:2; and 20:13.

[8] Probably a recently deceased member of the WCTU.

whoever devotes his time to useful pursuits belongs to a tabooed class, and you cannot be in Society unless you do the things that are of no mortal use to anybody and become the sort of person whose death would be no loss to the community, but oftentimes a gain." We know that this caste-law is supreme in aristocratic countries, and there must be a reason for it. That reason is not far to seek. The men and women who work for wages are generally those whose ancestors were also "working people," as we say, and for this reason they were as a rule shut out from the power to get much if any schooling, or to acquire those refinements of conduct that manifest themselves in graceful speech and attitude, attractive appearance and attire, accompanied by some knowledge of literature and art. But is it not the cruelest of injustices for those whose lives are surrounded and embellished by their work to have a superabundance of the money which represents the aggregate of labor in any country, while the laborer himself is kept so steadily at work that he has no time to acquire the education and refinements of life that would make him and his family agreeable companions to the rich and cultured? Now, the reason why I am a Christian socialist comes in just here: I would take, not by force, but by the slow process of lawful acquisition through better legislation as the outcome of a wise ballot in the hands of men and women, the entire plant that we call civilization, all that has been achieved on this Continent in the four hundred years since Columbus wended his way hither, and make it the common property of all the people, requiring all to work enough with their hands to give them the finest physical development, but not to become burdensome in any case, and permitting all to share alike the advantages of education and refinement. I believe this to be perfectly practicable, indeed that any other method is simply a relic of barbarism. I believe with Frederick Maurice of England, that it is infidel for anyone to say that the law of supply and demand is as changeless as the law of gravitation, which means that competition must forever prevail. I believe that competition is doomed, the trusts whose single object it is to abolish competition having proved that we are better without than with it the moment that one corporation controls the entire supply of any product; and what the socialist desires is that the corporation of humanity should control all products. Beloved comrades, this is the frictionless way, it is the higher law, it eliminates the motives of a selfish life, it enacts into our every-day living the ethics of Christ's Gospel; nothing else will do it, nothing else can bring the glad day of universal brotherhood. It will not come in our time, and those of us who believe that it will ever come shall be both cursed and laughed at; but let us work right on, investing the little increment of power that we possess to render this heavenly dream a little more likely to be realized.

Away down under the sea, the coral zoophytes begin their unseen work; they give their entire lives to the endeavor to make an island,

and dying bequeath their minute organism to the same work for which they have already given a life of toil. Other infinitesimal creatures, their descendants, work on in the same way through many ages, until at last a gleaming coral reef is seen above the water's edge. And now the birds come from happy homelands, and bring seeds to scatter where the ocean has already deposited from its gardens a film of soil, and later on the grass flings down its green carpet; gardens bloom, great trees lift themselves skyward with their coronal of leaves, man builds his home under their shade, and the smoke of his hallowed hearth-fire curls upward in the bright air. No one thinks about the little beings that wrought so sturdily and well away below there in the darkness, yet but for them there would have been no happy island with little children at their gladsome play, and women in their purity and joy.

RESCUE WORK

Bear with me, my sisters, while I suggest an addition to our general classification of methods. We call them the "preventive, educational, evangelistic, social, legal, and the department of organization." It is believed by many of our good friends, and especially by those who have reformed from the thraldom of drinking habits, that we are not as warmly interested in rescue work as once we were. In reply we remind them of our Evangelistic Department busy in every State; we point to our noon prayer meeting in Chicago, maintained so far as possible from the Crusade days, where the work of rescue is steadily carried on as it has been daily for so long a time in Baltimore by the W.C.T.U., and assure our brothers that nobody living has rescue work at heart more earnestly than we. It is in our plans to establish such a meeting in Washington, D.C., and I believe it could be successfully maintained there; also in New York, Boston, Philadelphia, San Francisco, New Orleans, indeed in all our large cities. The motto of such a work must be, "Not willing that any should perish,"[9] and its rallying song, "Rescue the Perishing." I feel confident that we should respond to the call of our brothers who urge us to give a larger place to Christian effort for the reformation of inebriates than we have done as yet, although the numberless prayer and testimony meetings and the personal work of our women in helping men enslaved, is far more extended than that of all other temperance societies combined. It is, nevertheless, not all it ought to be. If you approve, let us insert in our general classification of methods, evangelistic *and rescue* work, and set some woman whose heart God hath touched to render special aid and efficiency to this department.

---

[9] 2 Peter 3:9.

INEBRIATE INDUSTRIAL HOMES

Dr. Norman Kerr, one of England's ablest physicians, a thorough-going teetotaler, is the leader in a movement which has already found favor in the British Parliament, and the purpose of which is to send drinking men who are arrested to industrial homes instead of prisons, and to make it possible for those whose friends are given over to the drink habit, to secure to them the benefits of such an institution. The industrial feature will enable them to be self-supporting, at least in part. Before many years such institutions will undoubtedly be found in all countries, and it would be a great advantage if just one State would give us an object lesson in this line of reform.

HOW CAN WE CLEAR THE SLUMS?

We have no co-workers more trusty and loved than Commander and "Consul" Booth-Tucker, the leaders of the Salvation Army in the United States. They have recently brought forward a plan to relieve the congested districts of New York and other large cities by moving the unemployed industrial population to the south-west, say, Arizona, where, by means of irrigation, great tracts of land can be rendered productive and an independent life brought within the power of these wretched and despairing ones, who are mostly emigrants and who sought an Eldorado in this land where nothing is a positive drug in the market except man. I need not say that these noble friends can count on our auxiliaries to help to the utmost in carrying forward this great scheme, which is but one of the spurs of the "delectable mountains" to which many of our eyes are steadily lifted, and their name is Christian Socialism, "all for each and each for all"; the utilization of the utmost force of this earth for the corporate benefit of Man; the cherishing of his labor as the holiest thing alive, and the development of individual gifts of brain, heart and hand under the inspiration of that universal sense of brotherhood which will be, as I believe, the perpetual tonic that will some day render all coarser stimulants distasteful.

*   *   *

PERSONAL OPINION[10]

Now in these best days of the Son of Man, we see the axe laid at the foot of the tree, when the proposition is soberly made to abolish

---

[10] Personal Opinion is the forty-fourth section of Frances Willard's 1897 annual address.

poverty and make misery a phantom of the past. Now it is openly declared, and a great group of people in live earnest are grouped around the banner with a new device, *"Evil is not a necessity. "* But no material evil is greater than absolute and hopeless poverty. The pagan political economy, whose utmost wisdom has never reached higher than "the law of supply and demand," is fast becoming discredited in factory and shop, pulpit and pew, and the law of Co-operative Commonwealth looms up in place of it.

Nothing recurs to my mind with such frequency and joyous hope as this soliloquy (It was with me in the quiet woods and hills of New England; it kept time to the soft sea waves; it twinkled in my soul when I looked up into the sky's bright dome): "I wonder why we don't set at work and abolish poverty in this great generous land within the next half century. We manage our public schools and great universities as the equal property of all; we carry on our entire postal system, our water supply, our parks, streets and highways in the same manner. In some countries the railroads, telegraph and telephone lines belong to the Government, and in some cities the lighting is done by the municipality. All this works well. In the most progressive cities tenement houses are built to rent to wage-workers, and the old rookeries where private capital demanded the highest rents and the lowest standards of living are being torn down like the Bastile of old—both being parts of the same ungodly way of dealing with that holy thing called Life. Why should we practically give away the right to build railroads and street-car lines, to manufacture gas, erect great public buildings, and thus farm out the people's business to corporate groups of men? Why do we not make the money basis of the country, not a mound of metal, white or yellow, dug out of the ground and piled up in our treasury vaults at Washington, but the country itself with 'I promise to pay' gleaming across its breast from Mt. Katahdin to Mt. Shasta?"[11]

Beloved comrades, whatever subject we may talk of here, no other the wide world over tingles with life like this one. The nervous little Emperor William tries to keep back the rising tide of social democracy, and better dykes than his standing army of seven hundred and eighty thousand men are found in his laws whereby wage-workers must lay up a prescribed fraction of their money to which the employer is obliged to contribute and the Government to add a bonus, and his proposed endowment for all workers after sixty years of toil. England, under Lord Salisbury, that most inveterate of aristocrats, is dyke-building against the Fabian movement and London County Council, and the Trade Unions, with their clear-eyed leaders, and the Labor members of Parliament, led by John Burn. But though the Employers' Liability

---

[11] Mount Katahdin, Maine, and Mount Shasta, California.

Bill, whereby the expenses of injury and illness to the wage-worker must be met by the capitalist, has proved a soothing plaster to many wounds, it is no anodyne, but a good-sized "entering wedge" toward corporate ownership by the great firm of the people.

Meanwhile "Government by Injunction," in which peaceable processions are forbidden to march, and "Government by Massacre," whereby a sheriff shoots down unarmed marching miners, are all so many surgical operations, lifting off the scales from the eyes of rich and poor alike, and piling up the proof that politicians and moneymakers between them own what we have been fond of calling

"The land of the free and the home of the brave."

Ours is the day of experts in politics, and the application of "business methods," thanks to the "Rise," not of Silas Lapham,[12] but of the subtle politician who leads the party dominant, is now so exact that the single instruction required by the party devotee, otherwise known as the "honest citizen," is "you press the button—we'll do the rest!" The political boss, through his faithful and expectant henchmen, has registered every voter's name in hamlet and village, plied him with motives and led him to vote the ticket "just once more" that he may "save the country," unless he was already safely to be counted "among the faithful."

No feudal chief ever had in the peasantry dependent upon him for life and its necessities, a more solid following than "the Boss." In many of our States he is omnipotent, and now he has become nationally enthroned in the person of a leader whose audacity, overstepping all bounds of political warfare hitherto known, proved itself equal, in our last presidential campaign, to claiming the national flag as a party emblem and calling out demonstrations on land and water that involved a nation in his partisan campaign and organized the greatest movement since the Civil War. Sometimes it looks as if "the Boss" were greater than the President. What does it all mean? That old systems die hard, and whales make the most flurry when the weapon reaches nearest heart. What does it mean? That the present Klondyke quick-step tattooed by the business men on every pavement in the land is the precursor of a more reasonable philosophy of life because this is "the pace that kills." And what has this to do with the temperance reform and all the others grouped around it? Much every way. "Man shall not live by bread alone."[13] The renaissance is here; the "revival of religion" has taken new form. The Christ is being reincarnated before our eyes and we know it not. As of old, "the common people hear him gladly," and the Creed of the past becomes the Deed of to-day. Never were so many good heads and warm hearts pledged to each other for

---

[12] Referent unknown.

[13] Deuteronomy 8:3, Matthew 4:4, Luke 4:4.

the reign of Jesus Christ in Custom and in Law, for the literal adoption of His precepts as the only Code never to be outworn, and the grouping of Humanity around His Person as the one steadfast shining Light that "lighteth every man hath cometh into the world."[14]

"Government by Injunction" cannot cope with Christ as a Deed; the massacre of unarmed miners does but hasten the common people's reign; the lynching of men by infuriated mobs only precipitates the uprising of Golden Rule justice; the worthlessness of the idle rich and the wickedness of the idle poor offset each other. The tramp, who, on being asked to saw wood before eating breakfast, left this scrawl on the pile as he disappeared, was the representative of that large constituency of rich and poor who stand on the same level: "Tell them you saw me, but you didn't see me saw!"

Beloved comrades, an age is hustling to the front that will see them all saw or know the reason why, and that is the age of the carpenter's Son. We have worshipped Him with our words, but henceforth we must worship with deeds or be set down as infidels and hypocrites. We have murmured, "We beseech thee to hear us, Good Lord";[15] hereafter it is Himself *we* have to hear saying in the same tones in which He rebuked the money-changers in the temple: "WHY CALL YE ME LORD, LORD, BUT DO NOT THE THINGS THAT I SAY?"[16] We have consecrated our knees to Him when it was our hands He wanted; we have courtesied to a man-made altar when He asked our obeisance for humanity itself. Science is killing out superstition as disinfectants kill microbes; no set of men can make any other set believe that they are custodians of any charm that makes men free from sin save love to God and love to man, wrought out into the enduring form of every day work to help others be less miserable. A bad life is the worst of heresies. Conferences and synods, revival meetings and prayer circles will have written as their epitaph, unless they make direct, honest, hard work to help men in the daily business of life: *"Behold your house is left unto you desolate."*[17] We Christians must not sit by and let the fires of intemperance burn on; we must not permit poverty to shiver and squalor to send forth its stench and disease to fester in the heart of great populations. All this must be stopped, and we are the Christ-men and Christ-women to stop it, or else we are pitiable dreamers and deluded professors of what we don't believe. I say this as a loving and always loyal daughter of the Church, and I say it more to myself than to you, *"O that I were less*

---

[14] John 1:9.

[15] Psalms 118:25, Jonah 1:14.

[16] Luke 6:46.

[17] Matthew 23:38.

at ease in Zion![18] But by Christ's name and life I mean to be—so help me, God."

Doubtless the most cheering thought that can engage our minds is the return of the world to faith, and that this return is led by those apostles of nature who headed the wanderings of the curious-minded into the wilderness a generation back. Even Huxley,[19] in that famous Oxford lecture, not long before his death, closed with the hope that what Tennyson[20] had said was true, about the happy islands of the Hesperides[21] that might lie below the sunset's golden mystery.

Pasteur[22] was profoundly penetrated with the exquisite adaption of means to ends in the universe, and each fresh revelation of his microscope deepened his reverence. He said: "When one has studied much, he returns to the faith of the Breton peasant; and if I had studied still more, I should have the faith of the Breton woman."

Herbert Spencer,[23] the completion of whose wonderful work on the Cosmos, after thirty years of toil, marks the scientific culmination of the nineteenth century, insists on nothing so much as that he is not a materialist. To my mind, one of the sublimest sentences in the language is this from his great work (I quote from memory): "We live in the presence of an infinite and eternal Energy from which all things proceed."

No one who looks out broadly over the splendid field of human endeavor where bugles and trumpets call earnest souls to join in the unending strife, "Where ever the right comes uppermost and ever is justice done," can help feeling that the return of the world to faith the broad basis of that holy work to which our Crusade Mothers gave the early impetus of prayer and song—the "Gospel Temperance Movement."

I learn that Wilson Barrett, who wrote the "Sign of the Cross," a play that puts before the audience a picture of the life and martyrdom of the early Christians, has organized ten companies to present these scenes to the people, so that he estimates that twenty thousand persons in a day will have brought before them these blessed scenes that cannot fail to make all who behold them better. I saw this drama in London,

---

[18] A reference to Amos 6:1: "Woe to you who are at ease in Zion."

[19] Thomas Henry Huxley (1825-1895), British biologist and advocate of Darwinism.

[20] Alfred Tennyson (1809-1892), renowned English poet.

[21] Hesperides: in Greek mythology, the Isles of the Blest, which lie at the western end of the earth.

[22] Louis Pasteur (1822-1895), French chemist who made significant discoveries in immunology and microbiology.

[23] Herbert Spencer (1820-1903), British philosopher.

and wept and rejoiced that even I, with all my faults, had "like precious faith" with those glorious confessors of the Gospel. What an unlooked-for thing is this in an age in which doubt had made such inroads upon faith!

Another most cheering sign of the times is, that books like "Bonnie Briar Bush," the "Little Minister," and the stories of Silas Hocking,[24] should be read by millions, and carry to the heart, as well as the head, the conviction that our holy faith stands sure. Invention is destined to play a larger part than we can conceive of in the propagation of Christianity. One can now order in Piccadilly a wire to be sent to his house along which he can hear the discourse of any great preacher in London, and the phonograph brings to our very firesides the voices of the great and good; the mighty oratorios that exalt our faith even to the gates of Heaven, and the sacred home songs that make the name of Christ a household word.

The better concept of the universe that we are getting nowadays, helps to disarm death. We know that a cube of solid iron can be changed by heat into a fluid, then into a gas so fine as to become invisible; but the iron is there, only it has taken a more ethereal form. Why, then, should not the infinitely finer human body, in its disintegration, yield up the celestial body in which the potent human soul shall move right onward in its growth toward perfectness, "Forgetting the things that are behind, and pressing forward toward the things that are before."

The Rontgen [sic] rays[25] are invisible, but how great is their power, even to dividing asunder joints and marrow, and revealing the inmost intents of the very organs of life. A mighty faith has fallen on the heart of man since he knew about these rays. They reveal to us the invisible as the most real thing in the material world. Indeed it begins to dawn upon us that there is no supernatural because there is no natural world; all is the Present God whose mode of action means the Present Heaven.

Instead of accepting any belief as in itself a final formulation of truth expressed in words chosen by fallible human beings, I am learning, amid all the contradictory voices of this Babel century, to say in my deepest heart, "What Thou wouldst have me believe,[26] Son of Man who are the Son of God, that I believe. Thy heavenly words are oftentimes too great for me, they are telescopes through which I try to look; but my gaze is dimmed, sometimes because of tears." The white

---

[24] Silas K. Hocking (1850-1935): English clergyman and novelist whose works contained religious and moral themes.

[25] X rays, named here after the German physicist William Konrad Roentgen (1845-1923).

[26] A reference to Acts 22:10.

light of God's truth shines through the stained glass window of my brain, but I would it were white light and not discolored or refracted like a stick in water by the imperfect medium through which it has to pass. Christ is to me, as I move forward toward the bourn whence we do not return, more and more the vital centre of all that is worth cherishing in this or any world, and by His words that are life, I seek to be transformed into the spirit of His mind.

On my recent birthday it came to me that I could gain no truer concept of God than by holding to the presence of Him who is the Way, the Truth and the Life, as ever tenderly smiling on me and saying, "Receive My spirit,"[27] and that in the halo round His head I saw the words, "With what measure ye mete, it shall be measured to you again."[28] "Receive My spirit!" That is life's safest and most alluring voice, but there will come a day when we shall utter those great words back again, "Lord Jesus, receive my spirit," and then the mystery of life, its discipline, its joys and grief, will end, and the glad mystery of death will work out the transfer to other realms of the Infinite Power.

We shall never climb to heaven by making it our life long business to save ourselves. The process is too selfish; the motto of the true Christian is coming to be, "All for each and each for all," and in the honest purpose to realize its everyday meaning we acquire "A heart at leisure from itself," *and in no other way.*

When Lady Henry Somerset and I were working for the Armenians in the great port of Marseilles, where raw material of every kind was being landed from a thousand ships, and heavy freight teams were moving along the streets conveying it to those who would shape it into finer forms, I could but think of the analogy of what I saw to life itself.

We are all of us raw material, carried on long voyages, landed at strange ports, rattled over noisy pavements, always on our way to be made more useful and of higher value. If we could only remember how raw we are, and what a rudimentary world we live in, it would help to give us courage to go on; and there is this about it, we are always coming into finer forms, higher value, and better company.

The raw material seen by us in the great port was borne from the ship on heavy trucks, by immense horses driven by men of swarthy, ill-kempt looks; but I asked myself, as I watched the moving procession—Whither is it tending? Where will it be when it becomes the perfect product? Those fruits and grains will be placed in cut-glass dishes on carefully spread tables, those great blocks of costly wood will become artistic furniture, those dyes from the far East will make

---

[27] Acts 7:59, Galatians 3:2.
[28] Mark 4:24, Matthew 7:2, Luke 6:38.

brilliant many a gorgeous robe that will encircle the fairest forms of grace and beauty.

It is the perfect product of which account is to be taken, whether it be in the fabric of cloth or that of character. Trace your material to its ultimate, and either in the service of the many or the embellishment of the few, it has always come to something immeasurably greater that it was at first. You must not judge it on the way; and you must remember that, if you are loyal to the best opportunities you have, more and more as the years pass by, you will be dealing with the product, not in its crude beginning but in its moulded perfectness.

The later philosophy claims that the evolution of man is brought about by the same influences that create a sun in the heavens. According to this view each one of us is the sum of a succession of interrupted vibrations. There is nothing in the universe but matter and force, force being the most recent name given by scientists to Him whose constant presence moulds and fashions all that we see, even that God of whom the great apostle said, "In Him we live and move and have our being."[29] The struggle of matter in the mineral as well as the vegetable and animal world is to reach individuality, for by this route only can immortality become the possession of any being. Every atom, even the lowest, palpitates with the purpose of attaining immortality. The ether is a finer atmosphere extending throughout space, and will yet become the means of intercommunication between our planet and all other stars. Those who have put off the physical form dwell in a finer body, but it is like this one and is suited to beings who breathe ether instead of air. These are the latest theories and may or may not be true, but are accepted as a working hypothesis by as strong and earnest minds as are now devoted to the study of God's laws in nature. The relation of the hypothesis to the temperance movement is this: If we are working out our physical salvation through a knowledge of these laws and conformity to them, we shall with sedulous determination avoid forming such habits as will hinder us in our progress toward the highest realization of an equipoised and beneficent individuality. Alcoholic drinks introduce added friction into the machinery of body and mind; by their use the individual is handicapped in the race toward a higher and more perfect individuality, and what hinders one in this race hinders us all. . . .

POWER OF THE SPIRIT

Nothing less than uttermost devotion will ever carry the temperance reform, or any other, to its high place in the temple of victory.

---

[29] Acts 17:28.

The way of the Cross is the only way out for any life, or for the aggregation of lives, that makes up a group of reformers. "This kind goeth out but by prayer and fasting:"[30] "Without the shedding of blood there is no redemption."[31] That these utterances of our Divine Master are of universal application, we are beginning to perceive; that they are the underlying principles of the universe, science is beginning to reveal. When Mrs. Abby Leavitt knelt with her Crusade band on the cold pavement of a Cincinnati street, and while she was leading the great song of the Crusade, "Rock of Ages, Cleft for me," a policeman's hand fell on her shoulder with the words, "Madam, you are my prisoner," and she looked up with face untroubled and sang on, "Let me hide myself in Thee," the great group gazers of the street knew that something more than mortal was in her tones. When a lovely girl in an Ohio town faced a saloonkeeper's blunderbuss, and while he dared her to proceed, she sang, "Never be afraid to speak for Jesus," a new force for King Emanuel had come upon the field. When dogs were set upon one of our Crusade women in Cleveland, and as they rushed toward her, those who were looking saw her face "as it had been the face of an angel," even as that of Stephen was, and saw her hands placed on the heads of those savage beasts, while no harm came to her, they knew a power had been let loose not of this world.

Sisters beloved, it is only when we feel ourselves at the very core and centre of our consciousness, linked with the Spirit of God, that we can put life into the ingenious and varied machinery which thought, purpose and devotion have wrought out for us in the past twenty-four years. How often have we said these things to one another; how utterly do we believe them! If I did not know that they are the Bread of Life to us in all that is best of our lives and character, I should be hopeless for the holy enterprise in which we have embarked. But, by the light that never shone on sea or shore, yet transfigured the kneeling faces of those Crusade groups,

> "I have read a righteous sentence writ in blazing rows of steel,
> As ye deal with my contemners so with you my Grace shall deal;
> Let the Hero born of woman crush the serpent with His heel
> While God is marching on."

There will be other reforms and reformers when we are gone. Societies will be organized, and parties will divide on the right of men to make and carry deadly weapons, dynamite and other destructive

---

[30] Matthew 17:21.
[31] Ephesians 1:7, Hebrews 9:12.

agencies still more powerful, that human ingenuity will yet invent. They will divide on the question of the shambles, and there will be an army of earnest souls socially ostracized, as we are now, because they believe that the butcher should cease to kill and the sale of meat be placed under ban of law. There will be a great movement to educate the people so that they will use neither tea, coffee nor any of the numerous forms of anodynes and sedatives that are now tempting millions to deterioration and death, and which will more strongly affect the finer brain tissues of more highly developed men and women. Long after the triumph of the temperance reform has universally crystallized upon the statute books; long after the complete right of woman to herself and to the unlimited exercise of all her beneficent powers is regarded as a matter of course; long after the great trust of humanity takes to itself the earth and the fullness thereof as the equal property of all, there will remain reforms as vital as any I have mentioned, and on them the people will group themselves in separate camps even as they do to-day. And it is not improbable that the chief value of the little work that we have tried to do on this small planet, lies in the fact that we have been to some extent attempered by it, we have become inured to contradiction, and we may be useful either in coming invisibly to the help of those who toil in the reforms of the future, or we may be waging battles for God upon some other star.

Chronology of Speeches

Woman's Lesser Duties, speech to the Browning Association of Pittsburgh Female College, Pittsburgh, Pennsylvania, March 24, 1863. Reprinted in a booklet of the same name.

The New Chivalry, public lecture delivered at Centenary Church, Chicago, Illinois, March 21, 1871. Reprinted in *Glimpses of Fifty Years*, 576-589.

People Out of Whom More Might Have Been Made, fund-raising speech for Northwestern Woman's College, Chicago, Illinois, April 10, 1871.

First Home Protection Speech, delivered at Old Orchard Beach, Maine, August 1876, Woman's Congress, Philadelphia, Pennsylvania, October 1876, and WCTU annual convention, Newark, New Jersey, October 1876. Reprinted in *Glimpses of Fifty Years*, 452-459.

Speech on behalf of home protection given in testimony before the House Judiciary Committee, Washington D.C., February 1, 1878. Reprinted in a newspaper clipping, Scrapbook 6, WCTU Series, reel 30.

Speech at the presentation of the crusade quilt, WCTU annual convention, Baltimore, Maryland, 1878. Reprinted in *Woman and Temperance*, 77-79.

Speech in defense of suffrage articles appearing in *Our Union*, WCTU annual convention, Baltimore, Maryland, October 1878. Reprinted in *Minutes of the National Woman's Temperance Union*, 1878 convention, 27-30.

Valedictory Thoughts, speech upon leaving as president of the Illinois WCTU, 1878. Reprinted in *Woman and Temperance*, 380-384.

Home Protection, Woodstock, Connecticut, July 4, 1879. Reprinted in *Home Protection Manual*, 6-12; *Woman and Temperance,* 345-356, 370-377; and *The (New York) Independent* 10 July 1879: 11-13.

Annual Address to the National Woman's Christian Temperance Union, Boston, Massachusetts, 1880.

Speech at Lincoln Hall, Washington D.C., March 7, 1881. Reprinted in *Woman and Temperance,* 265-271.

Presentation of Lucy Hayes portrait to President James A Garfield, Washington D.C., March 8, 1881. Reprinted in *Woman and Temperance*, 280-281.

Address delivered at the National Temperance Convention, Saratoga Springs, New York, June 21, 1881. Reprinted in *Woman and Temperance*, 569-574.

Speech at Lake Bluff Temperance Convocation, Lake Bluff, Illinois, August 1881. Reprinted in *Woman and Temperance*, 392-396.

Annual Address to the National Woman's Christian Temperance Union, Washington D.C., October 26, 1881.

Personal Liberty, address delivered during the Iowa campaign for a prohibition constitutional amendment, spring 1882. Reprinted in *Woman and Temperance*, 486-495.

Address of the President to the National Woman's Christian Temperance Union, Louisville, Kentucky, October 25, 1882.

Address of the President to the National Woman's Christian Temperance Union, Detroit, Michigan, October 31, 1883.

Speech seconding the nomination of John St. John as Prohibition party presidential candidate, Pittsburgh, Pennsylvania, July 23, 1884. Reprinted in *Glimpses of Fifty Years*, 397-400.

Address of the President to the National Woman's Christian Temperance Union, St. Louis, Missouri, October 22, 1884.

President's Annual Address to the National Woman's Christian Temperance Union, Philadelphia, Pennsylvania, October 30, 1885.

President's Annual Address to the National Woman's Christian Temperance Union, Minneapolis, Minnesota, October 22, 1886.

President's Annual Address to the National Woman's Christian Temperance Union, Nashville, Tennessee, November 16, 1887.

Speech on behalf of woman's suffrage given in testimony before the Senate Subcommittee on Woman Suffrage, Washington D.C., April 2, 1888.

Decoration Day speech at the Prohibition party national convention, Indianapolis, Indiana, May 30, 1888. Reprinted in *Glimpses of Fifty Years,* 447-452 and *Our Day* 1 (June 1888): 505-510.

President's Annual Address to the National Woman's Christian Temperance Union, New York, New York, October 19, 1888.

Tenth Annual Address to the National Woman's Christian Temperance Union, Chicago, Illinois, November 8, 1889.

A White Life for Two, 1890. Reprinted in *A White Life for Two*, 3-15
and the *Chatauqua Assembly Herald*, 1 Aug. 1891: 5.
President's Annual Address to the National Woman's Christian
Temperance Union, Atlanta, Georgia, November 14, 1890.
Address of the President of the Woman's National Council of the
United States at its First Triennial Meeting, Washington D.C.,
February 22-25, 1891. Reprinted in a booklet of the same name.
President's Annual Address to the National Woman's Christian
Temperance Union, Boston, Massachusetts, November 13, 1891.
President's Annual Address to the National Woman's Christian
Temperance Union, Denver, Colorado, October 28, 1892.
Speech at Exeter Hall, London, England, January 1893.
President's Annual Address to the National Woman's Christian
Temperance Union, Chicago, Illinois, October 1893.[1]
President's Address to the National Woman's Christian Temperance
Union, Cleveland, Ohio, November 16, 1894.
President's Annual Address to the National Woman's Christian
Temperance Union, Baltimore, Maryland, 1895.
President's Annual Address to the National Woman's Christian
Temperance Union, St. Louis, Missouri, November 13, 1896.
President's Address to the World's Woman's Christian Temperance
Union, Toronto, Canada, October 1897.
President's Address to the National Woman's Christian Temperance
Union, Buffalo, New York, October 29, 1897.

Note: All of Willard's annual addresses to the WCTU may be found in
the appropriate *Minutes of the National Woman's Christian
Temperance Union convention*, WCTU Series, reels 1-5.

---

[1] The 1893 annual address was written by Willard, but delivered
in her absence by Lady Henry Somerset.

Bibliography

ANNOTATED BIBLIOGRAPHY

Primary Sources

Jimerson, Randall C., Blovin, Francis X., and Isetts, Charles A. *Guide to the Microfilm Edition of Temperance and Prohibition Papers.* Ann Arbor: University of Michigan Press, 1977.

An invaluable descriptive guide to the *Temperance and Prohibition Papers*.

Temperance and Prohibition Papers. Joint Ohio Historical Society-Michigan Historical Collections-Woman's Christian Temperance Union papers, microfilm ed. (Cited as WCTU Series in notes.) Original WCTU papers are available at the National Woman's Christian Temperance headquarters, Evanston, IL.

The WCTU Series is an invaluable resource for the researcher interested in either Frances Willard or the WCTU itself. Additionally, the papers are extremely accessible because an extensive and useful guide to the papers has been published (see Jimerson, above).
  Reels 1-10: Annual Meeting Minutes, 1874-1934. The Minutes of the annual NWCTU meetings include minutes of executive committee and subcommittee meetings, a directory of officials, president's annual address, resolutions, departmental reports, membership and financial reports, and miscellaneous statistics. Minutes of the annual meeting itself are irregularly reported (e.g., Willard's 1878 defense of her

editorship of *Our Union* is included, but other extemporaneous remarks
are not). Of particular interest for Willard scholars are reel 1: 1874-
1884; reel 2: 1885-1888; reel 3: 1889-1892; reel 4: 1893-1896; and
reel 5: 1897-1900.

Reels 11-25: Correspondence, 1858-1933. Letters, telegrams, and
postcards in these reels are both those sent to and from Willard, with
some additional correspondence of Anna Gordon. Significant letters
include two from Susan B. Anthony (September 1876), which
congratulate Willard for speaking on behalf of woman's suffrage; an
invitation from J. Heyl Vincent for Willard to speak at Chatauqua
(1877); a letter from Willard to Mrs. Dwight Moody (September 5,
1877) explaining why Willard left Rev. Moody's Boston revival; many
letters from local WCTU members congratulating and thanking her for
speaking at their town; Anna Gordon's description of Willard's
judiciary speech (February 1888); and Susan B. Anthony's letter asking
Willard to keep the WCTU out of the California suffrage campaign, for
fear of alienating many male voters (1896). Much correspondence is
also devoted to Willard's work with the Prohibition party, other reform
groups (e.g., Knights of Labor, Populist party, suffrage organizations),
and, in the 1890s especially, to directing the WCTU's internal affairs.
A note to researchers: because the correspondence is largely handwrit-
ten, the microfilm edition of these materials is of limited utility.

Reel 26: Biographical Material. This reel includes many childhood essays, poems, and a few later articles written by Willard. It also
includes biographical essays and other assorted genealogical material.
Of greatest interest is a synopsis of "The New Chivalry," and a
complete text of "Everybody's War." There is also a synopsis of an
undated speech or essay, "Prohibition Based on the Survival of the
Fittest."

Reels 27-29: Historical Files, Folders 114-129.
Folder 114: tributes and eulogies to Frances Willard.
Folder 115: centenary celebration of Willard's birth, 1939.
Folder 116: miscellaneous and unidentified manuscripts.
Folder 117: Willard Home Inventory.
Folder 118: Scientific Temperance Material, 1892-1907.
Folder 119: WCTU publications (pamphlets and articles) 1877-
1932.
Folder 120: Legislative material, 1917-1933.
Folder 121: newspaper studies of prohibition, 1920s.
Folders 122-124: Articles, speeches and lectures by assorted
        temperance reformers, 1867-1933.
Folders 125-126: WCTU and non-WCTU prohibition pamphlets.
        Includes Willard's *Home Protection Manual.*
Folder 127: leaflets for and against prohibition, 1920s.
Folder 128: photographs.

Folder 129: Minute Book of the Evanston Young Woman's Christian Temperance Union, January-December 1879. Includes some references to Frances Willard attending and participating.

Reels 30-44: Scrapbooks. These journals consist primarily of clippings about and by Frances Willard, collected by Mother Willard until her death and continued thereafter by Anna Gordon. The clippings are organized in roughly chronological order and do not always include full bibliographical information. There are numerous articles by newspapers across the country reviewing Willard's local lectures. Although the articles are not unconditionally positive, it is hard to determine to what degree Mother Willard edited the material included.

Willard, Frances E. *A White Life for Two.* Chicago, IL: Woman's Temperance Publishing Association, 1890. A reprint of Willard's 1890 "A White Life for Two" speech.

————. *Address of Frances E. Willard, President of the Woman's National Council of the United States, at its First Triennial Meeting, Albaugh's Opera House, Washington, D.C., February 22-25, 1891.* (N.C.: np, 1891). A reprint of Willard's presidential address to the Woman's National Council, 1891.

————. *Glimpses of Fifty Years: The Autobiography of an American Woman.* Chicago, IL: Woman's Temperance Publishing Association, 1889. Written in several months during the winter of 1888-1889, this 698-page memoir suffers some problems of organization and historical accuracy. The first half of the book—recollecting Frances's life up to 1874 and her work with the WCTU—is the best organized part of the book, and contains some relatively frank discussion by Willard about her shortcomings. Still, the book is written from Willard's point of view, and she cannot avoid putting controversies in the most favorable light. It is a testament to her writing that so many biographers have relied so heavily on these autobiographical recollections. Stories she tells here are often repeated in later works with little or no qualification. As with much of Willard's writing and speaking, much that is written here is repeated elsewhere. She reprints freely and voluminously from her childhood journals, articles, and speeches, others' speeches and letters, and *Nineteen Beautiful Years.*

————. *Home Protection Manual.* New York, NY: The *Independent* Office, 1879. A reprint of Willard's 1879 Home Protection speech, with accompanying organizational instructions for those establishing local WCTUs.

————. Nineteen Beautiful Years, or Sketches of a Girl's Life. New York, NY: Harper, 1864. Willard's biography of her sister, Mary, is primarily comprised of extracts from Mary Willard's journals, with some introductory and transition material written by Frances. While it sheds little direct light on Frances Willard's own life, it gives some indication of the Willards' home life and gives an early demonstration of Frances Willard's proficiency as a writer.

————. *Woman and Temperance.* Hartford, CN: Park, 1888. Reprinted by Arno Press, 1972. Originally commissioned to be a reprint of Willard's speeches and articles, she transformed it into a testimonial to the WCTU. She solicited autobiographical sketches from various leaders of the WCTU, and for those who were "too busy" or "modest," she had others write a piece or wrote the biographical eassy herself. There is some explanatory and transitional material interspersed throughout, and the book does contain several reprints of her speeches: "First Home Protection Address" (1876), "Valedcitory Thoughts" (1878), "Home Protection" (1879), "Address to the Saratoga convention" (1881), and "Personal Liberty" (1882).

————. *Woman in the Pulpit.* Chicago: Woman's Temperance Publishing Association, 1889. Reprinted by Zenger, 1978. This is Willard's defense of and arguments for allowing women to preach and for ordaining women for the ministry. It includes several letters from noted ministers, plus two essays——one against and one for——written by other ministers. This work is far and away Willard's best organized and most logically argued book. From her nonoratorical work, this piece is the most representative example of the use of masculine elements in her style, as discussed in Chapter Five.

————. *A Wheel within a Wheel: How I Learned to Ride the Bicycle, with Some Reflections by the Way.* New York: Fleming H. Revell, 1895. Willard's short book advocating the healthful value of bicycle riding, and providing some instruction on its practice.

————. *Woman's Lesser Duties.* Pittsburgh, PA: W. S. Haven, 1863. A reprint of Willard's 1863 "Woman's Lesser Duties" speech.

————, and Livermore, Mary, eds. *A Woman of the Century: Fourteen Hundred-seventy biographical sketches, accompanied by portraits, of Leading American Women in all Walks of Life.* Buffalo, NY: Charles Wells Moulton, 1893. Willard and Livermore felt that young American girls lacked sufficient role models who could demonstrate the possibilities for women beyond marriage and family. This book was their attempt to provide such models.

Biographies

Bordin, Ruth. *Frances Willard: A Biography*. Chapel Hill: University of North Carolina Press, 1986. In the most historically complete biography of Frances Willard, Bordin thoroughly investigates Willard's life, influence, and world in which she lived. Bordin does an able job of defending Willard's supposedly "conservative" position within the history of American feminism. In this book and her *Woman and Temperance,* Bordin takes to task those who would belittle the temperance andprohibition reform movement. If Bordin's book has a weakness, it is that, occasionally, when trying to contextualize Willard's life with her times, the author is willing to apply some historical theories which do not necessarily pertain to Willard simply because she falls within a "class" of Victorian women reformers. Typically, however, Bordin qualifies any such speculation, and, overall, the exploration is worth the risk of error.

Earhart, Mary. *Frances Willard: From Prayers to Politics*. Chicago: University of Chicago Press, 1944. Earhart's biography is a comprehensive, thorough work on the life of Frances Willard. Earhart discusses many aspects of Willard's life in greater detail than most other biographers: Willard's engagement to Fowler, her resignation as dean of Northwestern's Woman's College, her talent as a speaker, and pertinent events which occurred subsequent to Willard's death. Earhart's introduction is especially informative, because it details Anna Gordon's concerted public relations program for making a legend out of Willard's life. Bordin claims that Earhart's work reflects the belief prevalent at the time that "temperance was a discredited movement," and at times Earhart indeed sounds too much the defender of Willard the woman's leader against Willard the temperance leader, but the bias seems slight. More important, Earhart sometimes makes overly broad claims with little tangible substantiation, and, typical of her era, her use of footnotes is more sparing than the current standard.

Gordon, Anna Adams. *The Life of Frances E. Willard*. Evanston, IL: National Woman's Christian Temperance Union, 1912. Written by Frances Willard's personal secretary and issued by the WCTU's publishing house, this volume is generally considered the "official" biography. Organized roughly in chronological order, but with each chapter devoted to a single topic (e.g., "The Teacher,"

"Founder of the World's Woman's Christian Temperance Union,"
"Answering Armenia's Cry"). Despite twenty-two years of almost
constant companionship with Willard, Gordon's biography is
comprised largely of secondary, published materials, with quoted
passages occupying many pages. The first half is drawn solely
from Willard's autobiography, while the second half consists
primarily of excerpts from addresses, essays, and petitions written
by Willard. Gordon's most significant contribution comes in the
last four chapters. In the first two of those, Gordon recounts the
final seven months of Willard's travels in America and the various
memorial services which attended her death. In the final two
chapters, Gordon reprints excerpts from eulogies given at
Willard's funeral service and from addresses delivered at the 1905
dedication of a statue in her honor in Statuary Hall of the Capitol
Building in Washington, D.C.

Gordon avoids many of the controversial aspects of Willard's
career: the engagement to Charles Fowler, the fight over the
Temple project, the antilynching dispute, and Willard's turn to
labor causes and socialism, to name a few. Bordin rightly calls
the book "eulogistic," and it is as a piece of history itself that the
biography is perhaps most interesting.

Miller, Ida Tetreault. "Frances Elizabeth Willard: Religious Leader
and Social Reformer." Diss: Boston University, 1978. Miller's
dissertation provides a useful, though relatively terse, eighty page
biography of Willard. She then identifies the major themes of
Willard's philosophy: religion, temperance, suffrage, politics,
labor and the econommic system. Expanding on the theme of
religion, Miller compares Willard's philosophy with Walter
Rauschenbush's, whom Miller calls the "foremost exponent of the
social gospel in America" (p. 177). She concludes that, although
some differences of content and style exist, Willard foreshadows
Rauschenbush's work, and should be classified as an early
proponent of the Social Gospel.

Strachey, Ray (Rachel). *Frances Willard: Her Life and Work.*
London: T. Fisher Unwin, 1912. Inspired by her grandmother
Hannah Whitall Smith's recollections, Strachey wrote this
biography of Willard. Unapologetically favorable, Strachey says
in the foreword that she began as an unbiased observer, but
became "biased" during her study of Willard's life. The biography
is interesting for Strachey's use of Willard's journals and as an
oral history of her grandmother's stories. Otherwise, the book
relies heavily on Willard's autobiography for its pre-1889 material,
and is noticeably thin in its discussion of Willard's life post-1889.

Strachey's best discussion is probably in regard to Willard's engagement to Fowler.

SELECT BIBLIOGRAPHY

Books, Theses

Adams, Elmer C., and Foster, Warren Dunham. *Heroines of Modern Progress*. New York: Sturgis and Walton, 1913.

Algeo, Sara M. *The Story of a Sub-Pioneer*. Providence, RI: Snow and Farnham, 1925.

Bellamy, Edward. *Looking Backward: 2000-1887*. New York: Modern Library, 1917.

Berg, Barbara. *The Remembered Gate: Origins of American Feminism*. New York: Oxford University Press, 1978.

Birdsell, David Sinclair. "The Woman's Christian Temperance Union: A Study in Rhetorical Consistency." Thesis: University of Virginia, 1981.

Blair, William Henry. *The Temperance Movement: Or the Conflict between Man and Alcohol*. Boston, MA: William E. Smythe, 1888.

Blocker, Jack S., Jr. *Alcohol, Reform, and Society: The Liquor Question in Social Context*. Westport, CT: Greenwood, 1979.

―――――. *"Give to the Winds Thy Fears": The Women's Temperance Crusade, 1873-1874*. Westport, CT: Greenwood, 1985.

―――――. *Retreat from Reform: The Prohibition Movement in the United States, 1890-1913*. Westport, CT: Greenwood, 1976.

Bordin, Ruth. *Woman and Temperance: The Quest for Liberty and Power, 1873-1900*. Philadelphia: Temple University Press, 1981.

Buechler, Steven M. *The Transformation of the Woman Suffrage Movement: The Case of Illinois, 1850-1920*. New Brunswick, NJ: Rutgers University Press, 1986.

Buhle, Mari Jo. *Women and American Socialism, 1870-1920*. Urbana: University of Illinois Press, 1981.

Burstyn, Joan N. *Victorian Education and the Ideal of Womanhood*. London: Croom Helm, 1980.

Campbell, Karlyn Kohrs. *Man Cannot Speak For Her*. 2 vols. New York: Praeger, 1989.

Catt, Carrie Chapman, and Shuler, Nettie Rogers. *Woman Suffrage and Politics*. New York: Charles Scribner's Sons, 1923.

Clark, Norman. *Deliver Us From Evil: An Interpretation of American Prohibition*. New York: W. W. Norton, 1976.

Cott, Nancy. *The Bonds of Womanhood: "Woman's Sphere" in New England, 1790-1835.* New Haven, CT: Yale University Press, 1978.

Dannenbaum, Jed. *Drink and Disorder: Temperance Reform in Cincinnati from the Washington Revival to the WCTU.* Urbana: University of Illinois Press, 1984.

DeBenedetti, Charles. *The Peace Reform in American History.* Bloomington: University of Indiana Press, 1980.

Dorr, Rheta Childe. *Susan B. Anthony.* New York: Frederck A. Stokes, 1928.

DuBois, Ellen Carol. *Feminism and Suffrage.* Ithaca, NY: Cornell University Press, 1978.

Duniway, Abigail Scott. *Path Breaking: An Autobiographical History of the Equal Suffrage Movement in Pacific Coast States.* 2d ed. Portland, OR: James, Kerns and Abbott, 1914. Reprinted by Klaus, 1971.

Elshtain, Jean Bethke. *Public Man, Private Woman: Women in Social and Political Thought.* Princeton, NJ: Princeton University Press, 1981.

Engelmans, Larry. *Intemperance: The Lost War against Liquor.* New York: Free Press, 1979.

Epstein, Barbara Lee. *The Politics of Domesticity.* Middletown, CT: Wesleyan University Press, 1981.

Findlay, James F. *Dwight L. Moody.* Chicago: University of Chicago Press, 1969.

Fink, Leon. *Workingmen's Democracy: The Knights of Labor and American Politics.* Urbana: University of Illinois Press, 1983.

Fitzpatrick, Kathleen. *Lady Henry Somerset.* Boston, MA: Little, Brown, 1923.

Flower, B. O. *Progressive Men, Women, and Movements of the Past Twenty-Five Years.* Boston, MA: The New Arena, 1914. Reprinted by Hyperion, 1975.

Frankfort, Roberta. *Collegiate Women: Domesticity and Career in Turn of the Century America.* New York: New York University Press, 1977.

Freedman, Estelle. *Their Sisters' Keepers: Women's Prison Reform in America, 1830-1930.* Ann Arbor: University of Michigan Press, 1981.

Goodwyn, Lawrence. *Democratic Promise: The Populist Movement in America.* New York: Oxford University Press, 1976.

Gordon, Elizabeth Putnam. *Women Torch-Bearers: The Story of the Woman's Christian Temperance Union.* 2d ed. Evanston, IL: National Woman's Christian Temperance Union, 1924.

Gusfield, Joseph. *Symbolic Crusade.* Urbana: University of Illinois Press, 1963.

Handy, Robert T., ed. *The Social Gospel in America, 1870-1920.* New York: Oxford University Press, 1966.

Hardesty, Nancy. *Woman Called to Witness: Evangelical Feminism in the Nineteenth Century.* Nashville, TN: Abingdon, 1984.

Hayden, Delores. *The Grand Domestic Revolution: A History of Feminist Designs for American Homes, Neighborhoods and Cities.* Cambridge, MA: MIT Press, 1981.

Hicks, John D. *The Populist Revolt.* Minneapolis: University of Minnesota Press, 1931.

Hopkins, Charles Howard, and White, Ronald Cedric. *The Social Gospel: Religion and Reformation in Changing America.* Philadelphia: Temple University Press, 1976.

Jamieson, Kathleen. *Eloquence in an Electronic Age.* New York: Oxford University Press, 1988.

Kraditor, Aileen S. *The Ideas of the Woman Suffrage Movement, 1890-1920.* New York: Columbia University Press, 1965.

Leach, William. *True Love and Perfect Union: The Feminist Reform of Sex and Society.* New York: Basic Books, 1980.

Lee, Susan Earls Dye. "Evangelical Domesticity: The Origins of the Woman's National Christian Temperance Union Under Frances E. Willard." Diss, Northwestern University, 1980.

Lender, Mark, and Martin, James Kirby. *Drinking in America: A History.* New York: Free Press, 1982.

Lipow, Arthur. *Authoritarian Socialism in America: Edward Bellamy and the Nationalist Movement.* Berkeley and Los Angeles: University of California Press, 1982.

Longmate, Norman. *The Water Drinkers: A History of Temperance.* London: Hamish Hamilton, 1968.

MacKenzie, Norman, and MacKenzie, Jeanne. *The Fabians.* New York: Simon and Shuster, 1977.

McBriar, A. M. *Fabian Socialism and English Politics 1884-1918.* Cambridge, MA: Cambridge University Press, 1962.

McCarthy, Kathleen D. *Noblesse Oblige: Charity and Cultural Philanthropy in Chicago, 1849-1929.* Chicago: University of Chicago Press, 1982.

McDowell, John Patrick. *The Social Gospel in the South: The Woman's Home Mission Movement in the Methodist Episcopal Church South, 1886-1939.* Baton Rouge: Louisiana University Press, 1982.

Morison, Theodore. *Chatauqua: A Center for Education and Religion and the Arts in America.* Chicago: University of Chicago Press, 1974.

O'Neil, William. *Everyone Was Brave.* New York: Quadrangle, 1971.

Pivar, David. *The Purity Crusade: Sexual Morality and Social Control.* Westport, CT: Greenwood, 1973.

Powderly, Terence. *The Path I Trod.* New York: Ames, 1968.

Rauschenbush, Walter. *Christianity and Social Crisis.* New York: Macmillan, 1907.

Rorabaugh, William. *The Alcoholic Republic: An American Tradition.* New York: Oxford University Press, 1979.

Scott, Ann Firor. *The Southern Lady: From Pedestal to Politics.* Chicago: University of Chicago Press, 1970.

Shaw, Anna Howard. *The Story of a Pioneer.* New York: Harper, 1915. Reprinted by Klaus, 1970.

Sinclair, Andrew. *The Emancipation of the American Woman.* New York: Harper and Row, 1965.

————. *Prohibition: The Era of Excess.* Boston, MA: Little, Brown, 1962.

Solomon, Barbara Miller. *In the Company of Educated Women: A History of Higher Education in America.* New Haven, CT: Yale University Press, 1985.

Stanton, Elizabeth Cady, Anthony, Susan B., and Gode, Matilda Joslyn, eds. History of Woman Suffrage. Vols. 3 and 4. Rochester, NY: Charles Mann, 1886, 189xx.

Stewart, Eliza Daniel. *Memories of the Crusade.* 2d ed. Columbus, OH: William G. Hubbard, 1889. Reprinted by Arno, 1972.

Strachey, Ray (Rachel). *The Cause.* Port Washington, NY: Kennikat, 1969.

Stratton, C. C., ed. *Autobiography of Erastus O. Haven.* New York: Phillips and Hunt, 1883.

Taylor, A. Elizabeth. *Citizens at Last: The Woman Suffrage Movement in Texas.* Austin, TX: Ellen C. Temple, 1987.

————. *The Woman Suffrage Movement in Tennessee.* New York: Bookman, 1957.

Tyrell, Ian R. *Sobering Up: From Temperance to Prohibition in Antebellum America, 1800-1860.* Westport, CT: Greenwood, 1979.

Unger, Samuel. "History of the National Woman's Christian Temperance Union." Diss., Ohio State University, 1933.

Vandersloot, J. Samuel. *The True Path: Or, Gospel Temperance.* Cincinnati: OH: W. S. Forshee, 1878.

Vincent, Leon H. *John Heyl Vincent, A Biographical Sketch.* Freeport, NY: Books for Libraries, 1925.

Walkowitz, Judith. *Prostitution and Victorian Society: Women, Class, and the State.* New York: Cambridge University Press, 1980.

Wiebe, Robert H. *The Search for Order, 1877-1920.* New York: Hill and Wang, 1967.

Wiener, Carolyn. *The Politics of Alcoholism: Building an Arena around a Social Problem.* New Brunswick, NJ: Transaction, 1981.

Williamson, Harold F. and Wild, Payson S. *Northwestern University: A History, 1850-1975*. Evanston, IL: Northwestern University Press, 1976.

Winskill, R. T. *The Temperance Movement and Its Workers*. 4 vols. London: Blackie, 1892-1893.

CHAPTERS, ARTICLES

Bolton, Sarah K. "Joseph Cook's Symposium on Temperance." *The (New York) Independent*, 18 Mar. 1880: 5-7.

Brumberg, Joan Jacobs. "Zenanas and Girlless Villages: The Ethnology of American Evangelical Women, 1870-1910." *Journal of American History* 69 (1982): 347-371.

Buhle, Mari Jo. "Politics and Culture in Women's History." *Feminist Studies* 6 (1980): 37-41.

Caroli, Betty Boyd. "Women Speak Out for Reform," *The Rhetoric of Protest and Reform, 1878-1898*. Edited by Paul H. Boase. Athens: Ohio University Press, 1980. 212-231.

Dannenbaum, Jed. "The Origins of Temperance Activism and Militancy among American Women." *Journal of Social History* 15 (1981): 235-254.

"Death of Miss Willard," *The Review of Reviews*. April 1898: 407.

Dickinson, Mary Lowe. "Frances E. Willard." *The Arena*, May 1898: 658-669.

DuBois, Ellen Carol. "The Radicalism of the Woman Suffrage Movements: Notes toward the Reconstruction of Nineteenth Century Feminism." *Feminist Studies* 3 (1975): 63-71.

—————. "Politics and Culture in Women's History." *Feminist Studies* 6 (1980): 28-36.

Field, Kate. "An Enemy in the Field." *Chicago Tribune,* 9 Nov. 1889: 16.

"Frances E. Willard (obit.)," *Outlook.* 26 Feb. 1898: 514-515.

Freedman, Estelle. "Separatism as Strategy: Female Institution Building and American Feminism, 1870-1930." *Feminist Studies* 5 (1979): 512-529.

Gusfield, Joseph. "Social Structure and Moral Reform: A Study of the Woman's Christian Temperance Union." *Journal of Sociology* 61 (1955): 221-232.

Leach, William. "Looking Forward Together: Feminists and Edward Bellamy." *Democracy* 2 (1982).

Leeman, Richard W. "Believing and Make-Believing: Christian Metaphors For and Against Prohibition." *Metaphor and Symbolic Activity* 4 (1989): 19-37.

Little, Charles J. "Frances E. Willard," *Chatauquan* 27 (1898): 73.

Stead, W. T. "The Uncrowned Queen of American Democracy." *The Review of Reviews*, Nov. 1892: 427-444.
Welter, Barbara.   "The Cult of True Womanhood, 1820-1860." *American Quarterly* 18 (1966): 151-174.

Index

About the Author

RICHARD W. LEEMAN is Assistant Professor of Communication Studies at the University of North Carolina at Charlotte. He specializes in rhetorical criticism and public address.

Great American Orators

The Search of Self-Sovereignty: The Oratory of Elizabeth Cady Stanton
Beth M. Waggenspack

Richard Nixon: Rhetorical Strategist
Hal W. Bochin

Henry Ward Beecher: Peripatetic Preacher
Halford R. Ryan

Edward Everett: Unionist Orator
Ronald F. Reid

Theodore Roosevelt and the Rhetoric of Militant Decency
Robert V. Friedenberg

Patrick Henry, The Orator
David A. McCants

Anna Howard Shaw: Suffrage Orator and Social Reformer
Wil A. Linkugel and Martha Solomon

William Jennings Bryan: Orator of Small-Town America
Donald K. Springen

Robert M. La Follette, Sr.: The Voice of Conscience
Carl R. Burgchardt

Ronald Reagan: The Great Communicator
Kurt Ritter and David Henry

Clarence Darrow: The Creation of an American Myth
Richard J. Jensen